Intellectual Property Rights and the Financing of Technological Innovation

NEW HORIZONS IN INTELLECTUAL PROPERTY

Series Editors: Christine Greenhalgh, *Oxford Intellectual Property Research Centre, University of Oxford, UK*, Robert Pitkethly, *Oxford Intellectual Property Research Centre, University of Oxford, UK* and Michael Spence, *Vice-Chancellor, University of Sydney, Australia*

In an increasingly virtual world, where information is more freely accessible, protection of intellectual property rights is facing a new set of challenges and raising new issues. This exciting new series is designed to provide a unique interdisciplinary forum for high quality works of scholarship on all aspects of intellectual property, drawing from the fields of economics, management and law.

The focus of the series is on the development of original thinking in intellectual property, with topics ranging from copyright to patents, from trademarks to confidentiality and from trade-related intellectual property agreements to competition policy and antitrust. Innovative theoretical and empirical work will be encouraged from both established authors and the new generation of scholars.

Titles in the series include:

Intellectual Property Rights and the Financing of Technological Innovation

Public Policy and the Efficiency of Capital Markets

Carl Benedikt Frey

Research Fellow, Oxford Martin Programme on the Impacts of Future Technology, University of Oxford, UK

NEW HORIZONS IN INTELLECTUAL PROPERTY

Edward Elgar
Cheltenham, UK • Northampton, MA, USA

Published by
Edward Elgar Publishing Limited
The Lypiatts
15 Lansdown Road
Cheltenham
Glos GL50 2JA
UK

Edward Elgar Publishing, Inc.
William Pratt House
9 Dewey Court
Northampton
Massachusetts 01060
USA

A catalogue record for this book
is available from the British Library

Library of Congress Control Number: 2013930516

This book is available electronically in the ElgarOnline.com
Economics Subject Collection, E-ISBN 978 1 78254 590 3

ISBN 978 1 78254 589 7

Typeset by Servis Filmsetting Ltd, Stockport, Cheshire
Printed and bound in Great Britain by T.J. International Ltd, Padstow

Contents

Acknowledgements

I gratefully acknowledge the contribution made by a number of people and organisations. Without them the completion of this book would not have been possible. First and foremost, my supervisor Knut Blind provided tremendous support and shaped my way of thinking in a way that made me always question conventional wisdom. Furthermore, I thank my colleagues at the Chair of Innovation Economics, Technische Universität Berlin, where this doctoral thesis was submitted, for their unfailing advice and support. Particular thanks are due to Peter Neuhäusler, who contributed substantially to important parts of this book.

I was fortunate to spend two years as a doctoral student at the Max Planck Institute for Intellectual Property and Competition Law, where I received a great deal of support, especially from Reto M. Hilty and Frank Müller-Langer. I was equally fortunate to spend the final year of my doctoral studies at the Oxford Intellectual Property Research Centre, University of Oxford, which allowed me to gather ideas from various disciplines. I am most grateful to Robert Pitkethly, Graeme Dinwoodie, Christine Greenhalgh and Dan Awrey for the invaluable feedback and support they have given me.

Throughout my doctoral studies my research benefited from the vast experience of Alexander Wurzer and Stephan Hundertmark – I learned a great deal from them. Moreover, the completion of this book would not have been possible without the time and effort of the many survey respondents and the participation of my interview partners. Finally, the greatest contribution was made by my family and friends. It is to my parents that this book is dedicated.

Abbreviations

AIC	Akaike's Information Criterion
AICPA	American Institute for Certified Public Accountants
AIMR	Association for Investment Management and Research
ANDA	abbreviated new drug application
ASA	acetylsalicylic acid
BaFin	German Federal Financial Authority
BD	business development
BHR	buy–hold return
BIC	Bayesian Information Criterion
BilMoG	Bilanzrechtsmodernisierungsgesetz
BIS	Department for Business, Innovation and Skills
CAPM	capital asset pricing model
CDS	credit default swap
CRA	credit rating agency
CTD	common technical document
CTM	community trademark
DBF	dedicated biotechnology firm
DCF	discounted cash-flow
DNA	deoxyribonucleic acid
EBIT	earnings before interest and taxes
EBITDA	earnings before interest, taxes, depreciation and amortisation
EMEA	European Medicines Agency
EMH	efficient-market hypothesis
EPO	European Patent Office
EUR	euro
FASB	US Financial Accounting Standards Board
FDA	Food and Drug Administration
FDCA	Federal Food, Drug and Cosmetic Act
FTO	freedom-to-operate
GAAP	Generally Accepted Accounting Principles
GBP	British pounds
GCP	Good Clinical Practice
GDP	gross domestic product
HGB	Handelsgesetzbuch
IAS	International Accounting Standards

IASB	International Accounting Standards Board
ICH	International Conference on Harmonisation
ICT	information and communications technology
IFRS	International Financial Reporting Standards
IPO	initial public offering
IPR	intellectual property rights
IR	investor relations
LBO	leveraged buyouts
M&A	mergers and acquisitions
METI	Japanese Ministry of Economy, Trade and Industry
ML	maximum likelihood
NCE	new chemical entity
NDA	new drug application
NDA	non-disclosure agreement
NGO	non-governmental organisation
NPD	new product development
NPV	net present value
OECD	Organisation for Economic Co-operation and Development
OHIM	Office for Harmonisation in the Internal Market
OLS	ordinary least squares
OTC	over-the-counter
PE	price-to-earnings
R&D	research and development
rDNA	recombinant DNA
ROA	return on assets
ROE	return on equity
S&P	Standard & Poor's
SBA	Small Business Association
SD	standard deviation
SE	standard error
SEC	US Securities and Exchange Commission
SME	small and medium-sized enterprise
SPC	supplementary patent certificate
SPV	special purpose vehicle
TCE	transaction cost economics
TM	trademark
TRIPS	Agreement on Trade-related Aspects of Intellectual Property Rights
USD	United States dollars
USPTO	United States Patent Office
VIF	variance inflation factor
WTO	World Trade Organization

1. Introduction

1.1 BACKGROUND AND MOTIVATION

In developed economies, technological innovation is a primary driver of economic growth (see, for example, Romer, 2003; Solow, 1956). Intensified competition stemming from the deregulation and globalisation of markets has made tangible and financial assets more commodity-like. Simultaneously, growing investment in research and development (R&D) has led to an ever increasing pace of technological change in the sense postulated by Schumpeter (1962), when describing the creative destruction of technologies and markets (see, for example, Christensen, 1997). This trend has put pressure on firms to reinvent their business models (see, for example, Hamel, 2002). However, although both managers and investors increasingly perceive the importance of intangible assets – such as techno-logical innovations – to the commercial success of companies, they often lack knowledge of their economic characteristics and do not have instru-ments for their measurement and valuation (see, for example, Hand and Lev, 2003). For example, intangible assets are rarely reflected in official measures of economic performance, and most are not accounted for as investments in financial statements (see, for example, OECD, 2008). As a result, financial statements have lost explanatory relevance in relation to the market value of firms (see, for example, Ballow et al., 2004). This has severe implications for the functioning of capital markets.

While the link between tangible assets, such as plants and machinery, and firm value is relatively intuitive and well established in the literature, technology-driven firms have few tangible assets and often spend more on R&D than their annual earnings (see, for example, Chan et al., 2001). Capital markets are therefore often deprived when assessing their value. In essence this means that investors need new measurements to assess the future financial performance of firms in order to allocate financial capital productively (see, for example, Lev, 2001). At the same time technology-driven companies need to communicate their ability to materialise their investments in order to raise capital to finance innovation. The aim of the present study is to suggest ways of bridging the informational deficit in capital markets that stems from the increasingly intangible economy.

According to Lev (2001, p.5): 'An intangible asset is a claim to future benefits that does not have a physical or financial embodiment.' Intangibles can take various forms such as technologies, brands, strategic partnerships, customer relationships, and so on. This study, however, focuses on technology-based intangible assets – that is, technological knowledge being accumulated through R&D – some of which is protected by intellectual property rights (IPR).[1] The link between R&D, intangible assets and IPR is well established in the literature. For example, Mahlich (2005) shows how R&D results in new ideas that add to our accumulated knowledge stock. Moreover, research pioneered by Griliches and Mairesse (1981) and Clark and Griliches (1982) finds that R&D expenditures contribute positively to companies' financial performance. This implies that R&D generates not only new knowledge, but knowledge of economic value. Griliches and Mairesse (1981) thus argue that R&D expenditures provide investments in intangible technology assets – hereafter referred to as intangible assets.

To appropriate their investments, technology-driven companies rely on IPR (see, for example, Allegrezza and Guarda-Rauchs, 1999; Schankerman, 1998). Empirical studies have accordingly shown that IPR contribute to both their productivity and market value. This is true of patents as well as trademarks. For example, Sandner and Block (2011) find that patents, trademarks and R&D are all associated with higher firm value. Moreover, Greenhalgh and Longland (2005) find that firms investing in R&D, and filing for patent and trademark protection, are more productive, while other studies show that patents contribute to both productivity measures and companies' market value (Bloom and Van Reenen, 2002; Neuhäusler et al., 2011).

However, firms have been successful in designing around patents, rendering appropriation for the innovator. This implies that even though IPR are supposed to perfectly protect against imitation, they do so imperfectly in practice. For this reason, firms rely on more complex patent strategies to generate economic returns based on their innovations (see, for example, Blind et al., 2004), as well as the combination of different types of IPR to achieve more effective protection. For example, Jennewein (2005) shows how Bayer and Cisco Systems created synergies through patent and trademark protection, and thus sustained technology-based competitive advantages created under patent protection beyond patent expiry. In this sense, IPR are not only to be seen as outputs of R&D investments, but are rather to be considered in the wider context of companies' business models and competitive strategies. From a resource-based view, firms manage their IPR to secure competitive advantages in making technology assets imperfectly imitable (see, for example, Barney, 1991). IPR thus provide important isolation mechanisms, postulated as crucial to firm performance by resource-based theorists (see, for example Grant, 1991; Wernerfelt, 1984). In addition, firms manage their IPR to restrain the market power of suppliers and enhance the firms' bargaining power within the industry (see, Greenhalgh and Rogers, 2010). Hence, patents are used to counteract competitive forces within industries, described in environmental models pioneered by Porter (1985). Furthermore, by means of offensive blocking, firms actively prevent competitors from developing technological solutions to circumvent or substitute their proprietary technologies (see, for example, Cohen et al., 2000). Thus it is essential for pharmaceutical firms to prevent competitors from commercialising competing chemical substances by also protecting the surroundings of their products (European Commission, 2009), thereby overcoming the threat of substitution (Gassmann and Von Zedtwitz, 2004).

What Hall and Ziedonis (2001) describe as IPR management does not therefore merely relate to improved efficiency in the business process reengineering sense, but is rather a redefinition and extension of its objectives beyond firms' R&D management (Blind et al., 2006). Accordingly, IPR have received increasing attention in a managerial context among research scholars (see, for example, Frey and Wurzer, 2009; Gassmann and Bader, 2010; Harhoff, 2005; Reitzig, 2007), as well as practitioners (see, for example, Frey et al., 2008; PwC 2007; *The Economist*, 2007). A recent survey of 197 executives reveals that approximately 83 per cent consider IPR management to be important or even very important to the performance of their firm (PwC, 2007). Moreover, PwC (2007) finds that IPR management is most often the responsibility of c-level executives, underlining its strategic relevance. Another survey involving 405 executives supports this view in suggesting that the strategic importance of IPR is growing rapidly (*The Economist*, 2007). A similar tendency in perceptions has also been shown among small and medium-sized enterprises (SMEs) (Blind et al., 2009b).

From a capital market perspective, increasingly intangible economies and the changing role of IPR management provide new challenges. These relate to the informational efficiency of capital markets. To allocate financial capital to where it can be used most productively, investors assess the fundamental value of different real investments or securities. This requires that they have access to information that is relevant in explaining their value. The deterioration of the value-relevance of information provided in financial statements, however, suggests that investors lack important information, not least when it comes to the valuation of technology-driven firms which do not have any particular assets in place and largely consist of growth opportunities. For example, Aboody and Lev (2000) find that gains from insider trading are comparatively substantially larger in technology-driven firms. They conclude that due to asymmetric information regarding companies' R&D, public information fails to directly capture the productivity and value of intangible investments.[2] Similarly, Nakanishi (2007) argues that financial analyst reports as well as corporate annual reports to a large extent do not provide sufficient quantitative or qualitative information on intangible assets to the public domain, leading to asymmetric information.

Theoretical corporate finance models, such as pecking order theory (Myers and Majluf, 1984), as well as empirical research (see, for example, Aghion et al., 2004), show that the presence of asymmetric information has an impact on companies' capital structure as well as their ability to obtain funding. Carpenter and Peterson (2002) argue that this is due to the high attrition rates of R&D projects, leading to highly skewed returns on R&D investments.[3] This is especially problematic from a debt contract perspective. Because creditors do not share the upside of the firm's investments, they are only concerned with the bottom tail of the distribution of economic returns (see, for example, Stiglitz, 1985). Hence, as the borrower's returns are highly uncertain, the creditor will want to raise interest rates in order to compensate. However, Stiglitz and Weiss (1981) show that, as interest rates rise, the nature of debt contracts can ex post lead unmonitored borrowers to invest in higher-risk projects with potentially higher returns, and thus increase the probability of default without offsetting higher gains to the creditor in the event of success. This means that the debt financing of R&D projects comes with moral hazard complications (see, for example, Stiglitz, 1985). Moreover, asymmetric information related to risk and default probabilities potentially leads to adverse selection and a situation where lenders will ration credit rather than raise interest rates, because higher interest rates can cause low-risk borrowers to exit the application pool (Stiglitz and Weiss, 1981).

Equity, on the contrary, does not require any collateral, nor does it cap the upside of investors' returns. Furthermore, equity finance does not give managers incentives to substitute low-risk for high-risk projects because managers themselves most often have their wealth tied up in compensation according to firm performance, mitigating agency problems (see, for example, Jensen and Meckling, 1976). Accordingly, Aghion et al. (2004) find that the use of debt declines with companies' R&D intensity, and that firms with higher R&D intensity issue more equity. This suggests that firms mainly rely on equity to finance innovation. However, Eberhardt et al. (2004) find that the stock market consistently undervalues intangible investments, although R&D spending is associated with subsequent abnormal operating performance. In conformity with these findings, Hall

(2002) suggests that smaller firms in R&D-intensive industries suffer from considerably higher costs of capital compared with larger competitors, as well as companies in less R&D-intensive industries. In addition, Guo et al. (2005) find that the ratio of patented products has a negative impact on the buy–hold return (BHR) on firms' shares, suggesting that investors discount even for proprietary intangible assets.

According to pecking order theory, managers will not want to issue equity under such conditions (Myers and Majluf, 1984). This implies financing constraints for technology-driven firms. The market for venture capital is one response to this problem. However, Sahlman (1990) shows that venture capital is associated with high costs of capital, suggesting high costs for technological innovation. Moreover, venture capitalists react to information provided by public stock markets (Gompers et al., 2008), and try to time initial public offering (IPO) decisions by making an exit when stock market valuations are relatively high. Hence, Black and Gilson (1998) argue that informationally efficient stock markets are crucial for venture capital funding.

While research has revealed informational deficits in capital markets, avenues to bridge such information gaps have been suggested in the literature. According to Ehrat (1997) approximately 80 per cent of all technical knowledge is disclosed in public patent databases. Moreover, this information is disclosed as patents are filed up to three years before the invention is commercialised and returns are generated (see, for example, Ernst, 2001). This means that patent information is not only relevant for the assessment of firms' performance, but is also forward-looking.

The value-relevance of patent information has been confirmed empirically. For example, Ramb and Reitzig (2005a; 2005b) show that European patent applications have a stronger correlation with companies' market value than activated R&D investments on their balance sheet. Moreover, several studies suggest that patent information explains the market value of firms better than information provided in annual financial statements. This is evident from studies conducted by Hirschey and Richardson (2004) in relation to US firms, but is also found to be true for Japanese firms (Hirschey and Richardson, 2001) as well as German ones (Trautwein, 2007).

However, because the value distribution of patents is highly skewed, it is difficult for corporate outsiders to evaluate and distinguish valuable patents from the large number that are of low value (see, for example, Gambardella et al., 2008). Patent information is also relatively complex and cannot be easily assessed without specific knowledge about the patent system. Moreover, in focusing on patent information, past research has failed to link the managerial aspects of the intangible economy to its capital market implications. Although several studies show that both patents and trademarks are reflected in market values, they consider IPR as outputs of R&D investments, rather than in the wider context of firms' business models and competitive strategies. Because companies' ability to materialise their R&D investments depends on their IPR management, the present study claims that investors need to assess companies' IPR management as part of their investment analysis, which can only partly be done through published patent information.

The scientific objective of the present study is threefold. Firstly, it aims to enhance the understanding of how technology-driven companies use IPR to generate profits based on their R&D investments. This should enable investors to make better assessments of companies' profit potential, and thus their value. Secondly, it looks to examine to what extent companies' IPR management is reflected in their share price performance, and thereby to identify potential areas of asymmetric information. Thirdly, it intends to suggest ways in which such information asymmetries can be reduced in order to improve the informational efficiency of capital markets and to facilitate the financing of technological innovation. In this respect, the present study goes beyond the existing literature in the following ways:

Through the identification of value-relevant IPR management indicators.[4] Although a significant amount of important empirical research has been conducted on companies' patenting behaviour (see, for example, Blind et al., 2006; Cohen, 2005; Pitkethly, 2001), none of these studies has provided a holistic conceptualisation of companies' IPR management. Accordingly, theory development has lagged behind in explaining how firms integrate and organisationally implement IPR strategies to profit from their technological innovations. To bridge this research gap the present study develops a conceptual framework for how pharmaceutical companies conduct their IPR management, and also how that contributes to their financial performance. This framework serves as a starting point for the operationalisation of value-relevant IPR management indicators – enabling investors to better assess the ability of firms to systematically materialise their R&D investments.

By examining whether IPR management information is reflected in share prices. To my knowledge, there is no empirical research on the role of IPR management information in financial analysts' investment analysis, nor on valuations of stock markets. Although several studies have examined the impact of patent and trademark applications on companies' stock market performance (see, for example, Greenhalgh and Rogers, 2006;

Neuhäusler et al., 2011; Sandner and Block, 2011), the stock market's valuation of IPR within the wider context of companies' business models has so far been ignored. Instead, past studies have considered IPR to be the outcome of innovation activities. However, the patent behaviour of firms shows that IPR are no longer only a consequence of an invention, but that firms also have different strategic motives for patenting depending on their business model. The present study therefore looks at whether companies' IPR management – including the strategic use of IPR – contributes to their share price performance. In doing so, it assesses the informational efficiency of equity markets.

By examining whether IPR reporting can reduce asymmetric information. Companies sometimes conduct voluntary information disclosures to reduce information asymmetries, and thus their costs of capital (see, for example, Healy and Palepu, 2001). This also involves reporting on their IPR (see, for example, Seethamraju, 2003). In addition, research has shown that IPR reporting provides new value-relevant information for stock markets. For example, there is empirical evidence that patents which have received attention in the media (Austin, 1993), and the voluntary publication of information related to trademark acquisitions, both have a positive impact on stock market valuations (Seethamraju, 2003). Still, the ability of technology-driven companies to reduce asymmetric information through active IPR reporting has not received much attention in the literature, although frameworks for doing so have been suggested (see, for example, METI, 2004). Moreover, the context of companies' IPR management, which is likely to determine the value-relevance of the information provided, has been left out in the studies mentioned. The present study goes beyond past research in deriving IPR reporting indicators on the basis of how companies manage their IPR, and examining the ability of companies to reduce asymmetric information in stock markets through active reporting.

By examining whether credit rating agencies (CRAs) help reduce IPR-related asymmetric information. The role of CRAs has largely been neglected as a source of reducing informational deficits regarding technology-driven firms in capital markets. Because CRAs gather and process information from various sources, investors can reduce their own research activities and rely more on the information retrieval and analysis of CRAs. This, however, raises the question: do CRAs consider IPR information in their assessments and thereby help technology-driven firms emerge from the fog of asymmetric information? Since past research shows that patents are associated with lower risks of default (see, for example, Bittelmeyer, 2007), technology-driven firms which rely on patent protection should have lower costs of accessing debt markets, provided that CRAs incorporate patent information in their credit risk assessments. Still, empirical research on the impact of IPR information on ratings is rather limited. Czarnitzki and Kraft (2004) study the impact of R&D intensity, patent stock and newly developed products' share of sales on credit ratings given by a German rating agency. However, they do not differentiate between valuable patents and 'lemons', and thus do not consider the implications of strategic patenting. Moreover, their sample is limited to German firms covered by a national rating agency. Hence, consideration of patent information by international CRAs, such as Standard & Poor's, has to my knowledge not yet been assessed. Finally, past research on the value-relevance of patent information has largely focused on equity markets. Because credit ratings are mainly of concern to lenders, an assessment of CRA use of patent information also, at least implicitly, considers its reflection in debt security prices. In short, the present study aims to bridge this research gap by examining whether CRAs differentiate between valuable patents and lemons, and thereby communicate patent value to debt markets.

1.2   STRUCTURE OF THE STUDY

Chapter 2 consists of a review of the literature on the intangible economy and its implications for managers and investors. This is followed in Chapter 3 by an empirical analysis of the link between patent value indicators and corporate credit ratings. An exploration of pharmaceutical firms' IPR management practices, related information disclosures, and the perceived value-relevance of IPR management information among financial analysts is undertaken in Chapter 4. Chapter 5 presents an empirical study assessing stock market valuation of firms' IPR management, but also the role of voluntary disclosures in reducing stock market uncertainty. Finally, some policy implications and recommendations are derived in Chapter 6.

   Chapter 2 reviews the literature regarding the economic consequences of the intangible economy. From a managerial perspective, it reviews the literature on how companies manage their IPR to create and sustain competitive advantages. It goes on to look at the literature examining the relationship between the intangible economy and the deterioration of the value-relevance of financial statements. In doing so, it looks at sources of asymmetric information regarding technology-driven firms, and its implications for corporate finance. Finally, current disclosure regimes are reviewed to identify potential avenues for the reduction of IPR-related asymmetric information. The chapter thus identifies some sources of asymmetric information stemming from the intangible economy, but also potential ways of reducing them.

Chapter 3 addresses a specific problem related to the flow of information in capital markets and the contribution of CRAs to the reduction of asymmetric information in an intangible economy. In theory, information intermediaries provide an important function in producing and distributing information, enabling investors and creditors to reduce their own research and rely more on the analysis of CRAs. For accurate valuations and risk assessments of technology-driven firms, it is therefore important that CRAs capture information concerning their IPR. As it has been shown that patent data can be used to assess the value of patents, it provides a promising source of value-relevant information. Accordingly, Chapter 3 examines the contribution of information intermediaries to the reduction of IPR-related information asymmetries on the basis of some patent value indicators. It uses a panel dataset, comprising 191 US firms, receiving credit ratings from 1990 to 2001. The results show that patents are valued differently in CRA credit risk assessments than by stock markets. Patent flows have a substantial impact on corporate credit ratings, while patent family size only has a marginal effect. In addition, forward citations have a negative impact on firms' ratings. I argue that the negative impact of the forward citations variable is due to the increased risk of patent lawsuits, which seems likely for several reasons. I further argue that CRAs consider patents as insurance against lawsuits rather than in terms of innovation outputs. This finding suggests that CRAs do not contribute to the informational efficiency of capital markets as expected, in terms of communicating patent value as growth opportunities to investors.

Chapter 4 examines pharmaceutical firms' IPR management by means of exploratory interviews. A qualitative empirical approach was chosen in order to further specify the IPR management term and its dimensions. On the basis of this study, I develop a conceptual framework for how pharmaceutical firms conduct their IPR management that serves as the basic foundation for the operationalisation of IPR management indicators in the quantitative empirical study that follows (see Chapter 5). Notably, I find companies' IPR management to be attached to the product lifecycle, from R&D to marketing and sales. Hence, IPR management is not to be seen as a standalone task, but is rather to be considered within the framework of product management. Moreover, the IPR management experts interviewed revealed several ways in which their company's IPR management contributes to its financial performance. From a capital market perspective, I conclude that related information ought to be value-relevant.

This alone, however, does not enable me to draw conclusions on the availability of IPR management information in the public domain. Nor does it tell us whether capital markets request it. In addition, I therefore examine whether IPR management information is requested by capital market participants. Additional interviews were conducted with financial analysts to conceptualise the impact of IPR reporting on companies' share price performance. Interestingly, I find that analysts do not consider IPR as such. Rather they do so in relation to products, throughout their respective lifecycles, and in relation to technology flows in terms of patent in- and out-licensing deals.

Following the findings of Chapter 4, Chapter 5 examines two main questions: (a) do share prices reflect information on firms' IPR management? (b) Can firms reduce stock market uncertainty through IPR reporting? The chapter is based on a survey of companies' IPR management practices within the pharmaceutical industry from which I end up with a final sample of 73 companies. The first part of the chapter describes the sampling process in terms of how the data for the empirical study were gathered. Secondly, some descriptive statistics are displayed to create a better understanding of how firms manage their IPR, and which aspects they report on, but also to enhance the reader's understanding of the dataset, its benefits and limits. I then proceed to hypothesise some relationships between firms' IPR management and their share price performance, and examine these through a multivariate analysis. Finally, I turn to the relationships between firms' IPR reporting and stock market uncertainty, which are also examined through multivariate analysis.

My findings suggest that most IPR management indicators are not reflected in companies' share price, although some are. At first sight, it was troublesome to find a common denominator for the indicators exhibiting a significant impact on companies' share price performance. The general pattern, however, seems to be that the indicators with a positive significant impact are those for which related information presumably had been communicated more extensively to the stock market, probably upon request. Most notably, I find that stock markets systematically discount for firms generating their revenue on technology markets, as opposed to on product markets. I argue that this is due to asymmetric information attached to technology markets and find evidence that these asymmetries can be reduced by means of IPR reporting. I conclude that IPR reporting can help companies overcome stock market uncertainties due to asymmetric information and thereby reduce their costs of capital.

Finally, in Chapter 6, I derive some policy recommendations on how to enhance the informational efficiency of capital markets in an intangible economy, and thereby also the ability of technology-driven firms to raise funding to finance investments in technological innovation. I argue that more forward-looking financial reporting is essential, of which IPR reporting forms a part. I go on to propose the introduction of a *growth statement*, containing forward-looking information about the expected revenues and costs of the R&D projects the company pursues, to which IPR information is to be linked. In addition, I argue that companies ought to disclose more detailed information about their licensing deals, and especially the deal's financial aspects. This would make technology markets more efficient and simultaneously improve the ability of technology-driven companies to access capital markets. These suggestions are followed by some comments on the outlook for future research in this field.

NOTES

1. The present study focuses on patents and trademarks which are together referred to as IPR.
2. Insider gains refer to benefits for traders from having information that is unavailable in the public domain.
3. For example, Mansfield et al. (1977) show that only 27 per cent of R&D projects are financially successful.
4. Information that enables investors to determine the fundamental value of an investment is referred to as *value-relevant* information.

2. The intangible economy

This chapter reviews the literature in relation to the *intangible economy* – a term I use to describe the paradigm shift towards an economy in which growth is primarily driven by technological innovation. In doing so, the chapter touches upon several aspects of the economy – notably managerial and capital market-related implications – which I intend to bring together. This is because the problems of measurement and valuation that stem from the intangible economy, I argue, are best solved by: (a) creating an understanding of its managerial implications among investors, so that they request value-relevant information for consideration in their investment analysis; (b) creating incentives for managers to disclose such information by gaining knowledge about informational deficits in capital markets and their implications for corporate finance.

The first section of this chapter describes the background of these implications, stemming from the relationships between technological innovation, IPR and economic growth. These relationships are examined at firm level. Following this, I review the literature on companies' IPR management practices in terms of how they profit from technological innovation. I do so to identify the drivers of firm performance in an intangible economy, not least because related information ought to be considered by capital market participants in their investment analysis and subsequent investment decisions. I then turn to the implications for the financing of technological innovation, if value-relevant IPR management information is not sufficiently disclosed. This involves a review of the literature in relation to asymmetric information attached to technology-driven firms, the efficient-market hypothesis (EMH), corporate finance theory, and the available sources of funding for investments in technological innovation. Finally, I look at ways of reducing IPR-related asymmetric information within the framework of present disclosure regimes.

2.1 TECHNOLOGICAL INNOVATION AND ECONOMIC GROWTH

Back in prehistory, the only thing we could do with iron oxide – ordinary rust – was to use it as a pigment in painting cave walls . . . Today, we take the same iron oxide and spread it on a videotape, combine it with some aluminium, plastic, copper, and other things that go into making a VCR . . . So, those raw materials . . . can be arranged in ways that are dramatically more valuable than ever before. (Romer, 2003, p. 65)

Life in industrialised nations has become much more prosperous over the past decades and centuries. According to Romer (2003), this is due to the increasing pace of technological innovations that add to our current stock of knowledge, providing us with new ways to combine existing raw materials more effectively, ultimately contributing to economic growth. As described above in relation to iron oxide, the combined value of a certain set of raw materials can be much higher than the value of each separate material added up. This means that most of the value is not intrinsic to the raw materials as such, but rather lies in the underlying technological knowledge on how to combine them. Hence, most of the value is of an intangible nature. This would explain why fewer resources are needed today than 50 years ago to create the same, or even more, economic growth.[1] For example, in relation to manufactured goods, such as mobile phones and computers, new ideas about how tangible product characteristics may interact can add to product performance without the need for further material or tangible resources. Accordingly, the performance of a typical PC has increased substantially over the past decade, although it consists largely of the same tangible resources as ten years ago (see, for example, Romer, 2003). Moreover, only 8.5 per cent of a camera priced at 700 USD is needed to cover the cost of resources related to its physical embodiment (Lehner, 2009). Similarly, considering the evolution of the car industry over the period 1985 to 2005, one can observe an increasing value percentage related to software and electronics, growing from 4 to 33 per cent of each vehicle (ZVEI, 2006). This means that the quantity of tangible resources needed to perform the same economic functions has steadily decreased across industries, pointing to substantial productivity gains. Romer (2003) argues that this can be derived from the more intelligent use of resources, often referred to as technological innovation (see Schilling, 2009).

Several research scholars have found a link between technology and economic growth. In 1987, Robert Solow and Trevor Swan received the Nobel Prize for their contribution to growth theory, formalising labour, capital and technology as the input factors or drivers of economic growth. The Solow-Swan model, first published in 1956, assumes a standard aggregate production function with a fixed level of technology (Solow, 1956). An increase in the level of technology effectively implies improvements in the technology base, meaning that technology essentially provides a parameter for technological innovation. Hence, if the level of technology doubles, output increases by 100 per cent. On the contrary, additional labour and capital increase output at a diminishing rate, meaning that long-term economic growth essentially depends on technological innovation. This raises the question of what the drivers behind technological innovation are.

In attempts to identify these drivers, various research scholars have suggested a link to R&D spending. Nakamura (2001) finds that R&D expenditure in the US has more than doubled as a proportion of gross domestic product (GDP) since the 1950s, while investments in tangible assets, such as equipment or machinery, have remained stable. According to the European Commission (2007), R&D spending continued to grow by an additional 10 per cent in 2007 on a worldwide basis. Finally, at firm level, R&D expenditures in the USA, Japan, France and Germany surged by approximately 150 per cent between the early 1980s and the mid 1990s (see, for example, Kodama, 1995).

The OECD defines R&D as something which relates to: '. . . creative work undertaken on a systematic basis in order to increase the stock of knowledge and the use of this stock of knowledge in order to devise new materials, products, devices, processes, systems or services, or improving substantially those already produced and installed' (Van Reekum, 1999, p. 58). This implies that firms invest in R&D in order to generate new ideas that add to the current stock of accumulated knowledge. Some of these ideas can be applied and commercialised in new products and processes. Empirical studies support this view. For example, Mahlich (2005) reveals a positive correlation between R&D expenditures and the stock of knowledge, using patent applications as a proxy.[2] Furthermore, based on a sample of 1,600 technology-driven firms, Allegrezza and Guarda-Rauchs (1999) find a positive correlation between R&D expenditures and the number of trademark applications companies file. These findings indicate that R&D spending not only adds to the knowledge stock, but that the knowledge is also applied in the development of new products.[3] In addition, pioneering research by Griliches and Mairesse (1981) as well as by Clark and Griliches (1982) finds that R&D expenditures positively contribute to firms' productivity as well as their market value. This has also been confirmed by more recent studies. Using patent stocks as a proxy for the knowledge within a firm, Bloom and Van Reenen (2002) find that total factor productivity (TFP) increases by 3 per cent as the stock of patents doubles. Similarly, based on a sample of 6,757 observations for 1,216 publicly traded firms, Sandner and Block (2011) find that R&D expenditures contribute almost 20 per cent to the average company's market value. This implies that R&D generates not only new knowledge, but knowledge with an economic value. Hence, Griliches and Mairesse (1981) suggest that R&D expenditures are investments in intangible assets, in terms of providing a claim on future benefits through increased productivity and value, without having any physical or financial embodiment.

2.2   THE ECONOMICS OF INTANGIBLE ASSETS

Intangible assets have economic attributes which diverge from tangible ones. Firstly, intangible assets are not exposed to abrasion in the same way as tangible goods. On the contrary, a brand would to some extent rather gain in value as it is used and customers become more familiar with it, leading to increasing brand awareness (Aaker, 1992). Similarly, a technology becomes more valuable if it can be applied in several markets on different products (see, for example, Chiang and Mensah, 2004). This contrasts to, for instance, a car which decreases in value as it is used.

Secondly, transaction costs related to intangible assets are usually lower compared with tangible ones, not least because no physical transportation is required. Transaction costs in relation to intangible assets rather depend on the need to transfer related information or knowledge (see Wurzer and Frey, 2009). Information constitutes regularities residing in the data that agents attempt to extract from it, and can be easily transferred. Knowledge, however, is characterised by a set of expectations held by agents. These are modified by the arrival of information. This means that expectations embody the prior interactions that have taken place between agents, and hence the agent's prior learning (see Boisot et al., 2007). Prior knowledge is therefore needed to allow a contextual understanding of the message itself. For example, reading a formula will not enable an agent to use it without an understanding of its parameters. While information can be transferred without any particular contextual understanding, the transfer of knowledge involves an element of education. This means that, even if knowledge is codified, as in a computing algorithm or a chemical formula, its transfer will involve certain costs. These costs tend to increase with the tacitness of the knowledge (see, for example, Arora et al. 2002). While codified knowledge is standardised and generally easy to articulate, tacit knowledge is embedded in a context and is difficult to communicate. Hence, the more tacit the knowledge becomes, the more tangible its characteristics, at least in terms of higher transaction costs.

Thirdly, economists have often stressed the public goods characteristics of knowledge and thus of intangible assets (see, for example, Arrow, 1962; Hand and Lev, 2003). A public good is defined as a good which is either non-excludable or non-rival in use (see, for example, Burda and Wyplosz,

2005). Non-excludable implies that an agent cannot be easily blocked from using a good and therefore cannot effectively be excluded. Because intangible assets do not have any physical embodiment, it is difficult to exclude an agent from its use other than by means of secrecy or IPR. For example, the approach of secrecy has been successfully pursued by the Coca-Cola Company, in terms of not revealing its formula, for decades.

Non-rival, on the other hand, means that the consumer of a good cannot legally or physically prevent others from consuming it simultaneously. This means that the use of a public good by an additional agent does not affect its availability to other agents. Nor is the value to the first agent reduced when a second agent is present. Economically speaking, once a public good has become available, often through R&D in the case of intangible assets, the marginal cost of an additional user equals zero. Accordingly, R&D conducted by a firm spills over, meaning that related economic benefits can be internalised by a third party. This implies the presence of *positive externalities* – that is, a situation with unpriced effects – as R&D conducted by one firm contributes to the profits of other companies. The public goods characteristics of intangible assets hence render the appropriation of economic returns for the bearer of the initial investment. Assuming that it is only possible for a firm to charge a price of zero, it will have no economic incentive to invest and produce. The appropriability problem related to intangible assets would therefore lead to a situation in which innovation is under-supplied and to market failure.[4]

2.3 IPR, MONOPOLY POWER AND APPROPRIATION

Economic theory provides several potential solutions for how to correct market failure (see, for example, Stiglitz, 2008). In relation to the production and supply of intangible assets, IPR probably provide the most dominant and therefore also most debated solution. The idea behind IPR is to create incentives to innovate by restricting the appropriation of intangible assets to the innovator, allowing charges to be imposed on third parties for their use of the innovation. This enables innovators to generate economic returns on their intangible investments, preventing *free-rider problems* from occurring – that is, when third parties consume more than their share of the costs of an investment. Hence, by assigning property rights to externalities, the unpriced spillover is integrated into the market system. Economists such as Coase (1960) have therefore argued that property rights can be applied effectively to overcome externalities.[5]

Because IPR provide exclusion rights in relation to the use of an intangible asset, they are often said to assign monopoly power to the owner (see, for example, Stiglitz, 2008).[6] According to economic theory, this creates market inefficiencies as the price set for the good will be higher than the marginal cost of producing it. This means that there is a trade-off between creating incentives for innovation and higher market prices as a consequence of monopoly power (see, for example, Nordhaus, 1969). However, the question of whether, for example, patents in fact provide monopoly power is still being debated (see, for example, Pretnar, 2003), not least because the claims of a single patent most often do not cover all technological knowledge in a product. For example, a mobile phone can be protected by several thousand patents which are held by various companies. Although a single patent can provide monopoly power for its claims, it does not necessarily mean that it provides monopoly power for the product being commercialised.

Moreover, while a property right on a new technology excludes third parties from the appropriation of related economic returns, it does not prevent them from developing a competing technology – that is, making the property right irrelevant. Hence, while IPR can prevent third parties from consuming or making use of an intangible asset, it does not prevent them from affecting its value. This is referred to as *Schumpeterian competition*, and implies that competition in technological innovation leads only to temporary monopolies which are displaced as further innovation occurs and technological progress is made (see Stiglitz, 2008). Furthermore, because filing a patent involves the disclosure of information about the invention, the development of competing technologies is sometimes eased. Accordingly, firms have been successful in designing around patents, rendering appropriation for the innovator. This implies that, even though the idea of IPR is to perfectly protect against imitation, they do so imperfectly in practice. Finally, the uncertainties related to the legal boundaries of patents have led research scholars to refer to them as rights to try to exclude, rather than exclusion rights (Lemley and Shapiro, 2005).

For this reason, firms rely on additional strategies to generate economic returns based on their innovations. Empirical studies have found that firms prefer the use of trade secrecy and first-mover advantages to IPR. Still, 18–30 per cent of companies consider patents to be more important than secrecy, and 25–40 per cent consider them to be equally important (Arundel, 2001). However, this says nothing about the value of the innovation being protected. It could well be that patents are used to protect more valuable innovations than trade secrecy (see, for example, Greenhalgh and Rogers, 2010). Furthermore, empirical studies have shown that IPR contribute both to the productivity and market value of firms, indicating their importance for the appropriation of economic returns. This suggests that, although IPR in practice often do not provide monopoly power, they still contribute to the financial performance of firms, and thus provide incentives for investments in intangible assets.

2.4   IPR AND THE FINANCIAL PERFORMANCE OF FIRMS

Research on the firm-level contribution of IPR to economic growth was pioneered by Scherer (1965) and Comanor and Scherer (1969) in the 1960s, who found a positive correlation between companies' patent stock and their sales performance. More recently, Ernst (1995) found that patent active firms with a narrow technological focus outperform other companies according to various profitability and productivity measurements. In a subsequent study, he also found that patent applications are followed by increases in sales two to three years later, revealing a causal relationship between the two (Ernst, 2001). Similarly, using patent stocks as a proxy for knowledge within a firm, Bloom and Van Reenen (2002) show that companies' TFP increases by 3 per cent as their stock of patents doubles.

Besides patents, the performance relevance of trademarks and brands is also widely acknowledged. The link between the two is described by Sandner and Block (2011, p.3) as follows: 'Trademarks and brands are highly intertwined . . . The former represents the legal basis upon which the latter builds. Investments in brands, in particular advertising, would be useless if trademark rights did not prevent rivals from unfairly appropriating the value of an owned trademark through, for example, counterfeiting or imitation.'

Trademarks and brands are of interest to the present study, not least since past research shows that firms also rely on trademark protection to appropriate investments in technological innovation (Allegrezza and Guarda-Rauchs, 1999), and that the commercial functions of brands can be used to extend appropriation beyond patent expiry (see, for example, Jennewein, 2005). The performance contribution of trademarks is also shown by Greenhalgh and Longland (2005), who find that firms committed to R&D, and the filing of patent and trademark applications, are more productive than their counterparties. The increased productivity and profitability associated with both patents and trademarks are also reflected in companies' market value (Greenhalgh and Rogers, 2006; Neuhäusler et al., 2011). Similarly, Griffiths et al. (2005) find that patents and trademarks, as well as design rights, are associated with higher stock market valuations. They show that patents and trademarks exhibited the strongest impact, while the contribution of design rights was found to be relatively marginal. In a later study, Sandner and Block (2011) find that 8.1 per cent of publicly traded firms' market value can be explained by their trademark portfolios, and 4.7 per cent by their patent portfolios. Hence, the productivity gains related to IPR are also, at least to some extent, reflected in valuations by stock markets.

Strands of the literature have also focused on the value of trademarks beyond their function as legal right, in terms of their commercial function as brand, for which the trademark provides the anchor (Phillips, 2003). For example, Barth et al. (1998) find that valuable brands contribute to annual shareholder returns. Furthermore, Aaker and Jacobson (1994) examine the impact of brand changes on annual stock returns over the period 1989 to 1992. In conformity with the findings of Barth et al. (1998), they show that firms with the largest gains in brand equity on average outperformed other companies, with 30 per cent higher BHR, and that companies with the largest losses in brand equity averaged negative stock returns of 10 per cent. In a subsequent study, Aaker and Jacobson (2001) find that changes in brand attitude also have an impact on stock market returns and firms' financial accounting performance. However, awareness that did not translate into a positive brand attitude did not contribute much to the firm's market value. Finally, Lane and Jacobson (1995) find that branding strategies, in terms of brand extension announcements, positively contribute to firms' market value. This leads me to conclude that trademarks as such, but also how they are used, are relevant to the financial performance of companies.

How patents are used also seems to have an impact on how companies are valued. For example, Austin (1993) investigates the value contribution of patents, using the capital asset pricing model (CAPM). In doing so, he also accounts for the impact of competitors' patents. Using an event-study methodology, he finds the average performance impact of patents owned by the firm to be positive, while patents filed by competitors had a negative impact on its share price. Hence, competitor patents seem to be perceived as threats, restraining firms' possible competitive actions. This suggests that stock markets not only consider patents as means to protect techno-logical innovations, but also as important instruments to secure a company's competitive position. In addition, Austin (1993) finds that patents which are linked to products have a higher value than non-linked ones, as do patents which have received attention in the media. This finding implies that patents mainly contribute to firm performance when they relate directly to its business, and related information is communicated to the stock market. Accordingly, for patents to be comprehensively reflected in share prices, relevant information must be publicly available.

Finally, past studies have also investigated the explanatory relevance of patents, concerning firm performance, compared with traditional financial indicators. Notably Ramb and Reitzig (2005a; 2005b) find that European patent applications have a stronger correlation with the market value of firms than activated R&D investments on their balance sheet. That patent information explains the market value of firms better than information being published in firms' annual financial statements is also evident from studies conducted by Hirschey and Richardson (2004) in relation to US firms, but is also found to be true for Japanese firms (Hirschey and Richardson, 2001) as well as German ones (Trautwein, 2007). Accordingly, it has been suggested that patents can be used to signal future economic benefits to capital markets (see, for example, Blind et al., 2006) – a view that has also received empirical support.

2.5 PERFORMANCE-RELEVANT CONTINGENCY FACTORS

Although IPR contribute to the financial performance of firms, the effectiveness and use of different types of IPR vary across industries. For example, Arundel and Kabla (1998) show that the number of patentable inventions that turn into a patent, referred to as the patent propensity, varies from 8 per cent in the textile and clothing industry to 80 per cent in the pharmaceutical industry. The divergence in the use of patents among industries can be explained by differences in their effectiveness in allowing firms to appropriate economic returns.

Based on a survey among 650 firms, Levin et al. (1987) investigate the appropriability conditions regarding patents across industries. In doing so, they find substantial differences in the perceived effectiveness of patent protection. Both product and process patents were found to be least effective in the paper industry, while they were found to be most effective in the pharmaceutical industry. Similarly, Mansfield et al. (1981) find that patents have the strongest impact on imitation costs in relation to pharmaceutical products. In contrast to these findings, however, Schankerman (1998) shows that only about 5–10 per cent of R&D investments in the pharmaceutical and chemical industry were recovered by means of patent protection, compared with almost 15–35 per cent in the electronics and automotive industry. He argues that this is due to the stringent price regulations on pharmaceutical products in France, which undermine the effectiveness of patents.[7] This argument is consistent with the findings not only of Lanjouw (1998) – who studies the effectiveness of patent protection in the German pharmaceutical industry, where prices are largely unregulated – but also of Arora et al. (2002) and Bessen and Meurer (2008a).

In addition, it has been argued that the private value of trademarks varies greatly across industries, being notably higher in service sectors (Greenhalgh and Rogers, 2006), and some technology-driven industries, such as the sector for biotechnology and pharmaceuticals (Sandner and Block, 2011). The importance of trademarks in protecting pharmaceutical innovations is also pointed out by Malmberg (2005), who finds a positive correlation between trademark applications and new medicines. This suggests that trademarks relate to firms' innovation activities, and provide an important instrument for the appropriation of economic returns, at least in certain technology-driven industries. Following these findings, the factors driving the effectiveness of IPR protection are considered.

2.5.1 Technological Complexity

Industries differ according to whether they are dominated by discrete or complex technologies. Several studies investigating the effectiveness of patent protection across industries have differentiated these accordingly (see, for example, Arundel and Kabla, 1998; Cohen et al., 2000; Levin et al., 1987). Discrete technologies have few clearly identifiable features that are directly related to a specific product. Hence, only a few patents are required to achieve effective protection. This is true of the pharmaceutical and chemical industry where compounds can be sufficiently protected by single patents to enable immediate commercialisation without the need to access external proprietary technologies (see, for example, Cohen et al., 2000; Hussinger, 2006). In contrast, complex technologies consist of several subsystems, which are required for the commercialisation of a product. This creates interdependencies among firms as they need to rely on external proprietary technologies to be able commercialise their products without infringing third party patents (Hall and Ziedonis, 2001; Reitzig, 2004c). Complex technologies are common in the ICT industry where products, such as mobile phones, consist of several sub-technologies, developed by different companies. Because related patents are also often held by several competing companies, *patent thickets* may occur (see, for example, Cohen et al., 2000; Harhoff and Reitzig, 2001; Shapiro, 2001).[8] As a consequence, relatively speaking, many patent applications are filed in complex technology industries, as companies look to increase their bargaining power upfront in cross-licensing deals.

2.5.2 Product Lifecycle

It has also been argued that the effectiveness of patent protection depends on the length of the product lifecycle. For example, Gottschalk et al. (2002)

find that first-mover advantages are more frequently used as a means for appropriation in industries with comparatively short product lifecycles, such as in ICT and mechanical engineering, than in the chemical industry where product lifecycles are generally considerably longer. Because patents are granted 18 months after application is filed, they provide ineffective means of protection if product lifecycles are short. Accordingly, Hall and Ziedonis (2001) suggest that secrecy and first-mover advantages provide more effective protection if the time to obtain the patent is longer than the product lifecycle. This implies that patents are more valuable in industries with longer product lifecycles, not least because trade secrecy most often does not provide a sustainable means of effective appropriation (see, for example, Denicolo and Franzoni, 2004), as employees with important technological knowledge switch companies over time (see, for example, Cohen et al., 2002).

2.5.3   Product Characteristics

Trademarks are arguably of higher value in industries where search costs are high (see, for example, Gottschalk et al., 2002). This is because if search costs are low, which is usually the case in industries for specialised goods, trademarks are not such an important way for customers to identify a product as there are fewer or no competing products. Similarly, trademarks are more important in relation to product innovations, since these provide means of communication to the end-customer. Because process innovations most often relate to efficiency gains, which are not necessarily observed directly by the end-customer, trademarks provide more effective means of appropriating returns from product innovations, for which marketing is usually conducted.

   The patent propensity is also higher for products than for processes (see, for example, Arundel and Kabla, 1998; Arundel, 2001; Hussinger, 2006), since patents provide a more effective means of protection for products (see, for example, Cohen et al., 2000; Levin et al., 1987). This is not least because third party infringements are easier to detect for products than for rather complex processes, meaning that product patents are also easier to enforce. Accordingly, these studies claim that secrecy is often a more effective instrument for the appropriation of returns from process innovations.[9]

2.5.4   Complementary and Financial Resources

Financial resources are important for companies to achieve effective appropriation, both by means of patent and trademark protection. This is because IPR protection is expensive to obtain, but also to maintain.

For example, the costs attributed to a single patent application amount to around 23,000 USD in Europe, and approximately 34,000 USD in the US (Hall et al., 2004).[10] Trademark protection is comparatively less expensive, costing around 2,000 EUR for a European community trademark (CTM) (Greenhalgh and Rogers, 2006).[11] However, there are significant costs associated with the establishment of a strong brand, on which basis economic returns can be effectively appropriated, often amounting to several million EUR. According to Tauber (1998), the introduction of a product with a new brand name on average cost 150 million USD, and even the introduction via brand extensions cost approximately 50 million USD. Also, to achieve effective appropriation several patents and trademarks can be required (see, for example, Jennewein, 2005), which only larger firms often have the financial means to maintain. Furthermore, smaller firms generally do not have the financial resources to monitor competition in order to detect potential patent and trademark infringements (see, for example, Arundel and Kabla, 1998).

The costs of enforcement can be even higher. According to the European Commission (2007), the legal costs alone of pursuing patent ligation in four member states would amount to between 310,000 and 1,950,000 EUR.[12] This ignores a substantial part of the costs associated with patent lawsuits, which also involve additional indirect costs. For example, pending litigation can shut down production, sales and marketing, and even without a preliminary injunction consumers may stop purchasing the product. Additional costs can come as a consequence of managerial distraction and a higher risk of bankruptcy (see, for example, Bessen and Meurer 2008b).

Finally, larger firms have advantages in terms of being able to realise economies of scope and scale with their IPR. Because these possess additional complementary resources, such as distribution and marketing channels, they can apply their patents and trademarks to a wider range of products, markets and industries. Notably, Garcia-Vega (2006) shows a positive relationship between a firm's degree of diversification and the size of its patent portfolio. In addition, Chiang and Mensah (2004) find that firms which are highly diversified, and have a larger share of intangible assets, exhibit higher growth rates. This means that larger diversified companies are able to generate more value out of their IPR. Hence, the use of patents and trademarks increases with the size of the firm (Allegrezza and Guarda-Rauchs, 1999; Zimmermann and Schwalbach, 1991). For the above-mentioned reasons, SMEs often rely on informal means of protection, such as trade secrecy (Kuusito and Paallysaho, 2007).

2.6   IPR IN A MANAGERIAL CONTEXT

Intellectual property rights can help a firm gain competitive advantage in various ways . . . Combinations of patents and trademarks can help sustain IP-based competitive advantages. (Reitzig, 2004a, p. 35)

With an increasingly intangible economy, IPR management has become a subject of growing relevance, among both practitioners and research scholars. This chapter reviews the literature on how firms manage their patents and trademarks. It shows that firms do so commercially, from a resource-based view, in order to profit from technological innovation, but also strategically, from a market-based view, to secure their competitive position. In the present study, the systematic use of IPR, commercially and strategically, to gain and sustain technology-based competitive advantages will be referred to as IPR management.

2.6.1   Patents in a Managerial Context

2.6.1.1   The functions of patents

A substantial part of the strategic management literature has been devoted to the study of sources of sustained competitive advantage. In what can be described as a dichotomy, one strand of research scholars postulates the resources of the firm as the essential determinant of competitive advantages (see, for example, Barney, 1991; Prahalad and Hamel, 1990), while environmental or market-based models tend to focus on opportunities and threats outside the boundaries of the firm (see, for example, Porter, 1985). Within resource-based models, technological knowledge has gained recognition as a resource in itself (see, for example, Grant, 1996), essential to the development of new competitive technology-based products. However, although empirical research shows that patents, as proprietary rights on firms' technology resources, substantially raise imitation costs in technology-driven industries (Mansfield et al., 1981; Levin et al., 1987), IPR have generally been excluded from such explanatory frameworks. Meanwhile, firms manage their patents to protect products and technologies from imitation and obtain exclusivity in the appropriation of economic returns (see, for example, Blind, 2006; Pitkethly, 2001). This is true not least of the pharmaceutical industry, where product development costs have increased substantially in recent years (see Lehman, 2003). Hence, pharmaceutical firms heavily rely on patents to support their product market strategy in safeguarding their market share throughout the product lifecycle (Arundel and Kabla, 1998; European Commission, 2009).[13] From a resource-based point of view, this means that patents enable them to establish competitive advantages in making technology resources imperfectly imitable (see, for example, Barney, 1991). In doing so, they provide important isolation mechanisms, postulated as crucial to firm performance by resource-based theorists (see, for example, Grant, 1991; Wernerfelt, 1984).

Patents are also used strategically to defensively and offensively block competitors. The use of patents in a broader sense than the protection of technological inventions is suggested by the changing application behaviour of firms. Until the mid 1980s the relationship between patent applications and R&D investments remained fairly stable. However, by the mid 1980s a structural break can be observed from which the growth rate in patent application increased considerably faster than the respective growth rate in R&D investments (see, for example, Blind et al., 2003; Cohen, 2005). In other words, patent applications relative to R&D investments increased rapidly. A possible explanation is that firms have experienced substantial productivity gains in R&D. This is suggested by Janz et al. (2001), who argue that companies' R&D has become more efficient and differentiated, leading to a higher number of patent applications per unit invested in R&D, due to a larger number of inventions.[14] But Hall and Ziedonis (2001) find no empirical evidence of increasing efficiency in firms' R&D activities. Instead they conclude that firms increasingly use patents strategically in order to build a strong competitive position and access third party technologies, rather than as a means of appropriating economic returns.[15] The strategic dimension of the surge in patent applications is also shown by Blind et al. (2004) in relation to a tendency in companies' IPR management – moving towards more complex and comprehensive patent strategies.

A definition of strategic patenting is provided by Arundel and Patel (2003), distinguishing it from what is referred to as traditional patenting:

> An alternative and more precise definition of strategic patenting is based on a comparison with 'traditional' patenting. The traditional function of a patent is to provide firms with an exclusive right to commercialise or license a patented invention, although it is up to the firm to defend its patent rights in court. Strategic patenting, in contrast, covers patent strategies that are used by firms to extend the function of patents beyond exclusive use. (Arundel and Patel, 2003, p. 3)

A number of studies have also investigated the use of patents beyond their function as an exclusive right empirically, revealing several additional patent functions (see, for example, Blind et al., 2006; Ceccagnoli et al., 2005; Cohen et al., 2002). Firstly, firms use patents to defensively block competitors in terms of protecting technology resources that the firm currently does not use, but that might be of relevance to future business models (see, for example, Granstrand, 1999). By means of defensive blocking, firms can react to shifts in competition and preserve their technological edge in future markets or technological fields without being restricted in their product development efforts due to inadequate patent protection (see, for example, Blind et al., 2006; Cohen et al., 2002; Duguet and Kabla, 1998). For example, firms proactively block competitors to secure freedom-to-operate (FTO),[16] and thus reduce risks of infringing third party patents when the product is commercialised (Cohen et al., 2002; European Commission, 2009), or simply to enable the firm to move into new markets for which a technology seems promising. Patents can accordingly be seen as a real option that enables further strategic decisions in the future (see, for example, Pitkethly, 2003; Reitzig, 2002). Through such responsiveness, firms have the ability to develop new competitive advantages in environments of rapid technological change, referred to as dynamic capabilities (Teece et al., 1997). This implies a need for firms to adapt to changes in competitive forces and deploy technology resources accordingly to create new competitive advantages as old ones are being eroded.

Patents are also used offensively to actively hinder third parties from pursuing their product development activities (see, for example, Blind et al., 2006; Cohen et al., 2002; Pitkethly, 2001). Related motives can be to restrain the market power of suppliers and enhance the firm's bargaining power within the industry (see, for example, Greenhalgh and Rogers, 2010). Hence, patents are used to counteract competitive forces within industries, described in environmental models pioneered by Porter (1985). For instance, by means of offensive blocking, firms can prevent competitors from developing technological solutions that circumvent or substitute the firm's proprietary technology (Cohen et al., 2002). Thus, it is essential for pharmaceutical firms to prevent competitors from the commercialisation of competing substitute substances by also protecting the surroundings of their products (European Commission, 2009), thus overcoming the threat of substitution (see, for example, Gassmann and Von Zedtwitz, 2004). From a market-based view, this contributes to the financial performance of firms, since the threat of substitution determines the prices firms can charge within an industry (Porter, 1985).

Finally, companies rely on patents to acquire and commercialise technologies. For example, Arora et al. (2002) point to the increasing specialisation of firms in different stages of the R&D process, leading to the division of innovative labour. Firms, hence, collaborate in technology-based product development (Rothaermel and Deeds, 2004). In the pharmaceutical industry, this mainly relates to the integration of biotechnology into the development of pharmaceutical products, which has led to the formation of specialised dedicated biotechnology firms (DBFs), focusing on early stage product development. Because these firms rely on collaboration partners in order to finance their research activities, patent licensing provides an integral part of their business model (see, for example, Farag, 2009; Lerner et al., 2003). Sheehan et al. (2004) also find that the generation of licensing revenue is an important reason for companies to patent, enabling them to generate economic returns on the technology market without product commercialisation. Gassmann et al. (2010) accordingly argue that the competitive advantage of these firms depends on their IPR.

In addition, Chesbrough and Teece (1996) conclude that only a few firms can afford to develop all the technologies that might provide a competitive advantage internally, implying a need for firms to acquire external proprietary technology resources to maintain their technological edge. This is suggested by research showing a demand among established pharmaceutical firms for access to external technology resources. The pharmaceutical industry, for example, exhibits the highest share of firms perceiving patent in-licensing as increasingly important (Sheehan et al., 2004). In particular, pharmaceutical firms with relatively thin product pipelines are found more likely to license proprietary external technologies to bridge internal weaknesses as well as building new strengths through the accumulation of external technology resources (Higgins and Rodriguez, 2006). This requires the acquisition and integration of external technological knowledge (Leonard-Barton, 1995; March, 1991), but also of related patents (Bader, 2008; Lichtenthaler, 2006).[17]

2.6.1.2 Patent portfolio management

Past studies reveal different approaches towards patent portfolio management. For example, it is common that companies in complex technology fields use their patent portfolio to achieve a dominant market position (Bekkers et al., 2002). This strategy is based on an agglomeration of the firm's patent portfolio, with single patents related to diverse technology fields, rather than the creation of a coherent patent portfolio around core technologies. Accordingly, industry structures emerge where firms depend on each other's patents for the commercialisation of their respective technologies and products. The logic behind this can be better understood by looking at how Motorola used its patent portfolio to enhance its competitive position in the 1980s:

> By using the negotiation power that came with its patent portfolio, Motorola could dictate its licensing conditions to all firms. The company thus imposed a market structure by conducting exclusive cross-license agreements with a

selected number of other parties on the market . . . As a result, the importance of Motorola in the network of strategic alliances increased drastically in the late 1980s. (Bekkers et al., 2002, p. 1060)

And indeed, Motorola was acquired by Google for a colossal 12.5 billion USD in August 2011 – a deal which Google priced on a cost-per-patent basis (*The Economist*, 2011). In contrast, in discrete technology industries, companies tend to use their patent portfolio as a fence around important products and processes (Cohen et al., 2000), leading to a more coherent portfolio built around core technologies. For these firms *patent bulks* serve as fences around the core technology, whereas in complex technologies patent thickets lead to technological interdependencies among firms.[18] However, Reitzig (2004b) shows that firms in discrete technologies file more patents than are needed for the commercialisation of the actual product. It shall, however, be noted that the motive for doing so is quite different. Kingston (2001) argues that in discrete technology industries patents are primarily used offensively in order to actively prevent others from using an invention, thereby hindering substitution; while in complex technology industries strategic patenting rather focuses on securing FTO so that the company is not restricted from using a technology. Furthermore, Reitzig (2004b) finds that the value of complex technology patents that are used exclusively by their owners increases with the number of surrounding patents. On the contrary, the value of patents protecting discrete technologies have an inverse relationship with the size of the bulk, and hence decreases with the number of surrounding patents. This suggests that patent fences in discrete technologies are only value enhancing if substitute technologies are easy to obtain. For this reason, an extensive patent portfolio does not automatically contribute to these companies' financial performance (Reitzig, 2004b). Rather, some research scholars have suggested that in providing ineffective means for appropriation, an extensive patent portfolio mainly provides a cost-driver. For example, Bhatia and Carey (2007, p. 15) argue that: 'Today leading firms are finding they can make more profit with fewer patents by focusing on securing only the essential protections they need to exploit the innovation . . . for technology firms, a highly disciplined patent strategy, tightly connected to the overall business strategy, is becoming essential to long-run success.' This implies that patents are mainly of commercial relevance if they protect relevant products and technologies. Findings by Grindley and Teece (1997) support this view in showing that the value of firms' patents depends on the alignment towards technology fields where the firm possesses particular strengths. Otherwise, an extensive patent portfolio increases costs rather than enhances firm performance.

Finally, research shows that the value distribution within a firm's patent portfolio depends on the firm's motive to patent. By matching survey data with secondary patent data, Blind et al. (2009a) find that the patent strategy being pursued – that is, the company's motive to patent – is correlated with the value distribution of the company's patent portfolio. In their study, they consider three main motives to patent – protection, blocking and exchange. These motives were matched with well-established indicators of patent value, such as forward and backward citations as well as oppositions filed against the patent.[19] As expected, companies which rely on patents for protection against imitation had patent portfolios exhibiting a relatively large share of valuable patents, while firms using patents for defensive blocking and exchange purposes had a comparatively low share of valuable patents in their portfolio. Accordingly, the motive to patent, being the function the patent serves for a company's strategy, will have an impact on its value. This supports the argument that companies can achieve the same or better financial performance with fewer patents, by focusing on the protection motive. Still, a high share of low value patents can support a firm's strategy in creating additional bargaining power. It is therefore important to consider the managerial context in which the patent is being used.

2.6.2 Trademarks in a Managerial Context

2.6.2.1 The complementary function of trademarks

The protection of competitive advantages usually does not depend on a single patent but rather on a combination of different types of IPR (see, for example, Jennewein, 2005). This is suggested by Graham and Somaya (2006), who show how firms use different types of IPR, such as patents and trademarks, as complements rather than substitutes.

While patents provide a limited term exclusive right granted to an inventor in return for the disclosure of technical information about the invention,[20] the rights associated with trademarks, by contrast, have no maximum duration, provided they continue to be used in trade.[21] This means that since trademarks have no maximum duration, they can be used to sustain competitive advantages created under patent protection even after the expiry of the patent (see, for example, Teece, 1986). Accordingly, Parchomovsky and Siegelman (2002) argue that both patents and trademarks can be used in a complementary way to appropriate intangible investments. Patents protect technological advantages, while trademarks enable firms to establish sustainable goodwill that maintains the technological reputation created under patent protection among customers. This can enable patentees at least partially to preserve market share after patent protection expires. Hence, Mendonca et al. (2004) argue that a major strategic motive for establishing trademark protection is to extend appropriation beyond patent expiry.

Jennewein (2005) exemplifies this with two case studies – Bayer and Cisco Systems. When Bayer entered the pharmaceutical industry in 1899, one of the first tasks of the section for testing new drugs was to find a salicylic acid – commonly used for the treatment of infections and rheumatism – with fewer side-effects than those of current products. In pursuit of this objective, chemist Felix Hoffmann invented a method for producing a pure and durable form of acetylsalicylic acid (ASA) more effectively than earlier methods. Based on this method, Aspirin was developed. Bayer obtained trademark protection for Aspirin in almost every country in the world, and when it was launched in tablet form, each tablet was stamped with the Bayer-Cross, clearly stating the connection between Aspirin and Bayer. After the success of Aspirin in Europe, Bayer decided to launch it also in the US, where within four years they achieved almost 30 per cent of their sales. After realising the magnitude of Hoffmann's invention, Bayer tried to file for patent protection on its improved production process for ASA and trademark protection on the name Aspirin wherever possible. However, patent protection was only obtained in countries that disregarded the fact that the chemists Gerhard and Kraut had invented ASA years before. The US was, accordingly, the only country where Bayer obtained a patent. Although Bayer did not achieve patent protection in most countries, they were able to exclude competition through trade secrets, since it was extremely hard to produce ASA in large quantities, especially in tablet form, at a reasonable cost. When their US patent expired in 1917, Bayer had succeeded in establishing a strong brand so that when US competitors entered the market that year most customers did not know that they could buy identical products under another trademark, since they regarded Aspirin as a drug in its own right. Based on the synergies between patents, trade secrets, and trademarks, Bayer had established a dominant market position in the US. Accordingly, while patents were central to excluding competitors from the appropriation process and to gaining a technology lead, Bayer needed to rely on trademarks to extend appropriation by protecting brand equity generated under patent protection.

Cisco Systems had similar success, but under very different conditions. In the early 1990s the industry for network equipment was fast moving and uncertain. It was therefore almost impossible for Cisco Systems to provide a complete solution with the latest technology in all fields through internal innovation. They therefore started acquiring small R&D-intensive firms possessing technology-based competitive advantages, but which did not have the necessary marketing and distribution resources for successful product commercialisation. Their strategy combined the acquisition of external patented technologies with internal R&D to finish the development and integrate the technologies of the acquired firms, while keeping the firm's business units at the technological edge in their respective fields. Moreover, Cisco Systems created a number of strategic partnerships with firms that could complement their products but which were considered to be too far from their own core business. Following this strategy, by the end of 2001 the Cisco System brand for networking equipment and internet protocol was valued at 17 billion USD. In essence, these examples show how companies use different types of IPR to create and sustain technology-based competitive advantages.

2.6.2.2 Trademarks and brand equity

The sustainability of technology-based competitive advantages created depends, as we have seen, on the ability of the company to establish brand equity on this basis. While brands relate to the perception of a product among customers, trademarks confer exclusive rights to use a brand that enable firms to appropriate related economic returns (Mendonca et al., 2004). According to WIPO (2004, p. 13), a trademark is defined as a 'sign, or a combination of signs, which distinguishes the goods or services of one enterprise from those of another'. The sign may constitute words, graphics, figures, images and even sounds, shapes and colour that can be used as a distinctive feature. This means that trademarks provide an essential instrument of differentiation, allowing products to be distinguished from those in competition, and thereby enable firms to create brand equity by means of marketing. The trademark, accordingly, carries information about a certain product, which it delivers to the market. As suggested by Landes and Posner (1987), trademarks reduce customer search costs by distinguishing products and signalling consistency in quality, allowing firms to charge higher prices. In doing so, they represent a guarantee for the quality of the product which reduces risk for the customer in his purchase through trademark identification (Malmberg, 2005). This encourages firms to improve their offerings further – since advantages created can be sustained and appropriated – and to invest into brand equity. Hence, trademarks provide the legal anchor for the use of the commercial functions of brands (Phillips, 2003). According to Aaker (1995), trademarks thus enable companies to establish:

- brand loyalty;
- brand awareness;
- perceived quality;
- brand associations or image.

Brand loyalty refers to the way consumers relate to a brand, and is influenced by the satisfaction of the customer, but also by individual associations (Aaker, 1991). By building brand loyalty firms can create a loyal customer base, which raises customer switching costs – providing a barrier to entry for competitors (Aaker, 1995). In this sense, brand loyalty expresses the probability of the customer changing brand if the product or technology experiences a change in its performance, characteristics or price. Furthermore, Tsao and Chen (2005) show that switching costs increase with the differentiation of the brand, meaning that differentiation enhances brand loyalty. Accordingly, Bennett and Rundle-Thiele (2005) argue that: 'Differentiation is likely to be the key driver of brand loyalty.' This is also suggested by empirical evidence showing that loyalty intentions are largely a function of perceived value early in the product lifecycle (Johnson et al., 2006), which is related to the features and attributes of the product. These aspects provide the basis for premium pricing and make customers less sensitive to prices by creating a loyal customer base (Dall'Olmo et al., 1997; Reichheld, 1996). A high brand loyalty on the part of the customer consequently enhances trust in the brand relative to the competition, and thereby increases the customer base, which in turn reduces promotion and customer acquisition costs (see, for example, Jones and Sasser Jr, 1995; Reichheld, 1996; Uncles and Laurent, 1997). Accordingly, Fornell et al. (2006) find a positive correlation between companies' financial performance and customer loyalty. From a strategic point of view, this gives the firm time to react to possible market shifts, such as threats from competition (see, for example, Lane and Jacobson, 1995; Porter, 1991; Zeithaml, 1988).

Brand awareness, on the other hand, is the capacity of a potential buyer to recognise or memorise a specific brand in relation to the product. It is often an important influencing factor in the purchase decision process and is therefore crucial to the marketing and communication activities of a firm. Among potential customers, it represents an advantage with regard to competitors with less recognised brands, since unfamiliar brands are most often not even considered by customers in the purchasing process. For example, in a taste test, more than 70 per cent of the customers chose known brands, although in a blind test it was shown that they considered other products to be superior (Hoyer and Brown, 1990). Moreover, research shows that brand awareness is especially important in the purchasing decisions of inexperienced customers. According to studies by Hoyer and Brown (1990), 93.5 per cent chose familiar brands in initial purchases, and customers that are aware of one brand sample fewer brands in product trials. However, the awareness of potential customers about a certain brand should not be regarded as a guarantee of high sales volumes by itself. According to Bettman et al. (1991), various types of information are considered in purchasing decisions. Studies investigating the correlation between advertising – which can be seen as an investment in the creation of brand awareness (Macdonald and Sharp, 2003) – and sales, show mixed results. While studies by Bass and Clarke (1972) and Bass and Leone (1983) reveal a positive correlation between the two, Bogart (1986) could not confirm their findings.

Brand quality refers to the quality a current or potential customer perceives in a product. For example, studies conducted by Herrmann et al. (2007) show that the product has the strongest impact on brand equity. Theoretically, this is because the quality of products can be converted into perceived quality, related to the brand, which can be sustained long after the superior characteristics of the actual product have become obsolete. This can contribute to firm performance since the quality customers perceive to be associated with a specific brand is an important aspect of differentiation, and hence represents a key argument for the consumer to pay a price above that of comparable offerings (Aaker, 1991; Buzzell and Gale, 1987).

Several research scholars have also recognised the importance of brand image – that is, the degree to which a brand is associated with the general product category in the mind of the consumer – to create sustainable competitive advantages through brand equity (see, for example, Biel, 1992; Keller, 2000). According to Aaker (1992, p. 29): 'Brand associations or brand image is perhaps the most accepted aspect of brand equity.' Similarly, while Tommsdorff (1992) argues that brand image is a main driver of firm performance, Sattler (1997) finds it to be perceived as the main brand value driver across industries.

Finally, empirical research has also revealed synergies between different brand functions. For example, Li and Zhang (2008) have found that brand image positively affects relationship benefits for customers, which in turn enhances brand loyalty. This suggests several ways in which trademarks can sustain technology-based competitive advantages.

2.7 THE FINANCING OF TECHNOLOGICAL INNOVATION

2.7.1 Capital Markets and Economic Growth

> The financial system [is] the brain of the economy . . . it acts as a coordinating mechanism that allocates capital, the lifeblood of economic activity, to its most productive uses by businesses and households. If capital goes to the wrong uses

or does not flow at all, the economy will operate inefficiently, and ultimately economic growth will be low. (Mishkin, 2006, p. 342)

Firms need to invest in assets of both a tangible and an intangible nature. To fund their investments they mainly rely on internal funds in terms of earnings that they have retained.[22] However, most companies face periodic financial deficits, when they are unable to finance their investments internally. This is especially true for smaller technology-driven firms which often spend more on R&D on a yearly basis than their annual earnings, and sometimes even their annual revenues. To bridge such deficits, they rely on capital markets for external finance. A capital market channels financial capital from savers with surplus funds to other economic agents with deficit funds.[23] By allowing businesses to raise funding, it facilitates the transfer of financial capital from investors to firms with entrepreneurial or managerial talent, and thus provides an important mechanism for firms to finance growth opportunities, such as business expansions, new ventures and technological innovation.

Past research has also shown a positive correlation between the availability of private equity finance within an industry and its productivity, as well as employment levels (Bernstein et al., 2010). At national level, King and Levine (1993) show that economies with more developed financial systems also grow faster. Similarly, Levine and Zervos (1998) find that productivity gains are significantly correlated with financial development, suggesting a link between well-functioning capital markets and the performance of the real economy.[24]

This link was recognised early on by prominent research scholars such as Schumpeter (1939), who argued that technological development was dependent on the availability of financial capital. Perez (2003) also emphasised the role of financial capital in exploring the opportunities created by technological revolutions, such as new markets that drive investment in the further development of new technologies. Finally, Berger et al. (2003) find that, in both industrial and developing nations, efficiency rank, as well as market shares of domestically owned banks, is associated with higher economic performance. This implies that long-term growth – on a national level as well as on a firm level – depends on access to capital markets.

2.7.2 The Informational Efficiency of Capital Markets

Capital markets can be divided into private and public markets (see Figure 2.1). In private capital markets, capital is channelled either through financial intermediaries, such as banks and venture capital funds, or directly, for example, by angel investors. In contrast, firms in

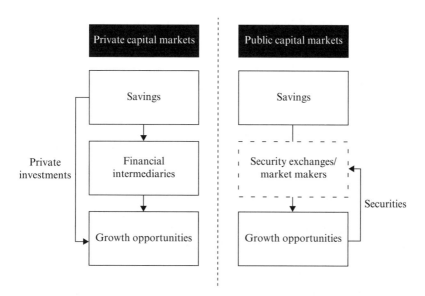

Figure 2.1   Public and private capital markets

public capital markets issue securities, which can be traded either on platform exchanges or through market makers in over-the-counter (OTC) markets.[25] This means that firms can access a broader base of investors through public markets.

A critical challenge for both private and public capital markets is the effective allocation of savings to growth opportunities. To allocate financial capital to where it can be used most productively, investors assess the net present value (NPV) of different real investments or securities. This requires access to relevant information. However, entrepreneurs and managers are generally better informed than outside investors about the value of a growth opportunity, and even have incentives to overstate its value, leading to an information problem (Healy and Palepu, 2001). In private capital markets, this is normally solved by due diligence, through which the investor acquires the relevant information to make an NPV assessment. This would be done under a non-disclosure agreement (NDA). Hence, the information does not spill over to other third parties, but solves the information problem between the investor and the firm. However, insider trading prohibitions hinder firms that are listed on a public stock market from providing information to particular investors only, in order that all investors have access to the same level of information (see Hopt and Voigt, 2004). This means that access to relevant information is mainly of concern in public capital markets.

It has often been argued that securities have a fundamental value, which is correctly known by some investors. They then purchase those securities that are undervalued and sell those that are overvalued, having compared their current price to their fundamental value. This in turn drives the price towards the fundamental value of the security (Hens and Schenck-Hoppé, 2009), on the assumption that investors have access to all value-relevant information. If this assumption fails, however, investors will systematically be unable to determine the fundamental value of the security, leading to an unproductive use of resources within the economy. The information problem is hence associated with a valuation problem. Consider, for instance, an investment decision where an investor has to decide whether to invest in a real estate project or the development of a new technology. In order to make a decision, the investor calculates the fundamental value of both projects based on the available information. Assume that sufficient information is provided for the investor to make a satisfactory assessment of the NPV of the real estate project, but that relevant information concerning the value of the technology is missing. This creates additional uncertainty related to the NPV of the technology, for which the investor will want compensation, leading to higher costs of capital for the firm wishing to finance the development of the technology.[26] This could even result in a situation where the investor underestimates the fundamental value of the technology and decides to invest in the real estate project instead, although the actual return on the technology would be comparatively higher, but insufficient information is available to make a satisfactory assessment. Consequently, financial capital will be allocated away from technological innovation, even when such investments actually yield higher returns. This means that to achieve efficient allocation of capital, markets must be informationally efficient in order for prices to reflect how capital can be most productively allocated. It is therefore important that the flow of capital is accompanied by a flow of information (see Figure 2.2). Hence, public firms disclose information to the capital market to enable investors to determine the NPV of their traded securities, and thus to overcome the information problem. This information can be communicated directly by the firm or through information intermediaries, such as financial analysts and CRAs (see Section 2.8).

2.7.2.1 The efficient-market hypothesis

The importance of information for the functioning of public capital markets has been widely acknowledged by research scholars, and even formalised into what is referred to as the efficient-market hypothesis (EMH). The EMH implies that capital markets are informationally efficient, meaning that prices on all traded securities already reflect all known

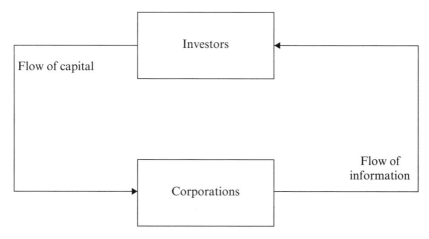

Figure 2.2   Flow of capital and information

information, and hence converge towards the fundamental value of the traded securities (Fama, 1965).

In a revised version of the EMH, Fama (1970) distinguishes between three levels of market efficiency, depending on the degree of information that is being reflected in security prices. On the first level – referred to as weak market efficiency – prices contain information about past prices' movements, meaning that it is impossible to outperform the market by studying historical prices, as prices follow a *random walk*.[27] On the second level – referred to as semi-strong market efficiency – prices, in addition, instantly adjust to reflect new information made available to the public domain. Such information can relate to earnings announcements, expansion plans, litigation issues, and so on, and may be published through a variety of information channels, including annual and quarterly reports, press releases, and conference calls. On the highest level – referred to as strong market efficiency – prices also incorporate all information that is privately held. This means that corporate insiders do not possess more information about the fundamental value of a security than outside investors. In such markets, above average returns can only be generated by chance, since it is not possible to identify superior investment strategies and insider gains cannot be made.

The EMH, however, has received considerable criticism since its development. For example, Grossman and Stiglitz (1980) have argued that strong market efficiency is impossible because if the price of a security equals its fundamental value, investors can earn no more than their cost of capital. This means that it is impossible for investors to make a profit – hence market transactions will not take place. If price and value diverged, profits could be generated by selling when the price exceeds the owner's value and buying when it is comparatively lower; while if the price equals the fundamental value there is no incentive for investors to gather costly information. The logical consequence is that, since there are no profits to cover the costs of gathering information, investors will simply not do so, meaning that all information cannot be reflected in prices. Empirical studies have also identified problems with the EMH, finding that equities with a low price-to-earnings (PE) ratio, and a low price-to-cash-flow ratio, consistently outperform other equities – something that would be impossible if the assumption that markets are always in equilibrium and perfectly arbitraged applied (see, for example, Basu, 1977; Rosenberg et al., 1985).

2.7.2.2   Asymmetric information in an intangible economy

The disruptive effects of informational inefficiencies are shown by Akerlof (1970), who illustrates how the interaction between quality, heterogeneity and asymmetric information can lead to the destruction of markets. As an example he uses the market for used cars, which he finds consists of both well-functioning and defective vehicles – the latter commonly referred to as 'lemons'. Because the seller generally knows more about the quality of the car than the buyer – meaning that there is asymmetric information between the seller and the buyer – the buyer is unable to distinguish the good cars from the lemons. This leads to a situation where sellers of good cars are unable to obtain a sufficiently high price to cover the costs of selling their cars. Hence, adverse selection occurs as the lemons drive the good cars out of the market.

Empirical studies show that asymmetric information exists also in capital markets, and especially in connection with technology-driven firms. For example, based on a sample of 253,038 purchase and sale transactions made by corporate insiders, Aboody and Lev (2000) find that gains from insider trading were comparatively substantially larger in technology-driven firms – measured by R&D intensity. Accordingly, they conclude that, due to asymmetric information regarding firms' R&D, public information fails to directly capture the productivity and value of intangible investments.[28] Moreover, findings by Daniel and Titman (2001) show that investors have difficulty in pricing intangible information compared with information on tangible assets. This is also suggested by Amir et al. (1999), who find that technology-driven firms are covered by comparatively more financial analysts, implying that they are more difficult to value. Similarly, Chung et al. (2003) investigate whether the number of analysts and the composition of the board have an impact on the valuation of R&D in equity markets.[29] Like Amir et al. (1999), they find that intangible investments are positively valued if the firm is covered by more analysts than average, and has an above average number of outside directors on the board. As previous research has shown that managerial monitoring by outside directors (see, for example, Cotter et al., 1997), as well as the number of financial analysts covering a firm (see, for example, Jensen and Meckling, 1976), reduce asymmetric information, this suggests that investors find it difficult to evaluate the commercial potential of R&D investments and the ability of firms to convert such investments into economic returns.

The literature points to at least three sources of asymmetric information, stemming from the intangible economy. These relate to:

- the characteristics of intangible assets;
- financial reporting standards and practices;
- non-transparent markets for IPR.

Various research scholars, such as Aboody and Lev (2000), have argued that the characteristics of intangible assets differ from those of tangible assets. For example, tangible commercial properties share common characteristics across firms, and hence are easily comparable for investors. In contrast, innovations are, by definition, unique. The difficulties of comparing innovations due to their uniqueness are especially troublesome because they also diverge substantially in value. Although patents and innovations are not the same, research on the value distribution of patents can be used to roughly predict the value distribution of innovations (Silverberg and Verspagen, 2007). This research shows that the value distribution is highly skewed.[30] Notably, Gambardella et al. (2008) find that, while the mean patent granted at the European Patent Office (EPO) has a value of 3 million EUR, the median is about one-tenth of the average, and the mode is only a few thousand EUR. Hence, it is difficult for investors to evaluate and distinguish valuable patents or innovations from the large number of lemons. Moreover, intangible assets are not exposed to abrasion in the same way as tangible ones. For example, a brand to some extent gains value as it is used and customers become more familiar with it, leading to increased brand awareness.[31] This means that the concept of amortisation does not apply, economically speaking, to intangible assets. Still, financial reporting standards state that intangible assets are to be amortised – something that is likely to have contributed to the deterioration of the information provided in financial statements.[32]

This leads on to the second point, which is that financial reporting standards have failed to adapt to the increasingly intangible economy. For example, Lev and Zarowin (1999) find that the decreasing informativeness of earnings releases is related to a higher rate of business change and increasing R&D intensity among companies. Accordingly, they conclude that change-drivers such as technological innovation also provide drivers for the declining usefulness of financial information. Similarly, Ballow et al. (2004) find a significant increase in companies' mean market-to-book ratio – from 1.0 in 1980 to about 5.0 in 2002.[33] Financial statements have hence lost considerable explanatory relevance concerning the market value of firms over the past 20 years. This can, at least partially, be explained by the treatment of intangible investments by accounting standards. In addition to advocating the amortisation of intangible assets, International Accounting Standards (IAS) require companies to expense all investments into research, and US Generally Accepted Accounting Principles (GAAP) advocate firms to expense both research and development outlays immediately, regardless of their economic benefits.[34] Research scholars, such as Lev (2001), have accordingly argued that corporate annual reports to a large extent do not provide sufficient quantitative or qualitative information on intangible assets to the public domain. In conformity with this view, Boone and Raman (2003) investigate the impact of changes in R&D expenditures on stocks' *bid–ask spread* and find that the off-balance sheet nature of intangible assets leads to considerable information asymmetries.[35] Moreover, in a study among 12 Italian banks, Ughetto (2007) shows that intangibles are not taken into account in a systematic way when assessing corporate credit risk. The majority of bank analysts do not even consider intangible assets as meaningful determinants in their assessments.[36] This suggests that the economic characteristics of intangible assets are not considered by financial reporting standards, nor are these assets considered to be value-relevant by financial intermediaries, often seen as important financiers for smaller technology-driven firms.

Finally, while tangible and financial assets are traded in organised markets – where prices provide information about asset values – markets for IPR are informal. Accordingly, there are no available market prices for IPR to derive information from (see Arora and Gambardella, 2010; Cockburn, 2007). While IAS allows capitalisation on the basis of the fair value of the asset, this is only permitted with reference to an active market for the asset. Küting et al. (2006) accordingly acknowledge fair value capitalisation of intangible assets to be problematic, since there are no transparent markets to derive information from (see, for example, Arora and Gambardella, 2010). For this reason, the IAS also expects markets for intangibles to be rare.

2.7.3   Asymmetric Information and Corporate Finance

The theory of corporate finance is commonly traced back to Modigliani and Miller (1958), who formalised the *capital structure irrelevance proposi-*

tion. Under the assumption of an efficient market – that is, without asymmetric information, taxes, and so on – this states that the value of a firm is unaffected by its capital structure. Decisions related to the proportions of debt and equity used to finance the firm's assets will therefore only have an impact on how cash-flows are divided among investors. The firm's costs of capital are, however, constant regardless of its leverage.

But empirical research shows that there is, in fact, asymmetric information between managers and investors, not least in an intangible economy. Theoretical models, such as pecking order theory, show that this also has implications for corporate finance decisions. The pecking order theory, proposed by Myers and Majluf (1984), assumes that a company has assets-in-place as well as a growth opportunity. To finance the growth opportunity, the firm is required to issue new shares. Due to asymmetric information, investors do not know the fundamental value of either the assets-in-place or the growth opportunity. This means that they cannot value the equity being issued (see, for example, Myers, 2003). Acquiring issued equity could be beneficial to investors if the growth opportunity turns out to have a positive NPV, but only if the new shares are not over-valued. On the other hand, if the shares turn out to be undervalued, and therefore are issued at too low a price, the value of the existing shares will be diluted. This has also been confirmed by empirical evidence showing that share prices fall by approximately 3 per cent after the announcement of an equity issue (Asquith and Mullins, 1986). Value is, hence, transferred from existing shareholders to new investors. If managers act on behalf of current shareholders – which Myers and Majluf (1984) assume – they will not issue undervalued equity unless the NPV of the growth opportunity more than covers the value being transferred away from the existing shareholders. However, in the derived equilibrium of the model, the equity issued is found to be undervalued, meaning that the losses incurred by existing shareholders – due to the bad news for the asset-in-place – will systematically outweigh the positive news of the growth opportunity. Accordingly, managers will not issue additional equity even if it means that a growth opportunity is lost.

If the firm can decide to issue debt or equity, the situation becomes slightly different. Because debt provides a prior claim on the firm's assets, while equity is a residual claim, debt investors are less exposed to valuation errors. Moreover, a debt issue will have a smaller negative impact on the firm's share price than the announcement of an equity issue – something that has also been found by empirical studies (see, for example, Eckbo, 1986; Shyam-Sunder, 1991). Managers who believe that their equity is undervalued will, therefore, prefer debt to equity. Only managers who are pessimistic about the future of the firm will rely on equity finance. However, if investors know that managers have the opportunity to issue debt securities when they are optimistic about the future, the issuance of equity signals bad news. Hence, in equilibrium, only debt will be issued. Equity is only issued if the debt is costly as a consequence of, for example, financial distress – stemming from too high a debt-to-assets ratio. In this case equity finance provides a last resort, meaning that the idea behind the pecking order is adverse selection. It shall be noted, however, that equity is not issued to finance a growth opportunity, but simply to reduce the probability of financial distress through an injection of fresh money (see, for example, Myers, 2003). The arguments stated above lead Myers and Majluf (1984) to derive the following pecking order:

- Because of asymmetric information between managers and investors, firms prefer to finance their investments through internal funds in terms of reinvested earnings or dividend cuts.
- If the firms' internal funds are inadequate, they will issue debt as a secondary option because financial managers prefer issuing debt to undervalued equity. According to pecking order theory, technology-driven firms with a high intangible-to-total assets ratio will prefer debt finance, since research has shown that their equity is systematically undervalued as a consequence of asymmetric information (see, for example, Eberhardt et al., 2004).
- Equity funding is used as a last resort to avoid financial distress, but not to fund growth opportunities.

In support of the pecking order derived above, there are other models that consider a situation with asymmetric information, but without any assets-in-place, and which also find that companies will turn to debt before issuing equity (see, for example, Ravid and Spiegel, 1997). However, pecking order theory has also received some criticism, which ought to be mentioned. It has often been suggested that public firms prefer internal funds, so as not to be controlled by capital markets (see, for example, Myers, 2003). But Myers and Majluf (1984) argue that they do so to maximise shareholder value. The assumption that managers look to maximise the value of the firm's existing shares, and thereby existing shareholder value, is however a topic of discussion (see, for example, Myers, 2003). Why should they, for instance, not act to maximise the value of the entire firm, regardless of the shareholder structure? Moreover, Myers and Majluf (1984) consider a setting in which only debt and equity is available. Other instruments such as mezzanine and convertible debt are not considered. Finally, properly designed managerial compensation contracts, in which

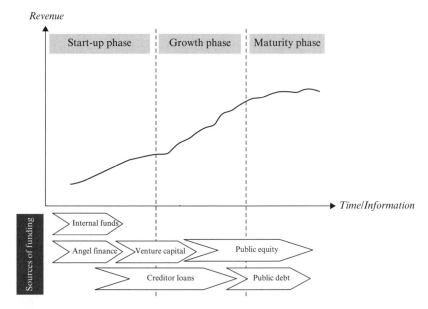

Figure 2.3   Sources of funding throughout the growth cycle

rewards are tied to firm value, could solve the adverse selection problem (Dybvig and Zender, 1991).[37]

2.7.4   Sources of Finance for Technological Innovation

The presence of asymmetric information related to technology-driven companies, and its implications for corporate finance, raises concerns about the sources available to finance investments in technological innovation. Berger and Udell (1998) illustrate how companies' financial preferences and options change as their businesses become more mature through the financial growth cycle (see Figure 2.3).[38] For example, smaller technology-driven firms initially rely on private capital markets, while larger firms with constant revenue streams and more tangible assets at the same time have better access to public capital markets. Berger and Udell (1998) argue that this is due to a higher degree of opacity and asymmetric information attached to smaller firms. Arguably financial intermediaries, who devote resources to tailoring contracts and the monitoring of firms, to produce additional information, are therefore essential for smaller firms to obtain funding (see, for example, Hadlock and James, 1997).[39] Hence, angel investors and venture capital firms are important in financing early stage technological innovation (see, for example, Kortum and Lerner,

2000; Wong, 2002). However, as the growth cycle suggests, a widely used strategy among venture capitalists is to exit through issuing publicly traded securities in terms of an IPO (see, for example, Jeng and Wells, 2000). This implies that private and public capital markets provide complementary sources for firms seeking to finance technological innovation. Accordingly, Berger and Udell (1998) highlight the interconnectedness of different sources of finance, showing that these can provide both substitutes and complements. Notable also is how information plays an integral part of their model, underlining that the sources of funding a firm can potentially access increases with the reduction of asymmetric information.

In general, past findings show that start-up firms mainly rely on insider funds (see, for example, Sahlman, 1990; Wetzel, 1994). Moreover, Rajan and Zingales (1995) find that profitability measurements are negatively associated with the debt levels companies exhibit. That more profitable companies exhibit lower debt levels is logical, because some earnings can be retained and reinvested. Accordingly, they can finance more operations internally – a finding that is in line with pecking order theory, suggesting that companies prefer to finance their operations through internal funds, at least in the presence of asymmetric information. This has been argued to be especially true for technology-driven companies, with a large share of growth opportunities to assets-in-place (see, for example, Bah and Dumontier, 2001). Notably Rajan and Zingales (1995) show that companies with a higher market-to-book ratio – implying a larger share of intangible-to-tangible assets – rely less on debt. This is presumably because greater leverage is likely to increase the risk of financial distress, and thus the company's marginal costs of capital. For example, Hall and Lerner (2010) argue that there should have been less pressure from the wave of leveraged buyouts (LBOs) in the 1980s on companies in R&D-intensive industries, as they relied more on internal funds to finance their investments. Reviewing the literature, they find empirical evidence suggesting this to have been the case. Studies by Hall (1993; 1994) as well Opler and Titman (1993) all show that R&D-intensive companies were much less likely to experience an LBO. Moreover, Opler and Titman (1994) find that R&D-intensive firms with higher leverage suffered more than less R&D-intensive companies from the event of financial distress. Hall and Lerner (2010) argue that this is likely as leveraged companies will not be able to pursue their R&D activities when internal funding dries up. This implies financing constraints in the sense that leveraged R&D-intensive companies face difficulties in tapping into capital markets compared with less R&D-intensive companies.

However, contrary to the view that smaller firms mainly rely on internal funds, Fluck et al. (1997) show that the proportion of external finance, including debt, exceeds internal funds as start-ups are formed. Moreover, internal funds increase over the first five years after firm formation, most likely because of the accumulation of retained earnings, and because equity is repurchased from family and friends who supported the firm initially. This suggests that younger firms are also able to obtain external funds, such as debt. However, economically speaking, Berger and Udell (1998) argue that such funding is not really external. This is because financial institutions often require guarantees by the owners of a start-up, meaning that they are held liable to cover the loan with their personal wealth. In certain cases, the owners even cover such loans with personal assets, which are used as collateral. External financiers are therefore often more concerned with evaluating the owners than the firm when making financing decisions. Moreover, it is generally easier to assess the creditworthiness of an individual, who has a longer credit history, than a newly established firm. This means, however, that the entrepreneur personally carries most of the risk. In terms of risk, such funding could thus be regarded internal (Berger and Udell, 1998).

The low debt levels exhibited by technology-driven companies can at least partly be explained by the fact that investments most often provide limited inside collateral value for creditors. Accordingly, financial institutions will typically constrain lending until the balance sheet of the firm contains more tangible assets which can be used as collateral. As argued by Hall and Lerner (2010, p. 13 f): 'Banks and other debtholders prefer to use physical assets to secure loans and are reluctant to lend when the project involves substantial R&D investment rather than investment in plant and equipment.'

Theoretically, the absence of collateral could lead to moral hazard complications as the entrepreneur may take more risk if he himself does not participate in the downside (see, for example, Stiglitz and Weiss, 1981). Extensive research pointing at the importance of collateral for debt finance suggests this to be an obstacle to funding intangible investments through debt. According to Bester (1987), the use of collateral enables creditors to separate high and low-risk borrowers. This means that collateral can be used as a signalling device, but also to confront moral hazard related problems. Hence, Berger and Udell (1990) find that approximately 70 per cent of all industrial debt is given on a secured basis. Although both patents and trademarks have been used as collateral, such practices are still not widely accepted among creditors. For example, Ughetto (2007) shows that banks do not even consider intangibles as meaningful determinants of credit risk. Moreover, the non-transparent market for IPR is likely to limit creditors' ability to make use of IPR as collateral, restricting the ability of technology-driven firms to acquire debt. This is because if the creditor becomes the legal owner of the IPR, he will face difficulties in finding a buyer.

Moral hazards are also likely to occur when the share of external finance is high relative to the share of internal funds. For this reason, in relation to technology-driven firms, angel finance or venture capital is often required before any additional external debt of significance can be acquired (Berger and Udell, 1998). Typically, angel finance is used to bridge financial deficits in start-up financing between internal funds and venture capital. This can take the form of equity investments or convertible debt contracts (Berger and Udell, 1998). Because of the high risk related to angel investments as well as the potential of dilution from future investment rounds, angel investors require comparatively high returns on their defined exit strategy, leading to high costs of capital for the entrepreneur.[40]

The term angel originates from Broadway, where it referred to wealthy individuals who provided funding for theatre productions (Wong, 2002). In the modern sense, angel investors typically consist of retired entrepreneurs or executives who provide finance, managerial advice and business contacts. Markets for angel finance are informal and are not intermediated (see, for example, Berger and Udell, 1998). As a result, search costs are typically high – although, in recent years, networks of angels have emerged in order to reduce the search costs of the entrepreneur (Kerr et al., 2010).

In the US the market for angel finance is, according to some studies, larger than the market for venture capital. A study by the National Venture Capital Association estimates it at approximately 100 billion USD, while the institutional venture capital market was found to be about 48 billion USD (Venture Economics, 2000). Moreover, estimations by the Small Business Association show that as many as 250,000 angel investors together commit 20 billion USD each year to more than 30,000 private companies (Small Business Association (SBA), 2009). Wetzel (1994) finds that the typical angel investment ranges from 50,000 to about 1 million USD. Similarly, Linde and Prasad (1999) reveal the average angel investor to have a portfolio of 335,000 USD invested over different companies. In the UK too, angel investors are found to have financed about five times as many small businesses as venture capitalists (Mason and Harrison, 1990). Finally, Kerr et al. (2010) find angel finance to be associated with higher survival rates for companies. This suggests that angel finance provides an important source of funding for smaller companies.

Venture capital is typically available in a second stage.[41] Gompers (1995) finds that venture capitalists largely focus their investments on technology-driven industries, and especially on smaller early-stage companies, where opacity due to asymmetric information is substantial, implying a need for the monitoring of investment targets. In addition, he shows that younger firms receive fewer financial resources per funding round and that longer financing durations come with higher asset tangibility as the need for monitoring is reduced. These findings are in line with the growth financing cycle of Berger and Udell (1998), suggesting that companies' access to funding improves as asymmetric information is reduced.

In contrast to the market for angel finance, the venture capital market is intermediated by venture capital firms. These pool capital from various investors and identify target firms, providing growth opportunities. Besides funding, venture capitalists provide managerial advice and actively partic- ipate in the recruitment of senior managers. Accordingly, venture capital firms act as a financial intermediary and advisory firm, providing funding to target firms in private ownership.[42]

Past research also reveals some other differences between angel finan- ciers and venture capital firms. While Wong (2002) finds that the majority of angel investors do not follow up their initial investments, Gompers (1995) shows that venture capital firms stage capital infusions in order to control agency costs. Moreover, Kaplan and Strömberg (2001) report that venture capitalists employ contractual clauses as control mechanisms, in a similar way to banks, while Wong (2002) finds that angels do not use con- tractual design to safeguard their investment, but rely on common equity claims, which do not offer any protection in case of bankruptcy. In con- formity with this finding, Casamatta (2000) reveals that angels typically conduct common equity investments. Venture capital firms, by contrast, use more complex securities.

Venture capital can be traced to the formation of American Research and Development in 1946 (see Kortum and Lerner, 2000). The industry boomed in the US during the late 1970s and early 1980s, mainly due to regulatory changes which allowed pension fund managers to invest in high-risk assets. In 1978, a total of 424 million USD was invested in venture capital funds, growing to 4 billion USD annually over the next eight years. In the late 1990s, US venture capital funding emerged as the major source of finance for technology-driven firms in private ownership (Kortum and Lerner, 2000). Even in bank-based financial systems such as Germany, venture capital has achieved a prominent role in the financing of technological innovation (Audretsch and Lehmann, 2004b). Hence, today it is widely regarded as a major contributory factor in the forma- tion of new businesses and economic growth. Especially with regard to high-risk projects, venture capital is considered to play a crucial role in financing the development of new technologies (OECD, 1996). This is suggested not least by Kortum and Lerner (2000), who show that venture capital has an influence on patented inventions in the US. Their estimates suggest that venture capital contributed to 8 per cent of all technological innovations during the decade ending in 1992, growing to approximately 14 per cent by 1998. Moreover, based on a sample from 16 OECD countries, Van Pottelsberghe and Romain (2004) find a positive and significant positive correlation between venture capital and a country's innovation activities – in terms of R&D investment, triadic patents, and the available stock of knowledge. However, Sahlman (1990) shows that venture capital is associated with high costs of capital, suggesting that it is an expensive way to finance technological innovation.

Empirical research shows that venture capitalists generate most of their profits by taking firms public (Venture Economics, 1988). This means that the cost and availability of venture capital also depends on active public equity markets. An informationally efficient stock market is hence also crucial for private capital markets, such as the market for venture capital. According to Jeng and Wells (2000), the potential to exit through an IPO provides the strongest driver for venture capital funding. Moreover, venture capitalists react to information provided by public stock markets (Gompers et al., 2008), and try to time IPO decisions by making an exit when stock market valuations are relatively high. For example, by investigating choices between public and private equity, Lerner (1994b) finds that venture capitalists take firms public when the stock market is peaking, and rely on private equity when valuations are low. In addition, Gompers and Lerner (1998) find that the ability of venture capital firms to raise funds depends on IPO valuations, meaning that the availability of venture capital in the first place depends on active stock markets. An active and informationally efficient stock market is thus important for venture capital funding.

The importance of stock markets for the financing of innovation is suggested by Aghion et al. (2004), who find that equity is more likely to be used to finance intangible assets, while firms rather rely on debt to finance tangible assets. However, empirical research shows that information asymmetries related to intangible assets lead to systematic underpricing of technology-driven companies, and thus higher costs of equity for the financing of technological innovation. For example, Eberhardt et al. (2004) find that the stock market consistently undervalues intangible investments, although an increase in R&D spending was found to be associated with abnormal operating performance within a five year window. Furthermore, Chung et al. (2005) examine the premium investors are willing to pay on the day of the IPO for the intangible assets of the firm. The intangible assets – considered as growth opportunities – are calculated as the market value of the firm's equity minus its book value. Their findings indicate that capital market uncertainty increases with the firm's share of intangible assets, leading to systematic underpricing. More specifically, they find that firms with intangible assets amounting to 56 per cent of firm value are on average undervalued by 16 per cent, while firms whose value consists of 96 per cent intangible assets are undervalued by 66 per cent. Accordingly, they argue that investors want a premium for the additional risk attached to the insufficient information provided on the company's intangible assets.

Moreover, based on a sample of firms that were listed on the NYSE, AMEX and NASDAQ between 1975 and 1995, Chan et al. (2001) investigate the impact of R&D related figures on stock market valuations. In so doing, they divide the sample of firms into five categories according to their R&D intensity – that is, R&D spending divided by the market value of the firm's equity. Their findings reveal that firms with high R&D intensity – which generally tended to have had poor past share price performance – are subject to underpricing. This means that stock markets systematically do not consider the value potential of R&D spending, leading R&D-intensive firms to experience unjustifiably high costs of capital. In addition, they find that R&D intensity has a positive significant impact on return volatility, suggesting substantial uncertainty associated with firms' intangible investments. Finally, Guo et al. (2005) examine whether product-related indicators, such as the share of patent-protected products, have an impact on the valuation of 122 biotechnology IPOs. They find that the ratio of patented products actually has a negative impact on stock market returns, suggesting that investors discount even proprietary intangible assets. In conformity with these findings, Hall (2002) argues that small firms in R&D-intensive industries suffer from considerably higher costs of capital compared with larger competitors or firms in less R&D-intensive industries.

2.7.5 Financing Constraints for Technological Innovation

> ... information asymmetries can preclude firms from being able to finance positive net present value projects. Even if the entrepreneur understands the value of the opportunity, if he cannot convey this information to a potential financier, the project may go unfinanced. (Lerner et al., 2000, p. 4)

Financial constraints refer to a situation where particular categories of firms which ought to receive funding are systematically unable to do so. This implies a capital shortage in the sense that the supply of funding is inadequate to satisfy the demand. According to Planès et al. (2002), this is mainly a concern of technology-driven firms, leading to delayed or abandoned R&D projects.

Hall and Lerner (2010) point to three main reasons why a funding gap between internal and external costs of capital may occur according to economic theory – namely, asymmetric information between the entrepreneur and the investor, moral hazard complications stemming from the separation of ownership and management and, finally, tax considerations that create a wedge between internal and external funding. As the present study is concerned with the informational efficiency of capital markets, I will focus on the potential for financing constraints to stem from the information problem.

During the 1980s, prominent theoretical models were developed, revealing how asymmetric information can result in financing constraints. Notably, Stiglitz and Weiss (1981) show how credit rationing occurs in debt markets when creditors have less information than entrepreneurs concerning the risk of an investment. In this case, they argue that creditors restrict the supply of debt although they have sufficient financial capital to lend, meaning that the supply of debt does not meet the demand of potential lenders. This is because interest charges on the debt do not equilibrate the demand for and supply of debt, as the creditor finds that raising the interest rate beyond a certain level reduces the profitability of lending, since lenders could default. Moreover, asymmetric information related to risk and default probabilities potentially leads to adverse selection, because higher interest rates can cause low-risk borrowers to exit the application pool. However, this situation is modelled in the absence of equity markets. DeMeza and Webb (1987) conceptualise equity and credit rationing through an integrated approach. They find that if information asymmetries relate to the expected return on an investment, investors will prefer debt to equity, and no credit rationing will occur. However, if there is asymmetric information concerning the risk of the investment, investors will prefer equity, prohibiting equity rationing. According to these findings, no rationing would occur as long as investors use the appropriate financial instrument. In their model, however, DeMeza and Webb (1987) did not account for asymmetric information related to both the risk and the expected return on the investment. On consideration of this scenario, Hellmann and Stiglitz (2000) show that both credit and equity rationing can occur simultaneously, meaning that firms can be restricted in their ability to obtain external funding, implying financing constraints.

A fundamental problem with the nature of debt contracts in the context of innovation finance should also be noted. According to Carpenter and Peterson (2002), this problem stems from the high attrition rates of R&D projects, leading to highly skewed returns on intangible investments. For example, Mansfield et al. (1977) show that only 27 per cent of R&D projects are financially successful. This has implications mainly for debt contracts. Because creditors do not share the upside of the firm's investments, they are only concerned with the bottom tail of the distribution of economic returns (see, for example, Stiglitz, 1985). Accordingly, as the borrower's returns are highly uncertain, the creditor will want to raise interest rates in order to compensate. However, Stiglitz and Weiss (1981) suggest that, as interest rates rise, the nature of debt contracts can ex post lead to the unmonitored borrower investing in higher-risk projects with potentially higher returns, and thus increase the probability of default without offsetting higher gains to the creditor in case of success. This means that debt finance of R&D projects comes with moral hazard complications (see, for example, Stiglitz, 1985).

Further implications associated with the debt funding of innovation stem from the limited collateral that intangible assets provide (see, for example, Lerner and Hall, 2010). This goes back to the point of Williamson (1988) that redeployable assets – that is, assets whose value is as high in an alternative use as their current value – are more suitable for financing through debt-type contracts. For example, Alderson and Betker (1996) find that R&D investments are associated with higher liquidation, implying that sunk costs for intangibles are relatively high. Indeed, Opler and Titman (1994) find that R&D-intensive firms with higher leverage suffered more than less R&D-intensive companies in the event of financial distress, implying financing constraints in the sense that leveraged R&D-intensive companies face difficulties in tapping into capital markets, compared with less R&D-intensive firms. Accordingly, Rajan and Zingales (1995) show that companies with a substantial share of growth opportunities relative to assets-in-place exhibit lower debt levels.

Equity, on the contrary, does not require any collateral, nor does it cap the upside of investors' returns. Further, equity finance does not give managers incentives to substitute low-risk projects for higher ones, because managers themselves most often have their wealth tied up in compensation based on the performance of the firm, mitigating agency problems (see, for example, Jensen and Meckling, 1976). Accordingly, Aghion et al. (2004) find that the use of debt declines with the R&D intensity of the firm. By contrast, they find that firms with a higher R&D intensity issue more equity – implying that firms mainly rely on equity to finance innovation. Interestingly, Brown and Petersen (2009) find that public equity has recently gained in importance for the financing of R&D in the US. This is despite the fact that the use of equity to finance technological innovation comes at substantial costs. According to Lee et al. (1996), the average costs of issuing equity amount to 13 per cent for seasoned equity of less than 10 million USD, and 10 per cent if the issue was between 10 and 20 million. Moreover, adverse selection problems related to asymmetric information lead to lemon premiums. Hence, firms can be forced to sell equity at a discount, leading to systematic underpricing. Indeed, several studies have shown that this is the case (Chan et al., 2001; Chung et al., 2005; Eberhardt et al., 2004; Guo et al., 2005).

According to pecking order theory, under the assumption of asymmetric information, companies will prefer to finance their operations by means of internal funds. This should also be true of R&D investments, which are found to come with asymmetric information – a view that also finds support in empirical studies showing R&D to be associated with internal funds. For example, Himmelberg and Petersen (1994) find a positively significant relationship between the two, as do Hall (1992) and Harhoff (1998). In a more recent study, Brown et al. (2009) find that internal cash-flows and public equity are important ways for younger companies to finance R&D, but not so much for more mature firms. This suggests, as does the financial growth cycle of Berger and Udell (1998), that companies gain access to more sources of funding as they mature.

But investments in technological innovation are often substantial and unlikely to be covered through internal funds. If internal funds turn out to be inadequate, under asymmetric information, pecking order theory suggests that companies will turn to debt markets as the secondary option. However, as we have seen, debt contracts for the financing of innovation come with moral hazard complications and potential adverse selection. Furthermore, external equity is expensive and tends to dilute the value of the assets-in-place. Hence, Harhoff (1998), for example, concludes that R&D investment in small German firms may be constrained in their ability to obtain funding.

The market for venture capital is one response to this problem, but comes with high costs of capital (Sahlman, 1990).[43] Moreover, Hall and Lerner (2010) note that the venture capital market only focuses on a few sectors at a time, and that venture capital investments are often too large for smaller companies. Finally, and most importantly for the present study, they argue that active stock markets for smaller companies are essential to provide an exit strategy for private equity investors. As shown, however, several studies find that stock markets systematically undervalue technology-driven companies, and that the costs of venture capital depend on the return that can be achieved in the stock market. This means that the high costs of venture capital can at least partially be explained by the absence of informationally efficient stock markets.

While a funding gap for technological innovation is difficult to establish, it has been suggested by several research scholars (see, for example, Hall, 2002; Hall and Lerner, 2010; Harhoff, 1998). The literature shows that it can, at its best, be argued that technology-driven companies only suffer from unjustifiably high costs of capital, much of it due to asymmetric information. Accordingly, certain NPV positive innovation projects may not be undertaken which would be profitable if financing costs were lower. Considering the importance of both efficient capital markets and technological innovation to productivity, a funding gap for technological innovation could certainly be argued to provide constraints, also on economic growth.

2.8 CORPORATE DISCLOSURE AND INFORMATION INTERMEDIATION

> Corporate disclosure is critical for the functioning of an efficient capital market. Firms provide disclosure through regulated financial reports, including the financial statements, footnotes, management discussion and analysis, and other regulatory filings. In addition, some firms engage in voluntary communication, such as management forecasts, analysts' presentations and conference calls, press releases, internet sites, and other corporate reports. Finally, there are disclosures about firms by information intermediaries, such as financial analysts, industry experts, and the financial press. (Healy and Palepu, 2001, p. 406)

Healy and Palepu (2001) argue that the demand for information disclosure, and thus financial reporting, arises from asymmetric information, creating agency problems between inside managers and outside investors. This chapter reviews the literature regarding institutions dealing with the informational efficiency of capital markets. It does so in relation to two main theories – namely, *signalling* and *screening* – that have been proposed to overcome asymmetric information and how these theories work within the framework of disclosure regimes.

The theory of signalling was pioneered by Spence (1973), who proposed that the informed party can reduce asymmetric information by signalling its type. This idea was first developed in relation to the labour market, in the context of an employer looking for individuals skilled in learning. For signalling to reduce asymmetric information, however, it must be costly for unskilled individuals to imitate the signal. Otherwise, adverse selection could still occur as all potential employees would claim to be skilled. To increase the credibility of the information communicated, Spence (1973) proposes that signalling one's university degree enables employers to differentiate between applicants.

Similar suggestions have been made in relation to signalling in capital markets. For example, Leland and Pyle (1977) find that firms with growth opportunities should always signal this to the market in terms of owning a substantial share of the firm. Financial reporting standards and other regulatory frameworks provide additional ways of making signalling more credible by increasing the costs of imitating the signal. Accordingly, firms publish annual and interim reports to provide investors with relevant information about the financial state of the firm in a standardised manner on a regular basis. Financial reporting standards thus provide a commonly accepted language of communication to corporate outsiders (see, for example, Healy and Palepu, 2001). In addition, publicly listed firms are obliged to conduct additional reporting under securities regulations without delay as insider information occurs. Because of the obligation to notify corporate outsiders, and the legal consequences of not doing so, such disclosures ought to provide credible signals in terms of being costly to imitate. Finally, firms may conduct voluntary information disclosures in order to meet the demand for further information and to mitigate agency conflicts between managers and investors by reducing information asymmetries. Extensive research shows that voluntary disclosures also provide credible signals to the capital markets (see Healy and Palepu, 2001).

Screening provides another technique for reducing asymmetric information (see, for example, Spence, 1973). In contrast to signalling, screening refers to the situation where the uninformed party moves first (see, for example, Rothschild and Stiglitz, 1976; Wilson, 1977). This means that the uninformed party extracts information from the informed party. For example, creditors screen potential borrowers in order to assess their creditworthiness and reduce information asymmetries. Similarly, in private capital markets, financial intermediaries would conduct a due diligence investigation of the target firm before making an investment decision. However, while screening reduces asymmetric information between the two parties to a transaction, it does not necessarily spill over into the public domain. In the case of due diligence, a non-disclosure agreement (NDA) would be signed upfront as a standard procedure. To support the informational efficiency of public capital markets, investment analysts such as financial analysts and rating agencies – specialised in screening – have established themselves as information intermediaries. However, in contrast with screening conducted by the financier in private capital markets, their screening typically results in a rating or some kind of recommendation, which they signal to the capital market.

Accordingly, this section will focus on financial reporting standards, securities regulations, voluntary information disclosures and, finally, information intermediaries, as potential avenues for reducing the asymmetric information attached to intangible assets (see Figure 2.4).

The objective here is not to provide a complete overview of the regulatory framework for corporate disclosures, which tends to differ across countries. I will instead focus on internationally established guidelines and regulations.

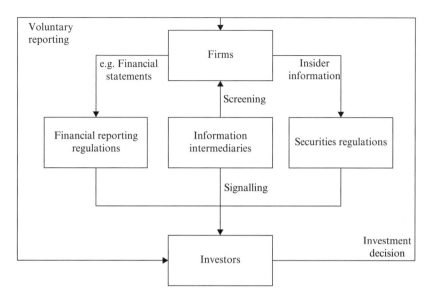

Figure 2.4   Framework of information disclosure

2.8.1   Financial Reporting and Intangible Assets

International Financial Reporting Standards (IFRS) are principle-based financial reporting standards promoted by the International Accounting Standards Board (IASB), which apply to all publicly listed firms in the EU since the implementation of Directive 2002/1606/EC in 2005, as well as most other countries.[44] Many of its standards are still known under the name International Accounting Standards (IAS), its predecessor, which since 2001 has formed part of the IFRS. The objective of these standards is to promote the disclosure of reliable information concerning the corporate affairs of firms, and provide external stakeholders with value-relevant and accurate information. An important task of empirical accounting research is therefore to investigate the accuracy and value-relevance of the information provided in firms' financial statements.

As previously discussed, the value-relevance of the information provided in companies' financial statements has deteriorated over the past 20 years, mainly due to the ever increasing pace of technological innovation (see, for example, Ballow et al., 2004; Lev and Zarowin, 1999). Accordingly, Ramb and Reitzig (2005a; 2005b) show that European patent applications have a stronger correlation with the market value of firms than activated R&D investments on the balance sheet. Moreover, several studies suggest that patent-related information explains the market value of firms better than the information in their annual financial statements (see, for example, Hirschey and Richardson, 2001; Trautwein, 2007). It has been argued that this is because, in treating a substantial share of intangible investments as expenses, accounting standards do not promote the full reflection of intangible assets on firms' balance sheets (see Hand and Lev, 2003).

According to IAS 38.8, an asset is a resource that is being controlled by the entity as a result of past events, including acquisitions or own developments, and from which future economic benefits are expected. IAS 38 goes on to state that an intangible asset is 'an identifiable non-monetary asset without physical substance' which needs to fulfil three criteria:

- identifiability;
- control;
- future economic benefits.

Examples of intangible assets are patents, licences, marketing rights, and so on (IAS 38.9). To meet the criteria of identifiability, an intangible asset needs to be either separable or to arise from contractual or other legal rights (IAS 38.12). Separable means that the asset can be sold, transferred, licensed and so on – individually or with a contract. Control refers to the ability of the owner to obtain benefits from the asset, and future economic benefits means that it must contribute to income or reduced costs. In addition, IAS 38 requires intangible assets to be recognised irrespectively of whether they have been generated internally or acquired at a cost, but only if these costs can be measured on a reliable basis and if it is probable that the future economic benefits of the asset can be internalised by the firm (IAS 38.21). The aspect of future economic benefits draws on assumptions about the conditions throughout the lifetime of the asset. These assumptions are required to be reasonable and supportable (IAS 38.22). However, the criterion of recognition is always fulfilled for acquired intangible assets (IAS 38.33). If this criterion is not met, the costs shall be expensed as they incur (IAS 38.68). Further, there is a distinction between research and development costs (IAS 38.54).[45] While research outlays must be expensed, development costs can be capitalised if the technical and commercial feasibility of the asset has been established for sale or internal use (IAS 38.57). Hence, it must be demonstrated that the asset will generate future economic benefits, meaning that the firm intends to complete the asset for one of these purposes. It shall, however, be noted that an R&D project that has been acquired from a third party can be capitalised on the basis of the price of the transaction (IAS 38.34).

In general, the capitalisation of development costs may be conducted on the basis of costs or the revaluation model. The cost model treats intangibles on the basis of costs, subtracted by conducted amortisation and impairment losses (IAS 38.74), while the revaluation model allows for capitalisation on the basis of the fair value of the asset.[46] This is only permitted by reference to an active market for the asset (IAS 38.75). However, Küting et al. (2006) describe fair value capitalisation of intangible assets as problematic since there is no active market for intangible assets to derive information from (see, for example, Arora and Gambardella, 2010). Also the IAS expects markets for intangibles to be uncommon (IAS 38.78).

Finally, intangible assets are classified according their expected lifetime. They can have an infinite life if there is no predictable limit to the period in which economic benefits can be internalised, or a finite life, and hence a limited period of economic benefits (IAS 38.88). On the basis of the best estimate of its useful economic lifetime, an intangible asset shall be amortised (IAS 38.79), and the amortisation period should be reviewed annually (IAS 38.94). However, intangibles with an infinite economic life shall not be amortised. This means that the method of amortisation should reflect the pattern in which the economic benefits of the asset are being used (IAS 38.88). Further, no residual value is normally presumed, if there is not a commitment by a third party to acquire the asset or there is an active market for this particular type of intangible asset (IAS 38.94).

2.8.2 Securities Regulations and Insider Information

The guiding principle for modern securities regulations is to enable investors to make informed investment decisions. According to this principle, securities law in the US, for example, developed from only prohibiting misrepresentations and the disclosure of misleading information to requiring the disclosure of insider information (see, for example, Bergmans, 1991). Hence, complementary to financial reporting standards, securities regulations are in place to promote the informational efficiency of public capital markets.[47] Both within the EU and the US issuers of securities are obliged to provide capital markets with as complete and correct information as possible in order for investors to make deliberate investment decisions (see, for example, Hopt and Voigt, 2004). More specifically, publicly listed firms are required to disclose any information that is essential for investors to be able to determine the current value of the firm. On the one hand, this principle governs the individual investor in terms of enabling him to make an assessment of the expected return and the risks related to a security. On the other hand, it enhances the informational efficiency of capital markets as such, and is hence fundamental to their functioning.

The disclosure of insider information applies to both primary and secondary markets. In primary markets – that is, where firms issue new securities – they are obliged to publish a prospectus containing all information considered to be relevant for an investor to make an informed decision. This prospectus is referred to as listing particulars and has become more or less globally mandatory across different jurisdictions (Hopt and Voigt, 2004). In contrast to financial statements, listing particulars also include economic forecasts in which issuers must quantify the development of their business, at least for the forthcoming year.[48] However, as forecasts are always uncertain, sufficient evidence needs to be provided in order to support the assumptions made. Still, the issuer should not be forced to disclose the complete informational basis for the prognosis as this would give competitors insights into sensitive data related its business. Moreover, the listing particulars must outline the risks that could have a negative impact on the prospects for the firm's business. Such information can relate to changes in competition, the expiry of important patents or contracts, as well as specific macroeconomic or industry-related factors, and so on (see Hopt and Voigt, 2004).

In addition to the listing particulars, firms in the EU and the US are obliged to report regularly – that is, without delay – when insider information occurs in the secondary market, to bridge informational deficits and prevent distortions in terms of unreasonable market prices (Hopt and Voigt, 2004). This is seen as essential to ensure trust among capital market participants and to facilitate the liquidity of secondary markets. To meet this principle, issuers in the EU are required to notify regulatory authorities as soon as possible after any *insider information* has occurred. According to Directive 2003/6/EC this comprises:

> ... any information of a precise nature which has not been made public; relating, directly or indirectly, to one or more issuers of financial instruments or to one or more financial instruments. Information which could have a significant effect on the evolution and forming of the prices of a regulated market as such could be considered as information which is indirectly related to one or more issuers of financial instruments or one or more related derivative financial instruments.

This means that information must be of a precise nature and have a significant impact on the price of a security in order to be considered as insider information. To be of a precise nature, the Commission Directive 2003/124/EC Art. 1(1), for the implementation of Directive 2003/6/EC, states that the information must indicate a set of circumstances or a particular event that has occurred or is expected to occur to be of a precise nature. Moreover, it needs to be specific enough to determine the potential impact on the price of a financial instrument.[49] If there are doubts about the occurrence of such circumstances or events, the prerequisite of a specific nature is not sufficient for the information to be seen as insider information, meaning there must be a certain probability of occurrence. It shall be noted that the need for information to be precise is not to be considered the same as having an impact on the price of a security. Rather, the prerequisite of preciseness provides a filtering function in determining if information is of an insider nature (see, for example, Eichner, 2008). Without this filtering function, issuers would need to raise the question of whether any type of information will have an impact on the price of the security. Hence, all information that is unavailable to the public domain would have to be tested in terms of its market price impact in order to exclude the possibility of unlawfulness related to not disclosing it.

Secondly, the issuer needs to determine whether a reasonable investor would consider it as relevant in an investment decision (see, for example, Barnes, 2008). Because there is no exact percentage change in a company's share price that could be regarded as indicating a significant effect, the issuer needs to assess whether the information would be considered by an investor, and thus would have an impact on the price of the security, provided the information is of a precise nature. A general catalogue of such information is not provided as it will depend on the business of the firm. However, the German Federal Financial Authority (BaFin) outlines a set of examples of insider information related to certain events, such as:

- divestiture of core businesses;
- merger agreements and corporate restructuring measures such as the spin-off or incorporation of certain divisions;
- major changes in previous publications such as annual and interim reports, as well as market forecasts;
- any litigation of particular relevance;
- major inventions, the grant of core patents and licences;
- etc.[50]

2.8.3 Voluntary Reporting

Information may be considered by investors, even if it is not of a precise nature. This is especially true of forward-looking information, for which the probability of occurrence can be difficult to assess. Because investors are generally concerned with determining potential future returns, forward-looking information can be critical to the functioning of capital markets and the ability of firms to obtain funding. For this reason, firms sometimes conduct voluntary information disclosures. Such information may be published in management forecasts, press releases, conference calls, publications on the firm's website or in other types of corporate reports (see, for example, Healy and Palepu, 1993; 1995). Hence, although intangible assets are not fully reflected in firms' financial statements, additional voluntary information disclosures can help reduce information asymmetries. Moreover, firms can disclose more detailed information about its intangible assets and IPR management on a voluntary basis.

The relevance of IPR management reporting has been recognised among policy makers. For example, the Japanese Ministry of Economy, Trade and Industry (METI) suggests that asymmetric information between firms and capital markets will become even larger as a result of companies systematically managing their IPR. The reason for this, they argue, is that information on companies' IPR management is generally not available in the public domain – something that will eventually lead to higher costs of capital for firms committed to IPR management. To deal with this problem METI (2004) proposed a pilot model with guidelines for the disclosure of IPR management information. Based on a survey conducted among institutional investors, METI (2004) proposes that firms should report on several aspects of their IPR management. These are summarised in Table 2.1.

Empirical studies have also examined the value-relevance of voluntary information disclosures about firms' IPR that cannot be derived from public patent or trademark databases. For example, Seethamraju (2003) shows that announcements regarding trademark acquisitions have a positive impact on stock market valuations. Moreover, he finds that additional voluntary information disclosures, of both a quantitative and qualitative nature, are associated with higher stock market returns. Especially quantitative information disclosures related to the size of the market the trademark covers, its growth potential and the price the trademark was acquired at, had an impact on investors' valuations. Accordingly, he argues that voluntary information disclosures reduce the uncertainty associated with the future profits of trademark acquisitions.

Similarly, by using an event-study methodology, Austin (1993) finds that patents which are linked to products receive a higher valuation than non-linked patents, but so do patents which have received attention in the media. This implies that patents mainly contribute to firm value when they relate directly to the company's business, and when patent information is communicated to the stock market.

Finally, some firms report on their patent licensing income (see, for example, Gu and Lev, 2004). Anecdotal as well as empirical evidence reveals the importance of patent licensing for a wide range of firms' business models (see Lichtenthaler, 2006). For example, according to Rivette and Kline (2000), aggregated royalty income from patent licensing has grown in the US from 15 billion USD in 1990 to more than 110 billion

Table 2.1   METI IPR management reporting framework

Item	Description	Investor purpose
Core technologies	Sources of competitive advantage according to R&D segments	Assessment of the firm's competitive position in each segment
Technology market potential	Analysis of the markets for the firm's core technologies in terms of their size and expected growth rate	Assessment of the firm's growth potential
R&D segment strategy	Explanation of how the firm's business, R&D and IPR strategies are aligned	Assessment of the firm's ability to materialise its R&D investments
IPR to R&D segment	An overview of the company's IPR according to its competitive advantages	Assessment of whether sufficient IPR protection has been acquired
R&D and IPR organisation	Description of organisational IPR management integration, including strategic R&D alliances and their respective objectives	Assessment of organisational IPR management efficiency
Technology leakage policies	Description of corporate policies to deal with knowledge spillovers	Assessment of ability to minimise the leakage of knowledge
Patent licensing activity	A statement on patent licensing income and licensing deal details	Assessment of ability to commercialise the firm's IPR and its financial performance contribution
Patent portfolio	Overview of the firm's patents and how they are used	Assessment of the strategic rationale behind each patent
IPR policies	Statement on IPR management objectives and related corporate guidelines	Assessment of the contribution of IPR management to firm performance
IPR risks	An overview of IPR litigation	Assessment of legal risks

in 1999. However, although licensing is essential to many firms' businesses, related external reporting has lagged behind. This is suggested by empirical research showing that reporting on royalty income contributes substantially to stock returns, but that most firms do not disclose such information.

Notably, Gu and Lev (2004) examine the stock market valuations of royalty income disclosures. They find that the multiple assigned by investors to royalty income is approximately three times larger than the earnings multiple. Despite the evident value-relevance of royalty income, however, they find that a substantial number of companies engaged in patent licensing choose not to report on this item. For example, when examining the royalty disclosure practices of 25 pharmaceutical and biotechnology companies, they find that approximately half of the firms provided quantitative information about royalty revenues. The remaining firms only provided a general discussion on patent licensing in their annual report, but without any figures on royalty income. Interestingly, they also find that royalty income conveys an important signal to investors about the quality and prospects of the generally uncertain outcomes of R&D investments.[51] To reduce the uncertainty associated with R&D investments, Gu and Lev (2004) find that companies with a high share of royalty income can communicate their ability to commercialise their patents through royalty reporting, enhancing investor confidence in their ability to turn their R&D investments into revenue. The existence and intensity of royalty income from patent licensing accordingly signal economic benefits to come, also from following R&D investments.

However, the considerable information asymmetries associated with technology-driven companies suggest that managers are reluctant to communicate information about their IPR. This raises the question of what drives managers' reporting decisions; Healy and Palepu (2001) find that managers' reporting decisions depend on six main circumstances. Firstly, managers who expect to issue debt or equity have incentives to reduce information asymmetries in order to reduce the firm's cost of external financing. This is in line with the pecking-order-theory argument that firms will not issue equity if there is asymmetric information. For example, Lang and Lundholm (2000) find a significant increase in disclosure beginning six months before new equity is issued, implying that firms are keener to conduct voluntary information disclosures before issuing new securities. Secondly, managers disclose additional value-relevant information to reduce the probability of undervaluation, and thus of hostile take-overs. Voluntary disclosures can be used to mitigate this risk by, for instance, explaining poor earnings performance. Because a substantial part of firms' investments in intangible assets is expensed in conformity with IAS, firms should therefore report on the future potential of R&D expenses through additional voluntary reporting. Thirdly, mangers are often rewarded through stock-based compensation schemes. This provides them with an incentive to correct any perceived undervaluation. Fourthly, litigation affects managers' disclosure decisions in two senses.

The risk of legal action against managers for not disclosing information in a timely manner encourages them to do so. On the other hand, litigation can also decrease managers' disclosure incentives, particularly in relation to forward-looking information, if they believe that this will affect analysts' forecasts negatively. Fifthly, managers may have incentives to disclose earnings forecasts to provide investors with information concerning their ability to anticipate and respond to the economic environment (Trueman, 1986). However, Healy and Palepu (2001) find no empirical evidence to support this hypothesis. Finally, and perhaps most importantly with regard to IPR reporting, managers are concerned about information disclosures potentially damaging their competitive position in product markets. Accordingly, several studies conclude that firms do not want to disclose information that could harm their competitive position even if their costs of capital will be higher (see, for example, Darrough and Stoughton, 1990; Verrecchia, 1983). Furthermore, METI (2004) finds that firms do not want to disclose too detailed technical information about their IPR that could potentially harm their competitiveness. However, they find that this is not the type of information investors request. Rather, investors are found to be interested in information about the firm's IPR management.

While firms will probably not want to conduct too detailed reporting about their IPR management either, the literature suggests other ways of increasing the credibility such information disclosures (Healy and Palepu, 2001). For example, independent third parties, such as auditors, can confirm the accuracy and quality of the disclosed information. Moreover, new voluntary information disclosures can be reinforced by earlier disclosure – for example, an earnings forecast for the forthcoming year can be verified by the end of that period. Similarly, the accuracy of voluntary IPR disclosures could be verified ex post.

2.8.4 Information Intermediaries

2.8.4.1 Financial analysts
Financial analysts consist of buy-side and sell-side analysts. Buy-side analysts are employed by institutional investment firms, such as mutual funds or hedge funds, for which they identify investment opportunities and provide internal recommendations accordingly. Hence, their recommendations are made for the benefit of the investment firm, and are not available in the public domain. In contrast, sell-side analysts work for brokerage firms and investment banks where they provide their clients with investment recommendations, which are also disclosed in the public domain. Because this requires specific knowledge about technologies and

industries, financial analysts are generally assigned to cover specific firms within a particular industry with which they have regular contact.[52]

To arrive at a recommendation, they gather information by analysing published records and engaging in discussions with firm representatives and other industry experts. The gathered information is then filtered down to what the analysts consider to be value-relevant information. Mostly, such information relates to the firm's financial aspects, its management, particular competitive advantages, as well as trends and market developments affecting the firm's competitive position. On the basis of this information, they make forecasts about the future prospects of the firm. These forecasts, in turn, provide the basis for the fundamental analysis conducted to estimate the firm's financial value. The value is then set in relation to the price of the security in order to identify market inefficiencies in terms of mispricing. Depending on whether they find the firm to be over- or underpriced, they provide a rating of the security, resulting in a buy, hold or sell recommendation. This means that sell-side analysts' recommendations potentially reduce asymmetric information. For this reason, the present study will focus on sell-side analysts, who are referred to as financial analysts.

Empirical studies have been conducted on the accuracy of analysts' research, showing that their earnings' forecasts are more accurate than time-series models (see, for example, Brown and Rozeff, 1978; Givoly, 1982). Another branch of the literature has focused on the informational contribution of their recommendations. In general, these studies show that financial analysts contribute to the informational efficiency of capital markets – both their earnings' forecasts and their recommendations have an impact on stock market valuations (see, for example, Francis and Soffer, 1997; Lys and Sohn, 1990).

However, the role of financial analysts brings with it conflicts of interest. Firstly, investment banks perform services such as the underwriting of securities, where they act as an intermediary between the issuer of the security and the investing public domain. Hence, if a firm makes an IPO, the investment bank will engage in facilitating the process of selling the issued securities. This means that positive forecasts for the issuers' stock – provided by the financial analysts concerned, who are also employed at the bank – are helpful in facilitating the selling process. Financial analysts therefore have incentives to make buy recommendations, which can undermine the objectivity of their analysis. Secondly, clients prefer favourable reports related to their firm, meaning that financial analysts can attract more business for their employer if they provide favourable reports. Empirical studies have also found that analysts are too optimistic in their recommendations (Brown et al., 1985), although there has been a decline in analysts' optimism during the 1990s (see, for example, Brown, 1997; Matsumoto, 2000). Financial analysts' forecasts are therefore becoming increasingly accurate – something that should contribute to the informational efficiency of stock markets.

2.8.4.2 Credit rating agencies

As financial analysts, credit rating agencies (CRAs) produce information for capital markets in the form of opinions. In doing so, White (2002, p. 43) suggests that they 'can help lenders pierce the fog of asymmetric information that surrounds lending relationships. Equivalently, credit rating firms can help borrowers (and their credit qualities) emerge from that same fog'. This implies that CRAs contribute to the informational efficiency of capital markets as lenders rely on their information retrieval, analysis, and opinions. It could of course be argued that investors could gather their own information and conduct their own analysis. However, although larger institutional investors also conduct their own research, they often still use CRA ratings as an input factor in their own analysis, and most investors do not have the time and resources to do so in relation to every single investment. Moreover, CRAs have access to certain private information about issuers, suggesting that they are also better informed than the average investor. Accordingly, investors reduce some of their own research efforts and at least partially rely on CRA opinions.

In contrast to financial analysts, CRAs provide opinions on debt issuers' creditworthiness – that is, the issuers' risk of default. In sum, while financial analysts are concerned with equity markets, CRAs focus on debt markets. Debt issuers can range from firms, to governments, to non-governmental organisations (NGOs), to special purpose vehicles (SPVs). For example, an SPV may take on a risky R&D project or hold a firm's IPR in order to mitigate the potential impact of related risks on the rating of the parent firm. In the present study, however, the focus is on firms issuing debt securities, to which CRAs assign credit ratings.

The two main CRAs – that is, Moody's and Standard & Poor's – have similar rating systems and procedures. The investment grade scale of Moody's ranges from AAA for the least risky debt to Baa3 for the most risky. Similarly, Standard & Poor's give ratings from AAA to BBB–. Lower ratings are given, but considered to be of non-investment grade. Supplementary to ratings, CRAs announce outlooks and reviews. After a rating has been given, the CRA announces an outlook regarding the likely direction of the firm's rating in terms of being positive, negative or stable. Most often these are outlooks for the following 12 to 18 month period. The outlooks can be modified without a change in the firm's rating. This is usually the case when the firm's risk of default has increased, but not to a level seen as permanent. Reviews on the other hand – sometimes referred to as credit watches – indicate future changes in a firm's rating, typically within a few weeks after publication. However, an up- or downgrade can be conducted without the CRA announcing a review upfront, meaning that issuers' ratings can be changed without any prior announcement of a review.

In theory, a favourable rating will attract more investors and enable the issuer to issue debt securities at a lower cost. The issuer will pay a lower interest rate on its debt if investors consider its default risk to be lower, meaning that CRA assessments have an impact on firms' costs of capital. However, empirical research on the contribution of CRAs to the informational efficiency of capital markets shows mixed results. For example, Holthausen and Leftwich (1986) as well as Hand et al. (1992) show that rating upgrades are already incorporated into both bond and share prices, but that rating downgrades provide new information to investors. Moreover, Goh and Ederington (1999) show a stronger negative reaction in the stock market to downgrades of issuers with already relatively low ratings. Similarly, Hite and Warga (1997) find reactions in the bond market to be more substantial in relation to downgrades to, as well as within, the non-investment grade category. These findings were also confirmed by Dynkin et al. (2002) in a later study.

In addition, researchers have studied the impact of ratings on *credit default swaps (CDSs)*, finding that spreads increase as a consequence of negative rating announcements.[53] Hull et al. (2004) find that reviews for downgrades contain new information, but that downgrades and negative outlooks do not. Micu et al. (2006) show that negative rating announcements have a highly significant impact on CDS spreads. The strongest impact is found for negative reviews and downgrades, while outlook changes have less impact. Finally, they find that positive events do not contain value-relevant information, although they argue that their sample contains too few positive events to be statistically meaningful. In sum, however, previous research suggests that CRAs do contribute to capital market efficiency, at least through their downgrades.

2.9   SUMMARY AND MAIN FINDINGS

The conducted review of the literature provides several notable insights, which ought to be considered in the following empirical study. Firstly, it shows that IPR contribute to the financial performance of firms. This points to the value-relevance of IPR-related information, indicating its potential to bridge informational deficits in capital markets. However, the economic attributes of intangible assets, such as IPR, are not considered by financial reporting standards, and thus are not comprehensively reflected in firms' financial statements. For example, as intangible assets tend to increase in value as they are used, the accounting concept of amortisation is not meaningful for these assets. Moreover, IAS 38 exempts research costs from being capitalised, and development costs can most often not be fully capitalised. In technology-intensive industries such as the pharmaceutical industry, where attrition rates are high and marketing authorisation is uncertain, only a fraction of the costs of product development can be capitalised. The rest are treated as expenses, which systematically reduces the net income of the firm. In addition, although research shows that there is a market for intangible assets, these markets are generally informal, meaning that there is little information on market prices. As a result, intangible assets are more likely to be activated on the basis of costs, while markets for tangible assets enable their activation based on market prices.

Past research also shows that IPR are no longer simply outputs from firms' innovation activities. Rather, firms manage their IPR in the wider context of their business models. This is not least suggested by the increasing pace of strategic patenting, requiring investors to consider IPR not as mere exclusion rights, but also as competitive weapons. Past studies also suggest that investors are primarily interested in information on firms' IPR in the context of their business models. This suggests limits to financial reporting standards.

In addition to financial reporting standards, securities regulations require some IPR information to be disclosed, provided it is of a specific nature and there is a sufficient probability of occurrence. Hence firms are required to publish information related to IPR litigation, the expiry of commercially relevant patents and major licensing deals. However, most IPR management-related information is not specific enough, and thus does not fulfil the criteria to be treated as insider information. This suggests that voluntary reporting is of particularly relevant way for firms to communicate information on their IPR management to capital markets. Furthermore, information intermediaries ought to incorporate such information in their assessments.

Not doing so could have severe implications for the financing of technological innovation. For example, past research shows that technology-driven firms' equity is systematically undervalued, leading to such firms facing higher costs of capital in order to obtain funding. In addition, some firms may even face financing constraints, meaning that they are systematically unable to obtain funding, although they provide productive investment opportunities. This indicates that financial capital is being allocated away from technological innovation, leading to an unproductive use of resources in the economy as a whole.

The review of the literature also revealed several research gaps. Firstly, past research examining asymmetric information related to technology-driven firms has focused on uncertainty stemming from R&D intensity. Only a few studies consider the potential of asymmetric information related to the IPR system. Furthermore, these studies do not consider IPR in its managerial context, but rather as legal exclusion rights or innovation output. Secondly, past research has tended to focus on private capital markets, and notably the role of venture capital funding in financing technological innovation. This is not surprising since public capital markets only become accessible later in the financial growth cycle, when there is proven commercial potential, and opacity is reduced. However, past research shows that the cost of venture capital depends on the informational efficiency of public capital markets, implying that a reduction of asymmetric information related to technology-driven firms would also reduce their costs of funding in the earlier stages of the growth cycle. I therefore decided to focus on this aspect. Finally, the implications of the intangible economy for public debt markets have been largely neglected. This is especially troublesome, as past research shows that technology-driven firms' equity is systematically undervalued – a problem that could at least partially be mitigated by informationally efficient debt markets.

NOTES

1. Economic growth is defined as the state when gross domestic product (GDP) per capita increases over time.
2. Several studies point to the need to address time-lags between R&D investments and profit generation. Research conducted by Zimmermann and Schwalbach (1991) investigates the relationship between R&D investments and patents in 33 industries and finds a time-lag between the variables of two to four years. A study by Pakes and Griliches (1984) finds a 1.6 year time-lag between R&D investments and patent applications.
3. Malmberg (2005) finds a positive correlation between trademark applications and the introduction of new products in the market.
4. *Appropriation* refers to a firm's capacity to benefit commercially from its investments in technology (Tidd and Bessant, 1997).
5. Property rights arrangements, however, can range from the right of use to the right of appropriation or the right to transfer partial rights to third parties (e.g. Burr, 2003; Dietl, 1993).
6. It shall be noted that different types of IPR – i.e. patents, trademarks, copyrights and design rights – have very different characteristics. For example, trademarks cannot be said to provide a limited exclusion right since they do not have any maximum duration.
7. The study was conducted for the French market.
8. 'The term in the literature established to describe the observation that several patents

together form bulks that may legally be separated into individual rights but cannot be exclusively assigned to an individual economic unit, such as a single product, and vice versa is the "patent thicket"' (Reitzig, 2004c, p. 459).

9. However, Cohen et al. (2000) emphasises that personnel fluctuations can have implications for secrecy when employees leave the firm with knowledge about its processes.

10. These figures include fees, legal costs and translation costs. For the US, the fees for a non-small entity were used.

11. A community trademark is a trademark that can be registered through the Office for Harmonisation in the Internal Market (OHIM), enabling registrants to obtain EU-wide protection.

12. This estimate is based on litigation in Germany, France, the Netherlands, and the UK.

13. Costs related to new product development (NPD) in the pharmaceutical industry are said to have grown from an annual average of approximately 54 million USD in the 1970s to about 800 million USD by the 21st century (see Lehman, 2003).

14. Further explanations offered by Kortum and Lerner (1999) suggest that the number of patent applications have been extended to new technology fields, such as software and biotechnology (Blind et al., 2006; Thumm, 2003).

15. Large firms in particular rely on strategic patenting (e.g. Blind et al., 2006; Cohen, 2005).

16. FTO refers to whether the testing or commercialisation of a product can be done without infringing valid patents of third parties. If so, FTO has been obtained.

17. Patents can also be used in several ways to enhance a firm's reputation, and thus to improve its technological image (Blind et al., 2006). However, these motives are found to be of comparatively little relevance.

18. Patent bulks are defined as a coherent group of patents needed to commercialise an innovation.

19. For further reading on these patent value indicators, see e.g. Scherer et al. (2000), Harhoff and Reitzig (2001), Harhoff et al. (2003), Lanjouw and Schankerman (2001).

20. See Agreement on Trade-related Aspects of Intellectual Property (TRIPS) Art. 33: 'The term of protection available shall not end before the expiration of a period of twenty years counted from the filing date'.

21. See TRIPS Art. 18: 'The registration of a trademark shall be renewable indefinitely'.

22. Retained earnings are earnings that have not been distributed as dividends.

23. Securities are fungible instruments with a financial value, and are commonly categorised into equities, debt and derivatives. The present study, however, focuses on debt and equity securities, which together are referred to as securities. Equities are also sometimes referred to as stock or shares. These terms are used as synonyms.

24. Debt and equity markets are together referred to as capital markets.

25. OTC markets are markets that are not intermediated by an exchange, in which trading is conducted directly between two parties.

26. The company costs of capital are defined as the expected return on a portfolio of all its securities (e.g. Brealey and Myers, 2002, p. 222).

27. The EMH is associated with the theory of random walk, which is used to describe a price series where all subsequent price changes represent random departures from previous prices – i.e. stocks take a random and unpredictable path. Random walk theorists accordingly argue that it is impossible to outperform the market without assuming additional risk (see Malkiel, 1973).

28. Insider gains refer to benefits for traders from having information that is unavailable in the public domain.

29. The composition of the board is operationalised by the ratio of outside directors.

30. This has been shown by several research scholars. Prominent among them, Pakes (1986) and Schankerman and Pakes (1986) examine the value of patents on the basis of patent-renewal data, describing the willingness of the patent holder to uphold his patent in exchange for a renewal fee. They argue that patent renewals provide an economic decision by the patent holder which can be used to approximate the private value of the

patent. However, Gambardella et al. (2008) argue that this approach does not capture the value of patents in the extreme right tail of the distribution, since renewal fees only provide a lower bound to patent value based on costs. By using patent citations as a value indicator as well as a small set of patent licensing revenue data, Silverberg and Verspagen (2007) find that the overall distribution of patent value appears to be log-normal, as suggested by Scherer and Harhoff (2000), but that tails are fat. Hence, the tails need to be analysed from the perspective of extreme value statistics. This approach is taken by Gambardella et al. (2008) in assessing the possibility of fat tails through a survey questionnaire in which inventors were asked about the private economic value of their patents.

31. See Section 2.2 for a detailed discussion of the economic characteristics of intangible assets.

32. This is if they do not have an infinite lifetime. See Section 2.8.1 for a more detailed discussion.

33. The study was conducted for companies listed on the S&P 500 index.

34. An exception is made for software R&D after technological feasibility testing.

35. The bid–ask spread measures the liquidity of stocks and reflect investors' transaction costs. As the spread increases, the firm's costs of capital will rise since investors will require compensation for higher transaction costs.

36. Internal credit ratings are provided by banks and provide an assessment of a debt issuer's risk of default. These ratings are mainly used for internal purposes.

37. There are also other theoretical foundations for firms' financing decisions. Trade-off theory, for instance, states that the optimal capital structure is a trade-off between tax benefits related to debt and the costs of default (Kraus and Litzenberger, 1973). However, because, according to trade-off theory, firms' financing decisions neglect the implications of asymmetric information between managers and investors, the theory is not discussed further in the present study.

38. The original figure has been modified to fit the context of the financing of technological innovation in particular. For this reason, funding sources such as trade credit have been excluded.

39. Extensive research has been conducted on how financial intermediaries look to over-come asymmetric information as well as agency problems, by means of requiring collateral and incorporating covenants into contracts (e.g. Boot and Thakor, 1994; Myers, 1977), by gathering and analysing information (e.g. Boyd and Prescott, 1986; Diamond, 1984), by staging funding (Bergemann and Hege, 1998; Sahlman, 1990), and by syndication of the investment (e.g. Admati and Pfleiderer, 1994). As the focus of the present study, however, is on public capital markets, most of these aspects will not be discussed in further detail.

40. See Berger and Udell (1998) for a more detailed discussion.

41. By analogy with venture capital, Lerner et al. (2003) show that smaller firms in the pharmaceutical industry rely heavily on the formation of strategic alliances with larger companies to finance innovation.

42. For a more detailed discussion see, for example, Kortum and Lerner (2000).

43. Government funding programmes provides another solution to the problem, but research on their effectiveness is so far inadequate (Hall and Lerner, 2010), and indeed in a recent book Lerner (2009) has argued that public efforts to support the funding of technological innovation have largely failed. Lerner et al. (2003) also find that companies in biotechnology therefore often rely on the formation of strategic alliances with larger companies for funding. But this is not an option for companies in most technology-driven industries.

44. In recent years there has also been more convergence towards International Financial Reporting Standards (IFRS). For example, the Norwalk Agreement, established by the IASB and the US Financial Accounting Standards Board (FSAB), aims to enhance the cooperation between the two bodies, and bridge major differences in accounting principles. Moreover, in 2007 the US Securities and Exchange Commission

(SEC) allowed foreign private issuers – i.e. non-US companies that are registered in the US – to conduct their annual report according to IFRS without offsetting and reconciliation. Similarly, in Germany the Bilanzrechtsmodernisierungsgesetz (BilMoG) was implemented in 2009 to approximate the Handelsgesetzbuch (HGB) towards IFRS, in much the same way as intangible assets are treated.

45. This contrasts with the US GAAP according to which all R&D is expensed, with the exception of software development costs (Hand and Lev, 2003).
46. In conformity with IAS 35, impairment applies also to intangible assets.
47. Within the EU this is regulated by the Insider Dealing and Market Abuse Directive.
48. For further details, see Hopt and Voigt (2004).
49. For further details, see Eichner (2008).
50. For a more detailed list see BaFin (2005).
51. For example, Kothari et al. (2002) find that the variance of earnings associated with R&D is substantially higher than the variance in earnings associated with tangible assets.
52. For further reading about financial analysts, see Healy and Palepu (2001).
53. CDS is a contract where the buyer makes periodic payments, referred to as the CDS spread, to the seller, and in turn receives a pay-off if the lender in the contract defaults.

3. Patent information and corporate credit ratings: an empirical study of patent valuation by credit rating agencies

While substantial research shows that that stock markets to some extent do differentiate between valuable patents and lemons (see, for example, Hall et al., 2005; Lanjouw and Schankerman, 2004; Neuhäusler et al., 2011), the role of CRAs in doing so has widely been neglected. As past research finds that CRAs provide value-relevant information to both stock and bond markets, their assessments of patent information should be essential to the efficiency of capital markets. This is because, if the value of patents is reflected in their ratings, firms with a high share of valuable patents will receive a higher rating. Hence, financial capital will be allocated to firms with patents of relatively high value, and thus used more productively. Moreover, the issuer will pay a lower interest rate on its debt if investors consider its default risk to be lower. This means that a more favourable rating will attract more investors and enable innovative companies to issue securities at a lower cost.

Because information on patent as well as trademark applications is available up to three years before the actual product is brought to market and revenues are generated (see, for example, Ernst, 2001; Jennewein, 2005), IPR management-related factors could be incorporated to forecast the future financial performance of firms. Moreover, empirical studies have shown a negative correlation between IPR and firms' risk of default – that is, what CRAs ultimately look to determine. These studies focus on the relationship between IPR and firm survival rates after an IPO. Based on a study of 341 firms listed in Germany, Audretsch and Lehmann (2004a) find that the probability of a firm's survival increases with the ownership of patents. In addition, Wilbon (2002) considers patents within the framework of firms' technology management. On the basis of data from the published IPO listing particulars, he creates a scoring system for the variables investigated. For example, firms are rated depending on whether they have IPR protecting their products (highest score), IPR licences from a third party, or no IPR (lowest score). Based on this scoring system, he finds that firms with a higher IPR score also have a higher probability of surviving the first five years after an IPO. A recent study by Helmers and Rogers (2010) also reveals that both patents and trademarks are associated with higher firm survival rates, although they find sectoral differences for patents. In addition, Bittelmeyer (2007) shows that patent information can be used to determine firms' default risk, finding that well-established patent value indicators – that is, patent age and the number of forward citations – have a positive impact on companies' survival rate. This suggests that CRAs ought to be concerned with patent information in their credit risk assessments.

In examining the link between patent information and corporate credit ratings, the present study goes beyond past research in several ways. To my knowledge, only one study has so far addressed the relationship between patents and ratings. In doing so, Czarnitzki and Kraft (2004) study the impact of R&D intensity, patent stock and share of sales of newly developed products on the credit ratings of a German rating agency. They find that all the variables investigated have an inversely U-shaped relationship with credit ratings. However, they do not differentiate between valuable patents and lemons, and thus do not consider the implications of strategic patenting. Moreover, their sample is limited to German firms covered by a national rating agency. Hence, consideration of patent information by international CRAs, such as Standard & Poor's, has not yet been assessed. Finally, past research on the value-relevance of patent information has largely focused on equity markets. Because credit ratings are mainly the concern of lenders, an assessment of CRA use of patent information also, at least implicitly, considers its reflection in debt security prices. In short, the present study aims to bridge this research gap by examining whether CRAs differentiate between valuable patents and lemons, and thereby communicate patent value to debt markets.

3.1   THEORY AND HYPOTHESIS

In this section, I will first briefly discuss the corporate credit rating methodology of Standard & Poor's.[1] In addition, a review of the literature on patent value indicators is conducted. Based on both discussions, some working hypotheses are derived.

3.1.1   Credit Rating Methodology

When assessing the risk of default for a firm, CRAs consider three pillars of risk. Firstly, they assess the risks in the country of the issuer. In general,

Table 3.1   Framework of corporate credit rating assessments

Business risk	Financial risk
● Industry characteristics	● Financial characteristics
● Competitive position	● Financial policy
– e.g. Technology	● Profitability
– e.g. Marketing	● Capital structure
● Management	● Cash-flow protection
	● Financial flexibility

a firm cannot receive a higher rating than the main country in which it operates. For this reason, the rating of the country is often referred to as the *sovereign ceiling* on a firm's rating. The second pillar is the industry in which the firm operates. Because the revenues a firm can generate depend on the size of the industry it is in and its growth potential, an evaluation of the industry is made. This involves analyses of the intensity of competition within the industry, as well as barriers to entry. In addition, industry-related risks, such as regulatory changes, the pace of technological innovation, as well as dependence on cyclical economic patterns, are considered. The importance of these factors differs according to industry (Standard & Poor's, 2008). For industrial firms, a review of business fundamentals, such as industry prospects for growth and vulnerability to technological change, is inevitable. However, when rating financial institutions, technology change will, for example, be a factor of less importance.

Finally, a firm-level analysis is conducted. On this level, CRAs assess the firms' financial and business prospects by looking at factors of both a quantitative and qualitative nature (see Table 3.1). To determine the firm's rating, each of these factors is given a score. How these are combined to arrive at a specific rating is, however, individual to each case (Standard & Poor's, 2008). Qualitative factors relate to business-oriented parameters such as the firm's competitiveness within the industry and the competence of the management team. These are assessments that require close collaboration between the firm and the rating agency.

Still, the fundamentals of the firm-level analysis relate to financial risks. The underlying reasoning is that profitability of the firm's business is required for future debt redemptions – that is, for companies to be able to service their debt, there must be prospects of future cash-flows. CRAs are therefore concerned with evaluating the probability of returns to debt security holders, which in turn depend on the generation of cash-flows by the issuer. The creditworthiness of a firm accordingly ultimately depends on the firm's ability to amortize its debt and fulfil its interest payments. If the probability that the firm will not be able to do so increases, the firm's rating will eventually be downgraded (Standard & Poor's, 2008).

3.1.2 Patent Information and Patent Value Indicators

Past research shows that patents have a positive impact on firm productivity (see, for example, Bloom and Van Reenen, 2002; Greenhalgh and Longland, 2002), but also contribute to companies' market value (Griffiths et al., 2005; Neuhäusler et al., 2011). Although large patent portfolios do not simply lead to more effective appropriation (see, for example, Grindley and Teece, 1997; Reitzig, 2004a), they can be strategically useful. For example, firms rely on patents to block competitors, for licensing purposes and to trade with other firms (see, for example, Cohen et al., 2002; Pitkethly, 2001). Furthermore, an extensive patent portfolio can send positive signals to the capital market (see, for example, Blind et al., 2006). Firms may therefore be tempted to inflate their patent stock with low value patents. This in turn will, however, eventually reduce their signalling effect.

Since patents differ substantially in economic value, patent counts (or patent stocks) can give a distorted impression of a company's value. From a debt market perspective also, this means that the potential for patents to be used as collateral for loans diminishes, if patents are not valued properly. For this reason, several patent value indicators which can be used for patent valuation purposes have been proposed in the literature (see, for example, Frietsch et al. 2010; Reitzig, 2002).[2]

Probably the most common and widely used indicator of patent value is patent forward citations (Harhoff et al., 2003; Narin and Noma, 1987; Trajtenberg, 1990). Since forward citations (citations a patent receives) relate to the prior art, conclusions can be made concerning the inventive step and novelty of the invention. A citation in this sense means that the patent is still of relevance since it provides an important part of the prior art. Theoretically, it has therefore been argued that this indicator measures the degree of technological significance related to a patent (Albert et al., 1991; Blind et al., 2009a; Carpenter et al., 1981).

However, several studies show that citations provide a noisy signal of patent value (Alcacer et al., 2009; Alcacer and Gittelman, 2006; Bessen, 2008; Hall and Ziedonis, 2001). Another promising indicator of patent value that is frequently used is family size (see, for example, Harhoff et al., 2003; Lerner, 1994a). The family size of a patent describes the number of countries in which the patent has been filed (Putnam, 1996). Applying for patent protection in a foreign country represents an investment, indicating that the company is prepared to bear the additional costs of the application and maintenance fees in order to secure an additional market to commercialise its invention. Theoretically, therefore, it is argued that companies only file for patent protection abroad if a corresponding profit is expected from the patent.

3.1.3 Hypothesis

Based on the above-mentioned theoretical arguments, the following hypotheses can be established:

H1:   The larger the number of patents a company files per year, the higher corporate credit ratings they receive.

H2a: The higher the average number of forward citations associated with a company's patent portfolio, the higher corporate credit ratings they receive.

H2b: The larger the average family size associated with a company's patent portfolio, the higher corporate credit ratings they receive.

3.2   DATA AND METHODS

3.2.1 Data and Sample Statistics

For the empirical study, a panel dataset, including 479 firms from 1990 to 2007, was constructed based on the DTI Scoreboard,[3] containing firm-specific data on amongst other things R&D expenditures, market capitalisation and revenues. The base year 2001 was taken – in which in total 500 companies were listed on the DTI Scoreboard – for the construction of the dataset. Data on preceding and following years were added. If any of the 500 companies were not listed in the years before or after 2001, the respective observations were treated as missing. Fortunately, each year's scoreboard provided information on R&D expenditures for the previous four years, so at least some information could be added to fill the gaps. Since some observation variables were still missing in some years, the panel is unbalanced.

In case of merger and acquisition (M&A) related activities between the firms listed on the DTI Scoreboard, the data for the respective firms were added up to produce one observation for each year. Using this method, the firms were treated as if they were merged from the beginning of the observation period.[4] This approach was chosen to preserve comparability over time, as no separation of information was possible after the merger.[5] M&A activities could not be controlled for when not all the companies concerned were listed on the scoreboard. However, since the DTI Scoreboard already contains the most important R&D performers, most firms should be listed, and thus distortions should be limited. These procedures left us with a sample of 479 companies.

In a second step, the patent data and various key financial statistics were added to the sample. Corporate credit ratings as well as additional financial indicators were extracted from Standard & Poor's COMPUSTAT North America database. All financial indicators were converted to British pounds (GBP) based on a yearly averaged exchange rate – which was taken from COMPUSTAT Global Currency database – in order to make the data comparable with the DTI Scoreboard data. Since the information on credit ratings was found to be available only for North American companies, firms from other countries had to be excluded from the sample. This reduced our sample size to 3,438 observations from 191 companies.

The relevant patent data was extracted from the EPO Worldwide Patent Statistical Database (PATSTAT), which provides published patent information from 81 patent offices worldwide. The companies were identified via keyword searches. The keywords also included the names of subsidiaries, where the parent company held at least 25 per cent of shares. This was done to match the patent data with the financial data. Information on the names of the relevant subsidiaries by firm were derived from LexisNexis (http://www.lexisnexis.com) and Creditreform Amadeus (http://www.creditreform.com). Following this, the annual number of patent applications filed by each firm at the United States Patent Office (USPTO) was derived. Furthermore, the patent value indicators for forward citations and average family size were added to the dataset. The priority date – that is, the year of the first filing worldwide – was used for all patent data. Since the data on corporate credit rating was only available for US firms, I restricted the analysis to USPTO data. This was done to be able to focus on one patent system and thereby ensure the consistency and homogeneity of the sample. However, due to a legal change in the US patent system, the USPTO publishes patent applications instead of granted patents from 2001 onwards. This leads to systematic distortions when comparing the information provided by the USPTO before and after 2001. The analysis was therefore restricted to the years 1990 to 2001. This left us with a final sample of 2,292 observations from 191 US companies.

3.2.2 Operationalisation

3.2.2.1 Dependent variable

Standard & Poor's employs a rating system ranging from AAA (highest rating) to D (lowest rating).[6] On the basis of this rating scale, I specify

Table 3.2   Detailed summary of the dependent variable

Corporate Credit Rating	Category	Frequency	Per cent
D	1	60	3.33
C	2	233	12.94
B−	3	340	18.89
B	4	365	20.28
B+	5	406	22.56
A−	6	165	9.17
A	7	88	4.89
A+	8	143	7.94

the dependent variable (see Table 3.2). Like Czarnitzki and Kraft (2004), I do so with a one-period lead. The lead is used to ensure that causality runs from the value indicators to the credit rating and not vice versa. Furthermore, Ernst (2001) has shown that it takes up to three years after a patent application has been filed before a technology is commercialised and revenues are generated. Taking this argument together with the fact that patents are published at latest 18 months after they have been filed and given that the CRAs do not adjust ratings immediately to changes in firm activities (Standard & Poor's, 2008), our specification of the dependent variable seems reasonable.

3.2.2.2   Independent variables

The hypotheses derived above were operationalised on the basis of the following indicators. In doing so, I draw upon several past studies examining the value of patents (see, for example, Harhoff et al., 2003; Lerner, 1994a; Narin and Noma, 1987; Neuhäusler et al., 2011; Reitzig, 2002; Trajtenberg, 1990).

Patent flows of a company   The number of patents a company issues at the USPTO per year (in thousands). By including this variable the possibility that older patents will already be reflected in the firm's rating is accounted for. On the contrary, newly issued patents are more likely to provide new information.

Patent stock of a company   The sum of all patents issued over the previous five years, depreciated by 15 per cent each year (in thousands). This takes account of the possibility that the signalling function of patents is cumulative.

Average number of forward citations   The number of forward citations at the USPTO in a four-year time window divided by the number of applications with forward citations (also in a four-year time window). I use this time window to ensure that all patents have the same amount of time to be cited. Not using this restriction would lead to higher citation counts for older patents, as they would have had a longer time period to be cited, causing a systematic bias.

Average family size   The average number of distinct patent offices at which a company's patents were filed. A prerequisite, however, was that one of the offices was the USPTO, since our focus is on companies operating in the US.

3.2.2.3   Control variables
In determining the control variables, I draw upon extensive past research (see, for example, Horrigan, 1966; Pogue and Soldofsky, 1969; Pinches and Mingo, 1973; Kaplan and Urwitz, 1979; Ashbaugh-Skaife et al., 2004; Kim, 2005), as well as the rating framework of Standard & Poor's. The following indicators are controlled for (see Table 3.3):

Firm size (annual revenue)   Firm size enters the empirical model in term of sales (in billions). This is because past research shows that larger firms exhibit a lower risk of default and thus usually receive a higher rating. For example, Ashbaugh-Skaife et al. (2004) employ total assets as an indicator of firm size and find a strong positive impact on corporate ratings (see also Horrigan, 1966; Kaplan and Urwitz, 1979; Kim, 2005). In my model, however, firm size in terms of sales is used, following Czarnitzki and Kraft (2004).

ROA (EBIT/total assets)   As indicated by Standard & Poor's (2008), profitability provides a litmus test for a firm's rating. Return on assets (ROA) provides a widely used measurement for the profitability of a company in terms of its ability to generate revenue on its assets. Past studies also show that ROA has a significantly positive impact on firms' rating (see, for example, Ashbaugh-Skaife et al., 2004). For this reason, ROA is controlled for in the model (see also Pogue and Soldofsky, 1969; Pinches and Mingo, 1973; Kaplan and Urwitz, 1979; Kim, 2005).

Leverage (total debt/total assets)   Firms with higher debt-to-assets ratios are more leveraged, imposing a risk that the company will not be able to service its debt. For example, Ashbaugh-Skaife et al. (2004) find that leverage has a significantly negative impact on a firm's rating. Accordingly,

CRAs employ leverage ratios to determine a firm's leverage (Standard & Poor's, 2008). Debt-to-assets therefore enters the model as a control variable (see also Horrigan, 1966; Pogue and Soldofsky, 1969; Pinches and Mingo, 1973; Kaplan and Urwitz, 1979; Kim, 2005).

Cash-flow adequacy (net debt/EBIT)   A main concern of CRAs is whether a firm will be able to service its debt. To assess this, CRAs look at the payback period over which a company will be able amortise its debt (Standard & Poor's, 2008). Taking EBIT (earnings before interest and taxes) over the firm's total debt provides an indicator of how many years it will take the company to do so. If a firm, however, holds significant amounts of cash, calculations on a net basis are essential (Standard & Poor's, 2008).[7] This is done by taking the firm's total debt and subtracting cash or cash equivalents. Accordingly, net debt/EBIT enters the model.

Subordinated debt (dummy variable)   Subordinated debt ranks after other debt instruments in case of liquidation during bankruptcy. This means that subordinated debt is associated with higher risks being imposed on lenders, as subordinated debt holders have claims on the firm's assets only after senior debt holders, while lacking the upside potential of shareholders. Not surprisingly Ashbaugh-Skaife et al. (2004) find that subordinated debt has a significantly negative impact on firms' rating. For this reason, a dummy variable controls for subordinated debt in the model (see also Horrigan, 1966; Pinches and Mingo, 1973).

Interest rate (net interest/total debt)   I also control for the interest a firm pays on its debt. This is because, if the risk of default related to a debt issuer increases, lenders will want a premium to compensate for the higher risk, usually in terms of higher interest (see, for example, Stiglitz and Weiss, 1981). While ratings are shown to have an impact on the interest a firm pays when refinancing its debt (see, for example, Hand et al., 1992), CRAs consider the interest that is currently being paid by an issuer in their assessments through various measurements (Standard & Poor's, 2008).

Short-term debt (debt due in one year/total debt)   Debt that is nearly due indicates a need for a firm to refinance itself. This imposes a risk that firms will fail to do so, or do so at a higher cost of capital (Standard & Poor's, 2010). I control for this risk by taking the share of a firm's total debt that is due within a year into the model.

R&D flows   Following past research, annual R&D expenditures (in billions) enters the empirical model (Czarnitzki and Kraft, 2004). This is

Table 3.3 Overview of the variables and summary statistics

Variable	Mean	Std. Dev.	Min	Max	No. of Obs.	No. of Firms
Corporate Credit Rating (1-year lead)	4.33	1.79	1.00	8.00	1800	172
Return on assets (ROA)	0.11	0.12	−0.76	0.48	2029	184
Total debt/Total assets	0.16	0.15	0.00	2.65	1956	184
Net debt/EBIT	3.59	48.37	−365.49	892.97	990	175
Subordinated debt dummy	0.09	0.28	0.00	1.00	1969	184
Debt due in 1 year/total debt	0.13	0.19	0.00	1.00	1735	173
Net Interest/total Debt	0.16	0.35	0.00	6.91	1676	171
Sales (in billions)	10.46	17.99	0.06	137.96	1136	191
R&D flows (in billions)	0.38	0.70	0.00	5.65	1638	191
R&D stock (in thousands)	1.68	2.72	0.10	18.41	691	180
Patent flows (in thousands)	0.15	0.32	0.00	4.58	1992	186
Patent stock (in thousands)	0.59	1.15	0.00	14.83	1041	166
Average family size	6.26	3.23	2.00	33.25	1902	182
Average no. of forward citations	8.14	8.16	1.00	140.00	1965	186

because new R&D expenditures indicate future growth potential that might not already be reflected in a firm's rating.

R&D stock I also control for the sum of the company's R&D expenditures in the last five years (in billions), depreciated by 15 per cent each year. This takes into account the fact that knowledge is cumulative. Therefore, it can be assumed that R&D stock could exert some additional influence on corporate credit ratings.

3.3   ESTIMATION METHODS

Since corporate credit rating is an ordinally scaled variable (credit ratings can be rank ordered, but uniform differences in categories cannot be assumed) and the data used for the analysis is in the form of a firm-level panel, the econometric specifications have to account for the typical peculiarities of this data structure.

Ordinal dependent variables violate the assumptions of the linear regression model (ordinary least squares – OLS). Using models that avoid the assumption of equal distances between the categories is a better choice. Therefore, we employ ordered probit models with maximum likelihood (ML) estimation to assess the effects of the patent indicators on corporate credit ratings. Ordered probit models start from a latent variable model with

$$y_i^* = x_i\beta + \varepsilon_i \text{ with } \varepsilon_i \text{ N}(0,1)$$

where x_i is a vector of explanatory variables, β is a coefficient vector and ε_i the normally distributed error term. The latent corporate credit rating variable is limited by thresholds with

$$y_i = \begin{cases} 0, & if -\infty < y_i^* \le \mu_0 \\ 1, & if \mu_0 < y_i^* \le \mu_1 \\ \vdots \\ N & if \mu_{N-1} < y_i^* \le \infty \end{cases}$$

where $n = 8$ for the last of our estimates since the corporate credit rating variable consists of eight categories.

As we use a panel dataset for our analyses, we are able to specify to which group each observation belongs and that we use data with repeated observations on firms. In other words, we can cluster the ordered probit model by companies. This allows us to control for unobserved heterogeneity in our models. In addition, we add time-dummies to the models to account for period-specific effects.

The coefficients of the ML estimation can be interpreted such that positive signs belong to a higher rating category, whereas negative signs of a coefficient are associated with a lower category.

3.4   EMPIRICAL FINDINGS

3.4.1   Descriptive Statistics

The bivariate analysis of the variables in Table 3.4 reveals several interesting insights. Firstly, and as expected, there is a positive and significant correlation between ROA and companies' credit rating. This is also true for the firm size indicator (sales), which, along with past findings, shows that larger firms exhibit a lower risk of default and therefore usually receive a higher rating. Moreover, in conformity with previous studies, I find a significantly negative correlation between the dummy for subordinated debt and the credit rating variable. A negative correlation is also found for the variable describing the share of short-term debt – that is, debt which is due within one year – indicating that the risk of refinancing affects a company's rating.

R&D expenditures are positively related to the credit rating variable, although for R&D stocks no significant correlation can be found. The number of US patents also has a significantly positive correlation with corporate credit ratings, which means that a larger number of patent applications are associated with higher ratings. The patent stock variable is also positively correlated with the credit rating variable. The high correlation between the R&D stock indicator and R&D flows should also be noted. The same is true for patent applications at the USPTO. I therefore decided to drop both stock variables in the following multivariate analyses.

Finally, as for the patent value indicator family size, a significantly positive correlation is found with the credit rating of firms, giving some support for H2b. Hence, a larger family size is associated with a higher rating. Theoretically, this could be explained by the fact that a larger family size indicates patent protection, and thus exclusivity in the appropriation of economic returns, for a greater geographical market. Surprisingly, however, patent forward citations are negatively correlated with ratings. An explanation for this would be the positive relationship between forward citations and the probability of patent infringement as well as invalidity lawsuits (Lanjouw and Schankerman, 2001). Accordingly, it could be that CRAs discount for the associated legal risks.

3.4.2 Multivariate Findings

Turning to the multivariate analyses, Table 3.5 shows the estimates on corporate credit ratings that result from ordered probit regressions. Starting from a model without innovation indicators (M1), several models have been calculated. R&D flows, patent flows and patent value indicators were added gradually. This approach was chosen because it allows me to assess whether the effects remain stable over different models. In addition, it enables me to observe if the added innovation and patent value indicators increase the explanatory power compared with the initial model.

It is, again, noted that the R&D stock indicator is highly correlated with R&D flows. The same is true for patent applications at the USPTO (see Table 3.4). For this reason, both stock variables are dropped in the following multivariate analyses.

Table 3.4 Pairwise correlations – 'patent value indicators'

	Corporate credit rating (1-year lead)	Return on assets (ROA)	Total debt/ total assets	Net debt/ EBIT	Subor-dinated debt dummy	Debt due in 1 year/ total debt	Net interest/ total debt	Sales (in billions)	R&D flows (in billions)	R&D stock (in thou-sands)	Patent flows (in thou-sands)	Patent stock (in thou-sands)	Average family size
Return on assets (ROA)	0.18***	1											
Total debt/ total assets	0.05**	−0.31***	1										
Net debt/ EBIT	−0.06	−0.02	0.07**	1									
Subor-dinated debt dummy	−0.05**	−0.10***	0.26***	0.01	1								
Debt due in 1 year/ total debt	−0.14***	0.02	−0.26***	−0.02	−0.03	1							
Net Interest/ total Debt	−0.03	0.07***	−0.23***	−0.02	−0.04	0.20***	1						
Sales (in billions)	0.23***	−0.01	0.08***	−0.01	0.24***	0.00	−0.04	1					

R&D flows (in billions)	0.10***	0.07**	−0.01	0.00	0.14***	−0.02	−0.02	0.70***	1						
R&D stock (in thousands)	0.06	0.13***	−0.02	0.01	0.20***	0.02	0.01	0.74***	0.95***	1					
Patent flows (in thousands)	0.09***	0.01	0.02	0.00	−0.00	−0.02	−0.02	0.21***	0.46***	0.41***	1				
Patent stock (in thousands)	0.10***	0.00	0.02	−0.01	0.04	0.01	−0.02	0.29***	0.51***	0.51***	0.95***	1			
Average family size	0.15***	0.09***	−0.03	−0.01	−0.08***	−0.02	0.00	0.05*	0.13***	0.16***	−0.12***	−0.13***	1		
Average no. of forward citations	−0.18***	0.08***	−0.19***	−0.04	−0.11***	0.14***	0.04	−0.13***	−0.05*	0.01	−0.12***	−0.13***	0.02	0.04*	1

Notes: Significance Level: ***p<0.01, **p<0.05, *p<0.1.

A look at the coefficients reveals that ROA exerts a consistent and significantly positive effect on the credit rating variable over all models. This finding is also consistent with past research (see, for example, Ashbaugh-Skaife et al., 2004; Kim, 2005). Hence, as expected, more profitable firms exhibit a higher rating. In conformity with previous studies, we also find that the dummy variable for subordinated debt has a strongly negative impact on firms' ratings (see, for example, Ashbaugh-Skaife et al., 2004; Pinches and Mingo, 1973). We therefore conclude that the riskiness of subordinated debt is reflected in corporate credit ratings. A similar effect can be observed for the interest rate variable, although only in the first model. To my knowledge, this control variable has not been used in past research on the determinants of ratings. However, as elaborated, there are good theoretical reasons for its inclusion. Firms that exhibit higher interest on their debt have a more difficult financial situation in terms of covering their interest payments as they need to generate higher operating profits than firms paying less interest to do so. They accordingly face a higher risk of default. Finally, I find that the firm size indicator (sales) has a consistently positive effect on the dependent variable, which again supports the argument that larger firms with more mature business models generally face a lower risk of default, and thus also receive higher ratings. The other controls, however, did not show any significant effects in the multivariate analysis.

As for the innovation indicators, I find that R&D expenditures are not significantly associated with corporate credit ratings. There are at least three potential explanations for this finding. A first and very straightforward argument would be that CRAs do not have any particular knowledge about the evaluation of R&D expenditures and therefore do not explicitly consider these. For example, in a study among Italian banks, Ughetto (2007) finds that intangibles are not taken into account in a systematic way in corporate credit risk assessments. The majority of the respondents did not even consider intangible assets as meaningful determinants for credit risk. A more refined explanation stems from past research, which shows that financial analysts find technology-driven firms more difficult to value (see, for example, Amir et al., 1999). In contrast to assets such as commercial properties which share common characteristics across firms, and thus are easy to compare, R&D projects are very specific. In addition, Kothari et al. (2002) find that the variance of earnings associated with R&D is substantially higher compared with the variability in earnings related to tangible assets. It could therefore well be that CRAs are reluctant to explicitly consider the value potential of R&D as a consequence of valuation difficulties stemming from the high uncertainty attached to related returns. Finally, in conformity with accounting standards, R&D

investments are – at least partly – instantaneous costs, reducing profits (see Section 2.8.1). It could therefore well be that the positive and negative effects that are reflected in the R&D indicator balance out, resulting in a non-significant effect.

The patent flows indicator shows a significant and positive effect on credit ratings, also when the patent value indicators are included in the model. Therefore, it can be concluded that companies which file a comparatively high number of yearly patent applications receive a higher credit rating than their respective counterparts with lower patenting activity. This finding strongly supports H1, meaning that more patents are associated with less credit risk. I find two potential explanations for this. Firstly, it may be that CRAs view patents as innovation output, and thus value more innovative firms positively and increasingly so. Against this argument, I hold that no such impact was found for R&D expenditures, which after all provide investment in technological innovation. However, although CRAs do not perceive the growth potential of investments in innovation, it may be that they perceive future economic benefits related to a large innovative output, as there is proven commercial potential and thus a higher probability of future returns. Secondly, it may well be that CRAs view patents not just as innovative output, but as competitive weapons (see, for example, Rivette and Kline, 2000; Reitzig, 2007). Clearly, past research has shown how companies use patents strategically in order to build a stronger competitive position (see, for example, Blind et al., 2006; Cohen et al., 2000; Pitkethly, 2001), and to reduce the risks of lawsuits (see, for example, Lanjouw and Schankerman, 2001). Accordingly, Lanjouw and Schankerman (2001) argue that portfolio size effects exist, meaning that firms with a larger patent portfolio are better able to settle disputes through cross-licensing agreements, without resorting to patent lawsuits. Since the costs of patent lawsuits can threaten the existence of a firm from one day to the next, it is likely that CRAs consider patents from this point of view.

In line with H2b, the average family size of a company's patent portfolio shows a significantly positive impact on the dependent variable. Hence, firms that have secured exclusivity for a larger number of markets receive higher ratings. Theoretically, it seems plausible that a larger average family size is associated with higher future cash-flows, as exclusivity may have been obtained for more markets. As shown, cash-flow adequacy is of major concern to CRAs in their credit risk assessments, providing a theoretical foundation for its positive impact. Still, the impact of the family size variable is relatively low, at least compared with the patent flows variable. It should also be noted that our findings do not tell us whether CRAs explicitly assess the average family size of a firm's patent portfolio, or if the positive impact is indirect, for example as a consequence of a larger family size being associated with firms that operate more globally.

In contrast to H2a, and consistent with bivariate analysis, the patent forward citations variable has a significant, but negative impact on corporate credit ratings. This is not in the least surprising since Hall et al. (2005) show that one forward citation represents a value of 210,000 USD. However, Lanjouw and Schankerman (2001) also find a positive relationship between forward citations and the probability of patent infringement as well as invalidity lawsuits. Similarly, Harhoff et al. (2003) show that more valuable patents are more often the target of opposition or litigation.

The costs of patent litigation can be devastating for any single firm. Bessen and Meurer (2008b) argue that the total costs of patent lawsuits are substantially large compared with legal costs, R&D expenditures, and even patent value. This is because patent lawsuits are associated with additional indirect costs such as distractions for management and loss of market share. For example, pending litigation can shut down production, sales and marketing, and even without a preliminary injunction consumers may stop purchasing the product. Additional costs may be related to managerial distractions, but also a greater risk of bankruptcy. Measuring the loss of wealth from Tobin's q, they find lawsuit costs for alleged infringers to be about 28.7 million USD in the mean and 2.9 million USD in the median.[8] Also the costs for patent owners were found to be substantial.

A theoretical reason for the negative relationship between forward citations and ratings could accordingly be that, although forward citations are associated with future economic benefits, CRAs still discount for the associated legal risks. I find this argument plausible, and not only because forward citations provide an indicator of patent value. This is also true for family size, which shows a positive impact on the dependent variable. Rather, I argue that because forward citations indicate subsequent research investments, and hence potential competition in R&D, they are associated with a higher probability of lawsuits. It is therefore only logical to discount for forward citations when assessing risk, including credit risk.

Finally, it should be noted that the patent value indicators only have a marginal effect on the dependent variable, compared with patent flows. This finding contradicts past research showing that these indicators have a stronger impact on both stock market valuations (see, for example, Neuhäusler et al., 2011; Sandner and Block, 2011) and firm profitability (see, for example, Neuhäusler et al., 2011). As past research shows a surge in strategic patenting (see, for example, Cohen, 2005), leading to a relatively high share of low value patents (see, for example, Blind et al., 2009a), CRAs should be concerned to differentiate valuable patents from lemons. This is because if the value of a patent relates to a strategic motive – for example its purpose is to increase the firm's bargaining power before cross-licensing negotiations (see, for example, Hall et al., 2005) – the patent is likely to have no economic value to a third party. The patent therefore has no potential of being used as collateral or of being commercialised to resolve financial distress. On the contrary, if the patent can be used to protect a product that generates income, it will have an impact on the default risk of a firm. However, I find that CRAs take another perspective, when it comes to patents, namely the perspective of litigation risks. I argue that the relatively low impact of the family size indicator, compared with the patent flows indicator, and the negative impact of the citations indicator, suggest that this perspective is predominant. Hence, the risks of litigation outweigh the potential benefits related to valuable patents. These effects, however, will be analysed in more detail below, when looking at the marginal effects computed at the means of the independent variables.

Turning our attention to the overall explanatory power of the models, that is, the R^2 values, it can be observed that adding the innovation and patent value indicators increases the explanatory power of the model. Hence, the innovation indicators explain some additional variance in corporate credit rating variable. Furthermore, I measure the overall fit of the models, using the Bayesian Information Criterion (BIC). The difference in BIC between two models shows which is better able to explain the variance in the dependent variable. BIC M1 – BIC M2 > 0 leads to a preference for M2 (Long and Freese, 2001). As we can see in Table 3.5, BIC takes a lower value when the innovation and patent value indicators are added to the model.[9] This means that M3 is best able to explain the variance in the credit rating variable.

To analyse the effects of the innovation and patent value indicators in more detail, Wald tests of the single coefficients for M3 were conducted (see Table 3.6). The tests show that the coefficients for R&D and patents are not equal to zero, meaning that I find that a combination of both indicators has a significant influence on the credit rating variable. The same is true when I add patent value indicators to the Wald test.

Finally, I analyse the effects of patent flows and value indicators' intensity on corporate credit rating in more detail across the categories of the dependent variable. This is done by calculating the marginal effects at the means of the independent variables (see Table 3.7).

The results show that patents are best able to explain the variance in corporate credit rating in the medium ranges of the dependent variable, that is, from rating 'C' to rating 'AA'. In the lowest and highest

Table 3.5   Results of the ordered probit models

DV = Corporate Credit Rating	M1		M2		M3	
	Coef.	S.E.	Coef.	S.E.	Coef.	S.E.
Return on assets	3.500***	0.998	3.486***	1.109	3.414***	1.134
Total debt/total assets	0.541	0.745	0.409	0.718	0.448	0.719
Net debt/EBIT	0.000	0.001	0.003	0.002	0.002	0.002
Subordinated debt dummy	−1.030***	0.296	−0.901***	0.255	−0.902***	0.231
Debt due in 1 year/total debt	0.459	0.517	0.577	0.536	0.654	0.540
Net Interest/total debt	−0.353*	0.204	−0.313	0.226	−0.324	0.218
Sales (in billions)	0.023***	0.011	0.023***	0.008	0.020***	0.008
R&D flows			0.000	0.000	0.000	0.000
Patent flows			0.427**	0.187	0.491**	0.193
Average family size					0.055*	0.032
Average no. of forward citations					−0.049*	0.028
Time dummies	YES		YES		YES	
Industry dummies	YES		YES		YES	
Observations	688		649		632	
No. of companies	135		133		129	
Pseudo R^2	0.165		0.179		0.192	
AIC	2289.38		2117.71		2032.46	
BIC	2461.66		2292.25		2214.86	

Notes:
Significance Level: ***p<0.01, **p<0.05, *p<0.1.
The difference in the number of observations can be explained by the fact that we use an unbalanced panel, in which data for some observations in the respective years could be missing.

Table 3.6   Wald tests for the innovation and patent value indicators

R&D flows, patent flows = 0	Chi²	6.6
	Prob > Chi²	0.04
R&D flows, patent flows, average family size,	Chi²	9.47
average no. of forward citations = 0	Prob > Chi²	0.05

categories of the rating variable, the patent flows do not play a significant role. One explanation for this could be that, in lower categories of the credit rating, other factors have a greater effect on credit risk. When evaluating distressed debt, this is regarded as highly likely as the immediate question will be whether the company can become more profitable in the short term to avoid bankruptcy. Profits related to innovation, however, usually lie further ahead and will therefore probably be seen as of less relevance in such situations. In the upper regions of the rating, where the top-performing firms are found, ceiling effects could be at work. This finding is also logical, since firms with many assets-in-place – that is, assets that already generate economic returns – can be assessed on the basis of their current cash-flow rather than their future profit potential.

What is surprising are the different effects of the patent value indicators across the different rating categories. While family size exhibits a positive cumulative impact on the dependent variable, it has a negative impact in the lower rating categories (from rating 'B' to rating 'C'), although the negative impact is only significant within category 'B'. While the reason for this is not known, a possible explanation would be that family size indicates investment in patent protection for additional markets, and hence is associated with higher instant costs. It could be that these costs are predominant in the future value potential of the patent in the lower categories, as these firms exhibit a higher default risk.

Also striking is the fact that the forward citations indicator, which had a negative cumulative impact on the dependent variable, has a positive impact in the lower rating categories. A potential explanation for this could be that forward citations are associated with R&D competition, and thus higher risks of patent lawsuits. This, however, also means that third parties have a commercial interest in the patent. In the case of financial distress, it is normal for a firm to look to sell assets to pay off some of its debt. It is, theoretically speaking, more likely that a firm will be able to find a buyer for a cited patent, and thus potentially, at least partially, be in a position to resolve its financial situation.

Table 3.7   *Marginal effects calculated at the means of the independent*
               variables

DV = Corporate Credit Rating	Rating D		Rating C		Rating B−		Rating B	
	dy/dx	S.E.	dy/dx	S.E.	dy/dx	S.E.	dy/dx	S.E.
Return on assets	−0.016	0.016	−0.331**	0.169	−0.395***	0.160	−0.612***	0.243
Total debt/ total assets	−0.002	0.004	−0.044	0.071	−0.052	0.084	−0.080	0.131
Net debt/ EBIT	0.000	0.000	0.000	0.000	0.000	0.000	0.000	0.000
Subordi- nated debt dummy	0.014	0.013	0.146**	0.066	0.110***	0.039	0.066*	0.038
Debt due in 1 year/ total debt	−0.003	0.004	−0.063	0.056	−0.076	0.067	−0.117	0.100
Net interest/ total debt	0.002	0.002	0.031	0.023	0.038	0.027	0.058	0.042
Sales	0.000	0.000	−0.002**	0.001	−0.002**	0.001	−0.004**	0.002
R&D flows	0.001	0.000	0.011	0.000	0.013	0.000	0.020	0.000
Patent flows	−0.002	0.002	−0.048**	0.025	−0.057**	0.027	−0.088**	0.040
Average family size	0.000	0.000	−0.005	0.004	−0.006	0.004	−0.010*	0.006
Average no. of forward citations	0.000	0.000	0.005	0.003	0.006*	0.004	0.009*	0.005
Time dummies	YES		YES		YES		YES	
Industry dummies	YES		YES		YES		YES	
Observa- tions	632							
No. of compa- nies	129							
Pseudo R²	0.192							
AIC	2032.46							
BIC	2214.86							

Note:
Significance Level: ***p<0.01, **p<0.05, *p<0.1.
For dummy variables, dy/dx represents a discrete change of dummy variable from 0 to 1.

Rating B+		Rating A−		Rating A		Rating A+	
dy/dx	S.E.	dy/dx	S.E.	dy/dx	S.E.	dy/dx	S.E.
0.464*	0.247	0.374**	0.175	0.237**	0.119	0.280	0.187
0.061	0.103	0.049	0.082	0.031	0.052	0.037	0.057
0.000	0.000	0.000	0.000	0.000	0.000	0.000	0.000
−0.176***	0.056	−0.078***	0.029	−0.042**	0.021	−0.040	0.029
0.089	0.077	0.072	0.064	0.045	0.043	0.054	0.057
−0.044	0.033	−0.035	0.026	−0.023	0.018	−0.027	0.026
0.003*	0.002	0.002*	0.001	0.001*	0.001	0.002*	0.001
−0.015	0.000	−0.012	0.000	−0.008	0.000	−0.009	0.000
0.067*	0.036	0.054*	0.029	0.034*	0.020	0.040	0.027
0.008*	0.005	0.006	0.004	0.004	0.003	0.005	0.004
−0.007	0.004	−0.005	0.004	−0.003	0.002	−0.004	0.003
YES		YES		YES		YES	
YES		YES		YES		YES	

3.5   SUMMARY AND CONCLUSIONS

The present study goes beyond past research in examining the contribution of CRAs to the informational efficiency of capital markets, in terms of communicating the value of intangible assets through their credit risk assessments. Previous studies showing that ratings provide new information to both stock and bond markets (see, for example, Holthausen and Leftwich, 1986; Hand et al., 1992) indicate that CRAs do play an important role in the informational efficiency of capital markets. I examine whether they do so also in today's more intangible economy, in which technological innovation has become the primary driver of economic growth (see, for example, Nakamura, 2001; Romer, 2003). My findings give a mixed picture.

Corporate credit ratings, as stock market valuations, reflect the future economic benefits related to patents, supporting H1. In addition, I find a positively significant, although relatively weak, impact of the patent portfolio's average patent family size on credit ratings, giving some support to H2b. This finding indicates that CRAs at least partially differentiate between valuable patents and lemons. They also seem to account for forward citations, but not in the positive manner I expected. Instead, I find a significantly negative impact on the rating variable, rejecting H2a. This finding shows that stock markets and CRAs value forward citations differently.

This is, however, not surprising, as stock market valuations and credit risk assessments are fundamentally different. While stock markets look to determine the future economic benefits of an investment, credit risk assessments focus more on the downside, which is of less interest to speculative stock markets. This is because of the different nature of debt and equity contracts. While a shareholder participates on the upside, creditors do not share upside gains related a the firm's investments, and thus are mainly interested in the bottom tail of the distribution of economic returns (see, for example, Stiglitz, 1985). For this reason, compared with shareholders, creditors are more concerned with determining the risks of an investment rather than the present value of potential future economic benefits (see, for example, Standard & Poor's, 2008). Still, past research shows that patents, as well as related value indicators, are also associated with higher company survival rates, meaning lower risks of default (see, for example, Bittelmeyer, 2007). Moreover, valuable patents can provide collateral to creditors (see, for example, Amable et al., 2008). Theoretically, the absence of collateral could lead to moral hazard complications, and thus credit rationing (see, for example, Stiglitz and Weiss, 1981). As most debt funding is given only on a secured basis (see, for example, Berger and

Udell, 1998), it is essential for innovative firms with few tangible assets to be able to provide some sort of collateral, and thereby enhance their creditworthiness, in order to finance innovation through debt. To assess whether an asset can properly serve as collateral, however, in terms of whether its value covers the secured debt, a valuation of the asset needs to be conducted (Standard & Poor's, 2006). This means that if intangible assets, such as patents, are not valued properly in credit risk assessments, creditors are likely to develop a distorted picture of the risks related to an investment. Hence, there are strong theoretical as well as practical reasons for CRAs to assess the value of a company's patents.

However, there is also another side of the patent coin – that is, the risk of patent lawsuits. The total costs related to such risks go well beyond legal costs, and can increase firms' cost of capital as a consequence of a higher risk of insolvency (see, for example, Bessen and Meurer, 2008b). Because patents of higher value are more likely to be subject to lawsuits (see, for example, Lanjouw and Schankerman, 2001; Harhoff et al., 2003), CRAs need to make constant trade-offs between the potential future benefits related to patents and the risk of lawsuits. Theoretically, from a creditor perspective, risks associated with patent lawsuits will generally outweigh potential economic benefits as creditors do not share the upside related to the firm's investments. At first sight, this may seem to contradict to our finding that patent flows are associated with higher credit ratings. However, like Lanjouw and Schankerman (2001), I argue that portfolio size effects exist, meaning that firms with a larger patent portfolio are better able to settle disputes through cross-licensing agreements, without resorting to patent lawsuits. Accordingly, I arrive at the conclusion that patents do contribute to higher credit ratings, not in terms of growth opportunities, but as insurance.

I believe this for two main reasons. Firstly, I find that R&D flows do not contribute to higher ratings, implying that CRAs do not explicitly consider innovation activity as a determinant of credit risk. Secondly, the impact of patent value indicators is only marginal compared to the impact of patent flows. My findings show that inflationary corporate patent policies under present conditions make it easier for firms to obtain debt funding, although most patents are of relatively low value and do not provide substantial collateral.

The relationship between my patent value indicators and corporate credit ratings can also be explained from the perspective of trade-offs between the economic benefits of patents and the risk of lawsuits. We argue that CRAs perceive the benefits related to family size to be relatively high, while the benefits related to forward citations are regarded as comparatively low. Our theoretical argument is that, while family size indicates exclusivity on a wider range of markets, forward citations not only indicate technological significance, but also the degree of R&D competition between firms, making patent lawsuits more likely.

Finally, my findings suggest some implications for the financing of technological innovation by means of debt. These are in line with past research revealing substantial informational deficits related to the valuation of technology-driven businesses, leaving both investors (see, for example, Aboody and Lev, 2000) and financial analysts (see, for example, Amir et al., 1999) deprived. The uncertainty about the boundaries of property rights under the current patent system is not likely to help solve this situation. The pace of strategic patenting has been ever increasing since the mid 1980s (see, for example, Blind et al., 2004; Hall and Ziedonis, 2001), leading to a relatively high share of low value patents (Gambardella et al, 2008; Harhoff et al., 2003). As argued by Lemley and Shapiro (2005): 'Under patent law, a patent is no guarantee of exclusion but more precisely a legal right to try to exclude'. This makes patent valuation more difficult, but also more important. Still, I find the number of patents to be a more important determinant of credit risk than their commercial value according to CRAs' current rating framework. This means that firms need to devote substantial financial resources to building and upholding a large patent portfolio as insurance or they will eventually face higher costs of capital. Hence, companies will experience higher costs of innovation either through increased costs of funding or increased patent portfolio costs – a finding that is especially troublesome for smaller technology-driven firms. I conclude that the financing of technological innovation through debt will be expensive either way.

NOTES

1. The discussion is limited to Standard & Poor's because the present study is based on their ratings. However, other CRAs, such as Moody's, adopt a similar approach.
2. For the sake of simplicity, all patent characteristics that could indicate patent value will be referred to as value indicators in the remainder of this study.
3. The DTI Scoreboard is provided annually by the Department for Business, Innovation and Skills (BIS). For the year 2008, the top 1,400 international companies were listed according to R&D expenditures by industry (the number of companies is smaller in preceding years). In addition to R&D expenditures, further firm-specific values, like sales and the number of employees, were provided. http://www.innovation.gov.uk/rd_scoreboard/.
4. For details of this method of dataset construction, see Frietsch et al. (2010).
5. Clearly, this treats merged companies as being the sum of their parts, which may be problematic if mergers and acquisitions caused, for example, synergy effects. Still, we think that this is the most suitable approach.
6. Ratings from AAA to BBB are considered as investment grade bonds.

7. This is because the firm could use its cash to immediately amortise a part of its debt, and thus reduce its debt burden.
8. This is measured in 1992 USD.
9. The same is true of Akaike's Information Criterion (AIC), which is a similar measure to BIC. All else being equal, a model with a smaller value of AIC can be considered as the model with the better overall fit (Long and Freese, 2001).

4. IPR management and company valuation in the pharmaceutical industry: an exploratory study

This chapter examines pharmaceutical firms' IPR management by means of exploratory interviews. A qualitative empirical approach was chosen in order to further specify the IPR management term and its dimensions. Moreover, research shows that industries differ according to whether they are dominated by discrete or complex technologies, and this is reflected in companies' patenting behaviour (see, for example, Levin et al., 1987; Arundel and Kabla, 1998; Cohen et al., 2000). While firms in discrete technology fields patent to protect their products from imitation, companies in complex technology fields rely more on strategic patenting (see, for example, Cohen et al., 2000; Hussinger, 2006). However, recent research reveals that strategic patenting has extended across technology fields (see, for example, Blind et al., 2006). Notably, a recent inquiry by the European Commission (2009) has shown that pharmaceutical firms develop more complex IPR strategies to enhance their financial performance. Unfortunately, however, the inquiry did not provide any holistic conceptualisation of how they do so. The objective of the present exploratory study was therefore to develop a conceptual framework for how pharmaceutical firms conduct their IPR management to serve as the basic foundation for the operationalisation of IPR management indicators in the quantitative empirical study that follows (see Chapter 5). General considerations for the holistic conceptualisation of IPR management are summarised in the following research questions:

- What are the motives for IPR protection in the pharmaceutical industry?
- Are there synergies between the different motives for patent and trademark protection?
- How do these motives fit into companies' overall business models?
- What are the dimensions of their IPR management?
- How is their IPR management organizationally integrated?
- Do they manage their IPR according to specific objectives?

- How does their IPR management contribute to their financial performance?
- Do they report on their IPR management to the stock market?

With these research questions in mind, I interviewed 21 IPR management experts. There followed interviews with 12 financial analysts, also within the pharmaceutical industry. The interviews with analysts were conducted in a second step – after the interviews with IPR management experts – to examine the role of IPR management information in company valuation. The fact that interviews with IPR management experts had been carried out upfront enabled me to ask the analysts more specific questions about how they valued companies' IPR management. More specifically, I developed the interview guidelines on the basis of findings concerning how companies manage their IPR. This was done because an examination of companies' IPR reporting practices alone would not have enabled me to draw conclusions about the availability of the information actually requested. As a main objective of the present study is to examine to what extent companies' IPR management is reflected in their share price performance, and thereby identify potential areas of asymmetric information, I decided to examine which kinds of IPR management information capital market participants request in advance of the quantitative study. Among other things, this will determine the ability of companies to reduce asymmetric information by means of IPR reporting. Taking together the findings from the interviews conducted with IPR management experts and financial analysts, I was able to conceptualise relationships between IPR reporting and companies' share price performance.

Although past research has shown that certain IPR information disclosures provide value-relevant information to the stock market, the extent to which IPR management information is considered by the stock market has, to my knowledge, not yet been investigated and conceptualised. Because financial analysts make investment recommendations related to pharmaceutical firms' shares on a continuous basis, they consistently analyse these firms, and thus information published by them. For this particular reason, analysts were considered an appropriate target group for the analysis in terms of addressing the following research questions:

- Do stock markets consider IPR management information to be value-relevant?
- What kind of IPR management information do they request?
- In what context is such information considered?
- Is the requested IPR management information sufficiently provided?

Chapter 4 is structured as follows: the first part of the chapter describes the methodology of the study, the sample, and how the data was collected. In addition, it gives a brief introduction to the evolution of the pharmaceutical industry and its regulatory framework. The section on the structure of the pharmaceutical industry, and its regulatory framework, is by no means complete – not least because regulations differ across countries. Rather it aims to provide an overview of the context in which pharmaceutical firms' IPR management occurs. Thirdly, I go on to describe the results of the interviews conducted among IPR management experts, on the basis of which I derive a conceptual framework for how pharmaceutical firms manage their IPR, and conceptualise several relationships between firms' IPR management and their financial performance. Following this, I describe the findings of the interviews with financial analysts and conceptualise a similar set of relationships between firms' IPR management reporting and their share price performance. These relationships form the basis for the indicators which are derived and operationalised in the quantitative empirical study that follows.

4.1   DESIGN OF THE STUDY

4.1.1   Method

For the empirical examination of pharmaceutical firms' IPR management, a qualitative research approach was taken. The main reason for this choice of method was the crucial characteristic of qualitative data – enabling a holistic contemplation and conceptualisation of a relatively complex phenomenon (see Eisenhardt and Gräbner, 2007; Miles and Huberman, 1994). Because the research questions concerning pharmaceutical firms' IPR management that ought to be answered are of rather an exploratory nature, a qualitative study was seen as the most appropriate research approach to derive some working hypotheses for the quantitative study.

The exploration was conducted my means of semi-structured interviews. More precisely, interview guidelines were used, containing broad questions related to the specific research questions. This enabled the interviewer to make sure that most areas of interest were covered, and to set the focus of the discussion, while still leaving room for respondents to freely explain their point of view, without being influenced by the interviewer. Moreover, as the interviewer learned more from the respondent, this enabled new aspects of interest to be picked up. This made it possible to gradually learn more about pharmaceutical firms' IPR management practices.

Like Pangerl (2009), I also initially worked with less detailed interview guidelines, and thus conducted more open interviews at the beginning. As I learned more from the experts, I added new questions to my guidelines (see Schnell et al., 2008). Hence, as the dimensions and scope of firms' IPR management became clearer, the interviews gradually became more focused. This approach does not create any bias as the issue is not whether there are standardised questions, but that there are no specifications leading the answers in a certain direction (see Hopf, 1995). The same approach was also adopted in the interviews with financial analysts. The interview guidelines were developed on the basis of the findings from the interviews with IPR management experts. This was done to assess the financial analysts' knowledge about IPR management in general and which aspects they perceived to be important from a stock market perspective.

4.1.2 Sample and Data Collection

In order to operationalise the IPR management indicators for the econometric study, semi-structured interviews were conducted with 19 originator firms in the field of pharmaceuticals and red biotechnology.[1] Generic firms, which rely less on patent protection, were excluded, although some of the firms interviewed also had generic divisions. The companies' IPR management was explored in relation to the development of pharmaceutical products. In addition, I explored companies' practices of disclosing information about their IPR to the public domain – referred to as IPR reporting.

The geographical scope of the sampled firms covered the main markets for pharmaceutical products in terms of the US and Europe, including Germany, Switzerland, the UK and Scandinavia. The annual revenue of these firms varied from less than 1 million EUR to more than 40 billion EUR. A categorisation of the sampled firms according to size in terms of annual revenues is illustrated in Figure 4.1.

The interviews were conducted with 21 IPR experts, involved in the firms' IPR management, between June and October 2009. The experts interviewed held various positions, underlining that IPR management is a cross-functional activity. They included three directors of IPR, seven directors of patents, one director of trademarks, one director of IPR and licensing, one director of IPR and business development, one director of IPR and R&D, one director of business development, one general counsel, one managing director, one CSO, one CEO, one chairman and one patent attorney. Nearly all of the experts had an educational background in chemistry or biochemistry.

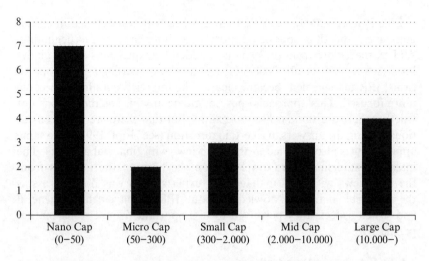

Figure 4.1   Distribution of firms according to annual revenues in MEUR

Finally, complementing the interviews with IPR management experts, additional interviews were conducted with financial analysts in a second stage. Because financial analysts cover specific industries and specific firms within these, the analysts could be identified through their annual reports. In total, 12 financial analysts were interviewed. The conversations lasted between 20 and 60 minutes. Similar to the IPR management experts, the financial analysts were located in the US and Europe, and were employed at some of the leading financial institutions.

4.2   AN OVERVIEW OF THE PHARMACEUTICAL INDUSTRY

This section describes how the pharmaceutical industry has evolved, its structure and regulatory framework. It is intended to provide the reader with an overview of the context in which pharmaceutical companies' IPR management occurs.

4.2.1   History and Evolutionary Patterns

Throughout its history, the pharmaceutical industry has undergone several radical changes. These evolutionary patterns have been described by various research scholars (see, for example, Chandler, 2005; Gambardella, 1995; Henderson et al., 1999; Malerba and Orsenigo, 2001). For example, according to Malerba and Orsenigo (2001), its evolution can be divided into three distinct epochs. Based on their findings, I briefly describe these epochs below.

The *early history* of the industry is marked by the emergence of the synthetic dye industry in Germany and Switzerland during the mid 19th century. Fifty years later the medicinal effects of the dyestuffs were discovered and applied by chemical companies – for example, Ciba, Beyer, Merck and Farbwerke Hoechst. While the development of pharmaceutical products tended to take place within larger chemical firms in Germany and Switzerland, specialised pharmaceutical firms such as Eli Lilly, Warner-Lambert and Pfizer gradually emerged in the US and the UK. Until the First World War, however, German firms were dominating the market, producing approximately 80 per cent of pharmaceutical output. During this period, pharmaceutical firms did not undertake any substantial formal research. Most new medicines were based on existing chemical substances or natural resources, such as herbs, and were not formally tested in terms of their safety and efficacy.

The transition towards a more science-based and R&D-intensive industry was marked by the Second World War, and more specifically by the development of penicillin. During the war, the US government allocated substantial resources to pharmaceutical research and the manufacturing of pharmaceutical products. This enhanced general technical expertise on chemical structure analysis and led to the development of new production techniques. Moreover, and perhaps even more important, the commercialisation of penicillin showed that the development of medicines could be highly profitable. Hence, pharmaceutical firms started to invest massively in building internal R&D capabilities, leading to a surge in R&D investments. By the 1980s, double-digit growth rates in earnings and returns on equity (ROE) had become the norm for pharmaceutical companies – largely because in the early post-war years numerous diseases existed for which there was no medicine.[2] For this reason, almost every therapeutic area provided an open research field for pharmaceutical firms.

Nevertheless, knowledge related to the biology of specific diseases was limited, requiring pharmaceutical firms to develop more systematic approaches to research, referred to as *random screening*. During the random screening epoch, very little knowledge was codified as chemists mainly relied on their intuitive sense for the links between a chemical structure and therapeutic effect, so that the creation of new compounds was mainly driven by individual scientists. Moreover, because screening capabilities related to internal organisational processes and the tacit knowledge of individual scientists, imitation was difficult for competitors, and thus provided substantial barriers to entry.

Thousands of chemical compounds were screened randomly for any potential therapeutic effect in experiments on laboratory animals, for which pharmaceutical firms created extensive libraries. Because researchers found it time consuming to synthesise new compounds, they tended to focus on synthesising variants of existing compounds, which had already shown promising therapeutic effects. It was therefore uncommon for firms to discover a medicine for one disease, while searching for a treatment for another. Hence, new chemical entities (NCEs) were rarely developed and only captured a fraction of firms' innovative efforts.[3] Furthermore, the creation of NCE-based products was most often followed by incremental innovation and imitation as firms started to specialise not in R&D, but in inventing around patents and imitating products. Accordingly, competition was mainly focused on improving existing products or replicating them as patent protection for the NCE expired. This created a highly skewed distribution of returns on innovation, as NCE blockbuster medicines were rare, but highly profitable.

At the beginning of the 1970s, the public funding of pharmaceutical research boomed, contributing to tremendous progress in various fields – especially in relation to the biochemical and molecular roots of many diseases.[4] These scientific breakthroughs had a significant impact on the process of drug discovery, offering scientists more effective means to screen compounds in terms of both accuracy and scale. Moreover, they added to the profitability of the industry. Consequently, firms started to apply biological knowledge in the design of new compounds. This opened possibilities for new targets as well as opportunities for new therapies, but also enabled scientists to design compounds with specific therapeutic effects more effectively. The shift from random screening to *guided search* and *rational drug design* was essential to the development of the pharmaceutical industry we know today, in which the role of biotechnology has a more prominent role.[5] For example, molecular genetics and recombinant DNA (rDNA) technology made it possible to use *genetic engineering* as a process technology to manufacture proteins in sufficient quantities to allow their use as therapeutic agents.[6] At the same time, genetics and molecular biology provided effective tools for the discovery of synthetic chemical medicines.

The discipline of biotechnology can be traced to the identification of deoxyribonucleic acid (DNA) by Oswald Avery, Colin MacLeod and Maclyn McCarty in February 1944. However, the first biotechnology start-up, Genentech, was formed decades later by Herbert Boyer in 1976 – one of the scientists who developed the rDNA technique – and venture capitalist Robert Swanson. Focusing on *diagnostics* and *therapeutics*, Genentech was applying its discoveries in the commercial development of new drugs.[7] Its scientists successfully developed the first chemically synthesised genes for human insulin, the first biotechnology product to be approved in 1982. In the 1980s several dedicated biotechnology firms (DBFs) followed Genetech's lead. However, the biotechnology industry remained modest in its impact on the pharmaceutical industry at this time. Between 1982 and 1992 only 16 biotechnology products were authorised on the US market. Furthermore, many of the new biotechnology firms never became fully integrated in terms of developing and marketing their pharmaceutical products by themselves. Often, they lacked crucial competencies for product development and marketing. Another obstacle was their inadequate experience concerning clinical trials and related procedures, such as the marketing authorisation process. Collaboration therefore provided the answer for those DBFs looking to survive and was found to be a source of substantial growth, allowing them to obtain the capital they needed to finance R&D, but also to develop the organisational capabilities for product development and marketing.

The relevance of scope and scale in pharmaceutical research is demonstrated by Henderson and Cockburn (1996) as well as Cockburn and Henderson (2001), in relation to transaction cost economics, providing theoretical justification for the benefits of being a vertically integrated firm (see Williamson, 1979). According to transaction cost economics (TCE), both institutions and markets provide potential forms of organisation to coordinate economic transactions. If costs of external transactions on the market are higher than internal transaction costs, firms will expand their boundaries by conducting more transactions internally. In contrast, if internal transaction costs are higher than external transaction costs, the firm will be downsized as more of its activities are outsourced. Williamson (1971; 1981) shows how the structure of the modern firm developed as a result of TCE, making multi-divisional firms increasingly profitable, as transaction costs within the firm's boundaries became more efficient compared with market transactions. Accordingly, Demsetz (1991) argues that the extent of a firm's vertical integration is reached when the costs of acquiring and managing specific information or knowledge to produce highly complex products is no longer economically beneficial. This also determines the boundaries of the firm. For this reason, it can be more efficient for a pharmaceutical firm to collaborate with a DBF possessing specialised knowledge, which is expensive to acquire, than to develop a particular product internally. Consequently, integrated pharmaceutical firms started to approach DBFs in order to gain new scientific knowledge, and thus enhance their productivity in the drug discovery process.

The adoption and integration of biotechnology turned out to work more smoothly in firms that had not experienced the epochs of *random* and *guided* drug discovery, as the tools of genetic engineering required a much broader range of skills to be employed. This, in turn, requires scientists to be tightly connected to the firms' organisational structures, but at the same time also to the scientific community, in order to promote the exchange of scientific knowledge (Gambardella, 1995; Cockburn and Henderson, 1994). For firms which had undergone random and guided drug discovery, the use of genetic engineering implied radical organisational changes, redefining processes as well as divisional structures, but also boundaries within laboratories, as the advantage of interactions with the scientific community could only be captured if external knowledge could be absorbed and integrated it into the internal R&D process (Arora and Gambardella, 1994). Collaborations between integrated pharmaceutical companies, DBFs and universities proved to be strongly complementary, leading to the establishment of collaborative networks in which DBFs positioned themselves as upstream technology suppliers and providers of R&D services, while integrated pharmaceutical firms positioned themselves as downstream buyers, providing funding and access to complementary assets.

From a resource-based view, this enabled pharmaceutical firms to develop dynamic capabilities, in terms of the ability to adjust and renew the firm's capabilities in order to respond to the increasing pace of technological change, competition and the development of new markets (see, for example, Teece et al., 1997). Moreover, from a market-based view, different types of entities, which specialised in different stages of the innovation process in which they were relatively efficient, transformed the structure of the industry. In the first stage, universities were integrated in the production of new scientific knowledge. In the second stage, DBFs applied this knowledge to product development, and in the final stage the pharmaceutical firm produced and marketed the product. Accordingly, this led to the division of innovative labour within the industry value chain, and to the increasing importance of technology transfer (see, for example, Arora et al., 2002).

Although there were substantial costs attached to the transfer of tacit knowledge between organisations, no firm could in the short run develop all the capabilities required for bringing innovative products to the market, as knowledge became more fragmented and dispersed. Moreover, patents, as legal rights to the use of certain technological knowledge, allowed discoveries to be transferred more efficiently. Also, structural developments in technology markets contributed (Arora et al., 2002). This is particularly true of the biotechnology industry in which the general transferability of technology could effectively be decomposed into independent tasks and commoditised.[8] In addition, recent developments in bioinformatics have substantially improved the transferability of platform technologies, which are important to the efficiency of drug discovery. DBFs therefore represented an opportunity for pharmaceutical firms to find an alternative approach to drug discovery and the development of new products (see, for example, Orsenigo et al., 2001).

Strategic alliances were soon found to provide an effective mechanism for technology transfer (Arora et al., 2002). This is best illustrated by the surge in strategic alliances of 28 per cent between 1990 and 1996, although this was followed by a decline of 3 per cent between 1996 and 2001 (Rasmussen, 2004). It has been argued that the surge of the early 1990s was a response to innovation deficits within pharmaceutical firms, which made it necessary for them to acquire external technologies to extend their product pipelines and increase productivity (see, for example, Dres and Ryser, 1996). Further, Rasmussen (2004) argues that the declining growth rates during the second half of the 1990s can be traced to the strategy of DBFs to use strategic alliances as a temporary financing mechanism, meaning that they relied less on strategic alliances as they gained access to further sources of funding. Typically, strategic alliances involve licensing agreements according to which the DBF receives upfront and milestone payments for product development. Moreover, if successfully commercialised, the DBF receives additional royalty payments on the basis of product sales. The type of licensing deals associated with platform technologies can differ, particularly depending on the commoditisation of the technology. For example, alliances can range from co-development projects to R&D services for which non-exclusive licence agreements can be made. Either way, technology markets today play an important role within the pharmaceutical industry – something that has implications for pharmaceutical companies' IPR management (Bader, 2008).

4.2.2 Industry Structure

The structure of the pharmaceutical industry is complex and highly regulated. On the demand side it is characterised by an extensive number of relationships between doctors, patients and hospitals, but also reimbursement systems and insurance providers.[9] Often the end-customer or the patient is not the decision-maker in the purchase process as medicines are usually prescribed by doctors. This means that pharmaceutical firms mainly have to convince doctors about their products. Accordingly, detailing is an essential activity for firms in the industry.[10] Hospitals, however, buy medicines directly from the manufacturer, although sometimes also through wholesalers. Because prices are typically determined in public tenders, companies have more flexibility in price-setting when selling to the retail segment. Moreover, most prescription medicines, at least in the EU, are covered by public health insurance systems – meaning that most patients do not directly purchase their own medicines. Under certain systems, co-payments take place, where the patient pays part of the price, although the typical patient cannot directly choose among products, and generally pays indirectly through taxes.

On the supply side there are two main types of firms; originator firms and generic firms. Originator firms invest in the development of innovative medicines, which are usually subject to patent protection. Between 2000 and 2007 originator firms in the EU on average spent about 17 per cent of their annual revenues on R&D and between 20 and 25 per cent on marketing (European Commission, 2009).[11] As patent protection expires, the originator firm loses its exclusivity in the production and marketing of the medicine, or more specifically the protected chemical composition.[12] This enables generic firms to enter the market with an equivalent to the medicine being produced and provided by the originator.[13]

Generic medicines are also tested for safety, efficacy and quality. However, since generic firms do not have to provide any detailed information from clinical trials – if they can show that their medicine is equivalent to the product of the originator – less investment in R&D is required. Generic medicines can therefore be sold at significantly lower prices (see, for example, European Commission, 2009), which in turn reduces the costs of public health budgets. Accordingly, generic firms put more pressure on originator firms to recoup their R&D investments within a shorter time-frame, requiring more effective IPR management.

4.2.3 Regulatory Framework

The main concern of the regulatory framework of the industry is to ensure the safety of pharmaceutical products. For this purpose, most countries have established government agencies to monitor and evaluate the drug development process. For example, in the US this function is performed by the Food and Drug Administration (FDA). Similarly, in the EU the European Medicines Agency (EMEA) and its predecessor, the European Agency for the Evaluation of Medicinal Products, was established in 1995 for this purpose (EC Regulation No. 726/2004). International initiatives have also been taken to regulate the industry (Wright, 2001). The International Conference on Harmonisation (ICH) – established by regulatory authorities and industry associates from the US, Japan and the EU – has continued to standardise the clinical testing of prescription medicines across nations (ICH Harmonised Tripartite Guideline, 1997).

The following section will accordingly focus mainly on the European regulatory framework.

4.2.3.1   Clinical trials

The authorisation of prescription medicines requires originator firms to conduct *clinical trials* to assess the safety and efficacy of the medicine.[14] Accordingly, the development of prescription medicines involves several phases. Before entering clinical trials, originator firms typically conduct basic research to identify a candidate medicine – that is, molecular targets for a certain disease. In a second step the molecular target is validated to demonstrate that it is therapeutically relevant. To do so, comparisons between different potential targets are made in which scientists carry out tests to identify and assess whether a molecular target is suitable for therapeutic application. Following this, further tests are made to find molecules with the highest potential for and probability of safe and effective treatment, typically resulting in the identification of a candidate medicine or a lead compound.

When a lead compound has been identified, by means of basic research, the safety and efficacy of the compound is examined throughout the development phase. The development phase, in turn, has two distinct phases – that is, the pre-clinical and clinical phases. In the pre-clinical phase, toxicity testing on animals is conducted to allow scientists to estimate a safe starting dose for the clinical trials in which the medicine is tested on humans. For authorisation, a medicine then needs to pass four clinical phases (European Commission, 2009):[15]

- Clinical phase I: Scientists test the medicine on a small group of healthy volunteers in order to determine a safe dosage range as well as identify potential side effects.
- Clinical phase II: The medicine is tested on actual patients for the first time – hence disease effects can be determined. This also includes parallel tests with placebo preparations to provide a control group.
- Clinical phase III: Involves tests on a substantially larger group of patients for a longer period of time. In doing so, information is gathered on the effects of the medicine on various populations. This information is essential for the assessment of the medicine's safety by the relevant government agency, and hence for market authorisation.
- Clinical phase IV: After the market launch, products continue to be monitored in relation to possible adverse reactions as well as new side-effects. This is sometimes referred to as Phase IV, although the product has already been authorised.

Only a fraction of all compounds being tested are authorised and successfully commercialised. According to the European Commission (2009), one out of 5,000–10,000 compounds tested makes it through the clinical trials and is actually brought to market. Attrition rates, however, fall throughout the development phase, while R&D costs follow the opposite trend.[16]

4.2.3.2   Marketing authorisation

Within the EU, medicines are only authorised if safe, effective and of high quality. For this reason, a marketing authorisation process verifies all prescription medicines based on the data provided by clinical trials. Market authorisation can be granted either centrally by the EMEA or nationally. Regulation 726/2004/EC provides a centralised procedure for market authorisation of pharmaceutical products, which has the advantage of providing authorisation for all EU member state markets. Applications for Community authorisation need to be submitted according to a specific format referred to as the EU common technical document (CTD). This document must contain information including the name of the medical product, particulars of all its constituents, its therapeutic indications, its side-effects, details about the manufacturing process, the results of pre-clinical and clinical tests, and a summary of product characteristics.[17]

The Community procedure can also be used for generic applications.[18] Generic medicinal products submit abridged applications, in which they must establish that the generic product is based on the same substances, in quantitative as well as qualitative terms, as the reference originator product. Accordingly, the abridged applicant refers to the tests and trials conducted by the originator firm. This means that generic firms are not required to conduct pre-clinical and clinical trials. Instead, abridged applications ought to include data and the results from *bioequivalence* studies,[19] which demonstrate the quality and, most essentially, the similarity of the generic product to that of the originator.[20] However, such applications can first be made after the expiration of marketing and data exclusivity.

4.2.3.3   Marketing and data exclusivity

At the time of marketing authorisation, originators obtain eight years of data exclusivity within the EU (see, for example, European Commission, 2009). Data exclusivity protects clinical test data – which is submitted to the regulatory agency to prove the safety of and efficiency of a new medicine – but does not directly prevent generic firms from commercialising their products. Rather it prevents regulatory authorities from approving a subsequent application by a generic firm, based on the data submitted by the originator. However, because the production of own data is expensive and time consuming, data exclusivity does provide a barrier to entry for generic competition.

In addition to data exclusivity, originators obtain ten years of marketing exclusivity, with the possibility of obtaining one additional year for new therapeutic indications within the EU.[21] In the US, five years of data exclusivity is given, and three additional years can be obtained for new indications of existing medicines (see 21 USC § 355(c)(3)(E)(ii, iii)). Although generic firms are not permitted to enter the market during the period of marketing exclusivity, preparation measures can be taken after data exclusivity has expired.

4.2.3.4 Supplementary protection certificates

The lengthy marketing authorisation process in the pharmaceutical industry has implications for patent protection. For example, past research in the US shows that it takes on average 1.3 years between patents being granted and the beginning of clinical trials. Moreover, the clinical trials take an additional 3.8 years followed by an FDA review of 2.6 years (Lourie, 1989). In the US, the Hatch-Waxman Amendment (the Drug Price Competition and Patent Term Restoration Act, 1984) copes with this by granting a patent extension of up to five years for products that lose some of their patent life during the FDA regulatory approval process. Further, according to TRIPS Art. 33: 'The term of protection available shall not end before the expiration of a period of twenty years counted from the filing date', which leaves open the possibility of patent term extensions. Accordingly, several countries also provide for extended patent terms for pharmaceutical products, including Australia, Japan, Korea, Israel, the US, as well as the EU member states (Ministry of Economic Development, 2003).

4.3 IPR MANAGEMENT IN THE PHARMACEUTICAL INDUSTRY

Turning to the conducted exploratory study, I find that pharmaceutical originator firms pursue two distinct business models. Firstly, there are integrated pharmaceutical firms, which cover the entire value chain, from R&D to sales and marketing (Farag, 2009).[22] The IPR management of these firms ultimately has an end-customer focus, since economic returns are generated on the basis of product commercialisation. I call this a product-based business model. DBFs, on the other hand, specialise in R&D for specific therapeutic areas. As pointed out by Chesbrough and Teece (1996), these firms do not have the required financial resources to maintain an in-house sales force and carry the costs related to product development. Instead, they license-out[23] their proprietary technology resources for further development and product commercialisation (Pisano and Mang, 1993).[24] Hence, DBFs commercialise their R&D results on the technology market rather than on the product market. I call this a licensing-based business model. Since their customers consist of pharmaceutical firms, DBFs' IPR management is more focused on attracting potential licensing partners who can conduct or take part in the development required to commercialise the product.[25] Because returns are generated through out-licensing, the firm's IPR management is concerned with meeting the requirements of potential licensees, who aim to commercialise a product based on the licence taken. Accordingly, one of the IPR management experts interviewed at a DBF states: 'As every company, we need to meet the requirements of our customers. This is also true of the patent situation ... Before essential patent applications are filed we look for potential customers and evaluate their needs.' This implies that the IPR management of DBFs has similar objectives to pharmaceutical firms. The main difference is that their returns are generated on the basis of licensing deals instead of product sales.

Irrespective of their business model, the conducted exploration reveals four main IPR management objectives – all aimed to enhance the financial performance of the firm. Firstly, companies manage their IPR to secure freedom-to-operate (FTO) before marketing authorisation, to be able to commercialise the new product development (NPD) without infringing third party patents. To do so, they conduct regular FTO analyses throughout the R&D phase, providing risk assessments of their NPD projects. All the firms in the study pursued this objective. Its importance is underlined by one of the respondents: 'Without having freedom-to-operate, you cannot pursue a development project. Patent litigation is far too expensive to take that risk, and pharmaceutical firms monitor each other very tightly.' The second objective concerns the appropriation of economic returns based on the firm's investments in NPD (see, for example, Blind el al., 2006). The role of IPR management is therefore to maximise exclusivity in the appropriation of returns related to a product. This involves analyses of the patent landscape in order to assess whether exclusivity can be obtained. Such assessments are crucial to determining the potential profitability of a product, and thus whether to go on with an NPD project. Seventeen interviewees involved in firms' IPR management were concerned with meeting this objective. Thirdly, the profitability of NPD investments depends on the duration of exclusivity (European Commission, 2009). This means that IPR management is focused on protecting the product throughout its lifecycle, in terms of enforcing the firm's

IPR, but is also concerned with prolonging the lifecycle as such through branding strategies and additional patent applications. This is referred to as extending the duration of exclusivity – an objective pursued by 16 of the firms explored. Finally, firms are concerned with using their R&D budget effectively. As one firm puts it: 'We only have so much money for each development project . . . Patent protection can be very expensive, especially if you need it on a worldwide basis, which is the case for most companies in the industry . . . This is why we constantly evaluate the commercial benefits of each patent in our portfolio.' This objective, however, was mainly of concern for DBFs.

4.4 IPR MANAGEMENT IN THE NPD PROCESS

The firms investigated reveal that to achieve the objectives stated above, the main task of their IPR management is to support the firm's NPD throughout their products' respective lifecycles. In doing so, their IPR management involves several sub-tasks which vary in relevance according to the different phases of the product lifecycle. These tasks can be categorised according to three main subject areas – R&D support, technology transfer and portfolio management. It should be noted that not all firms conducted all of these tasks, especially not DBFs, which focus on the early phases of the product lifecycle.

4.4.1 R&D Support

4.4.1.1 Patent landscape analyses
Initially, firms' IPR management is mainly focused around supporting their internal R&D. Before an NPD project is undertaken, patent searches are conducted, which provide the basis for analyses of the patent landscape in terms of the prior art. Based on the patent landscape, assessments are made concerning the therapeutic area in question and related competitor projects. This enables firms to evaluate the technical and commercial viability of an NPD (Moehrle et al., 2005).[26] Technical viability, on the other hand, refers to the project's innovativeness in relation to the state of the art and involves analyses of competitors' patent applications in order to identify recent technology trends and competing NPD projects. Commercial viability refers to whether sufficient patent protection can be obtained to secure FTO and obtain exclusivity. Related considerations include whether licences will need to be applied for in order to secure FTO, or whether the firm can design around a blocking patent to prohibit the infringement of third party patents. Accordingly, the IPR management

needs to ensure that projects are not started unless they are financially beneficial.

One of the IPR management experts interviewed in my study explains how the economic viability of a project is evaluated: 'Before a project is started, a valuation is conducted in which a quite complex valuation model is developed including all sorts of factors such as market size, expected growth . . . whether patent protection can be obtained, for which markets, and what the freedom-to-operate situation looks like.'

4.4.1.2   The stage-gate-process and patent information

When an NPD project has been approved, project milestones are deter-mined. According to these milestones, the product is regularly evaluated in terms of its technical progress and commercial feasibility. The milestones often relate to the clinical phases and provide the gates in what can be described as a stage-gate product development process (see Cooper, 1985). If the criteria determined at each gate are not met, the project is aban-doned. Typical questions raised at each gate relate to whether the firm will be able to obtain sufficient exclusivity for a sufficient duration of time and what the exposure to competition is. Competitors are therefore continu-ously monitored in terms of what protection they have, when they will reach the market, how long their protection will last, and whether their products or patents interfere with those of the firm.[27] Hence, assessments made relate to the IPR management objectives of securing FTO, maximis-ing exclusivity and its duration.

4.4.1.3   Patent portfolio generation

In relation to the discoveries made throughout the NPD process, a patent portfolio is built around the product. These patents are positioned to secure FTO and maximise exclusivity according to analysis of the patent landscape. This means that firms identify relevant technology spaces which are not in the prior art, and position their patents beyond the actual R&D embodiment in order to obtain the highest possible financial benefit. The claims of the patent can relate to the therapeutic indication, the basic manufacturing process, as well as the surroundings of the compound to secure FTO and prevent competitors from commercialising products based on modified versions of the compound. Hence, firms initially file patents of broader scope in order to maximise exclusivity, but also to leave research options open. The hierarchy of patents in terms of the exclusiv-ity they provide has been described by practitioners, such as Voet (2008). This hierarchy is largely confirmed by the IPR management experts interviewed, revealing compound patents to be most important. This is because the compound patent covers the medical product regardless of its formulation, its manufacturing and its use, and hence gives the broadest scope of protection. A medical use or indication patent for the treatment of a specific disease or condition – which can be filed on the use of known compositions, provided a new therapeutic application has been discovered – in contrast, only enables firms to obtain exclusivity for a field of medical use. Thirdly, patents can be filed on the pharmaceutical formulation of the medicine. Formulation patents relate to how different chemical substances – including the active drug agent – are combined into a final medicine. Developing a formulation involves studies on the medicine's acceptability to the patient. If the medicine is to be taken orally, the development of a formulation includes incorporation of the medicine into a tablet or capsule. The patent on the formulation typically covers the active agent for use in the body. However, these patents most often do not enable firms to obtain exclusivity since they can be designed around by using a different formulation. One of the experts explains: 'You cannot gain exclusivity on the basis of a formulation patent . . . To obtain exclusivity you need protection for the chemical substance because most substances have many different formulations.'

However, within the context of generic entry, formulation patents can provide important barriers to entry. This is because equivalence needs to be proven, meaning that if a generic firm enters the market based on another formulation, this may require it to conduct clinical trials in order to establish equivalence, although minor changes are permitted. For this reason, formulation patents can be very valuable to originator firms. Moreover, they can be important to ensure FTO and, in certain cases, also to prolong the duration of exclusivity if the formulation provides a competitive advantage.[28] Finally, it should be noted that firms which develop medical devices, rather than medicines, file for medical device patents, which can relate to diagnostic, therapeutic and surgical devices. Typically, relatively many patents are required for these firms to obtain exclusivity, compared with patents protecting medicines.[29]

Companies focused on the development of medicines generally first file for patent protection on the compound. Throughout the clinical phases further patent applications are filed as more discoveries about the capacity of the product are made. Such secondary filings can relate to improvements in the manufacturing process for the medicine or therapeutic effects for additional fields of medical use. Accordingly, a cluster of patents is built up around the product. The scope of the patents filed narrows throughout the clinical phases as more specific features are patented – hence secondary filings are less important in terms of exclusivity.

During clinical phase I, when studies on a smaller group of healthy volunteers are conducted in order to determine potential side-effects, additional data is obtained, which is added to the compound patent during the priority year. Here further areas of medical use can also be discovered for which additional patents are filed. In clinical phase III the interaction between the medicine and patients is generally known, but the commercial formulation as well as the packaging is not yet finalised. Accordingly, patent protection for the commercial formulation is filed in this phase. Since the commercial formulation of a medicine is often first determined in clinical phase III, the patent related to the formulation expires years after the compound patent, which has normally been filed for already during the research phase. Patenting of the formulation, therefore, provides the best option for firms wishing to prolong exclusivity, although most often there are several technical formulation options for a medicine. Finally, at the time of marketing authorisation, supplementary patent certificates (SPCs) can be filed. These can enable firms to gain compensation for patent protection lost during the marketing authorisation process.

4.4.1.4   Trademark portfolio generation

Before marketing authorisation, firms need to secure uniform trademark protection for the branded product on a worldwide basis. This is essential to prevent third parties from selling counterfeit products.

The trademark generation process is usually conducted by staff from the trademarks department, the marketing department and sometimes an external branding agency. The branding agency or the marketing department is responsible for the creative part of the trademark generation. This includes the generation of a name that is commercially viable in terms of appearance, being easy to remember and easy to pronounce; and hence provides a link in the mind of the public between the product and the trademark. Accordingly, the names are checked linguistically, in terms of whether they are free of connotations in the most important languages. Approximately three to five hundred names or trademark proposals are generated. An identity search is performed before a proposal is submitted to the trademark department. The trademark department then needs to filter a high percentage of the proposals, which are evaluated according to certain criteria. These include whether the trademark can provide worldwide protection, if it is likely to be approved by health authorities as well as other legal considerations related to its distinctiveness. To assess whether a trademark is available for worldwide protection and to evaluate its distinctiveness, trademark searches are conducted for countries which provide the firm's main markets. In doing so, the trademark proposals are filtered down to approximately ten. Finally, perception related to the trademark among physicians and pharmacists is evaluated. This provides the most important commercial aspect in the trademark generation process, since they are to prescribe the trademarked medicine.

Based on these assessments, two to three trademarks are filed. The filed trademarks are evaluated by the health authorities, which assess the possibility of confusion among patients and prescribers. As health authorities perform their own trademark examination with regard to safety risks attached to confusion – and hence from a different viewpoint from the trademark offices – it is not predictable which trademark will be accepted. Normally, the registration of a trademark takes two to three years, meaning that companies need to have alternative trademarks so as not to lose time-to-market if one trademark is not accepted. If the first-choice trademark is rejected for a main market, companies rely on back-up trademarks.

The relevance of trademarks, I find, depends on the indication – that is, the market for the product. In fragmented markets with only a few players, differentiation is less important and therefore so too is trademark protection. In contrast, in markets for consumer health care, where there are several competing products, trademarks are of greater relevance. This is especially true of over-the-counter (OTC) products, which are sold directly to the patient. Finally, the relevance of trademarks also depends on where the firm is located within the value chain. For example, for firms that do not commercialise products, trademarks are not a major concern. As one DBF explains: 'Most of our customers prefer to use their own trademark rather than acquire one . . . They do their own market research and have more resources for marketing purposes than we do . . . because trademarks are not requested by our customers, there is just no point for us to invest in one.'

4.4.2   Technology Transfer

In addition to supporting a firm's internal R&D, the IPR management is concerned with supporting its technology transfer activities. In technology acquisitions, firms absorb existing technological knowledge from a third party, mostly to extend their product pipeline and commercialise new products. This often involves the acquisition or in-licensing of patents in order to obtain exclusivity and secure FTO for the technology absorbed. Hence, in conformity with Ernst (1996), I find that firms' IPR management supports their technology transfer efforts. This can take various forms, including assignments, mergers and acquisitions, or patent licensing (see, for example, Lichtenthaler, 2006). The present study will focus on patent licensing.[30]

4.4.2.1   Patent out-licensing

Past research shows that firms' IPR management is concerned with the identification of technology commercialisation opportunities (Ashton and Sen, 1988). Similarly, I find that, before a licensing deal is conducted, firms screen the relevant therapeutic indication for potential licensing partners. If a partner is identified, it is ascertained whether it already has an NPD project in the pipeline, similar to the technology the firm intends to license-out. The product pipeline of specific firms is accordingly assessed in a second step. If no similar NPD project is identified, an evaluation is made of how much the firm can and will be willing to pay for the licence. This is done by screening the latest licensing deals conducted within the relevant therapeutic indication and more specifically by the firm under consideration. However, if the firm is looking for a third party to manufacture its NPD, companies will assess the licensee's manufacturing capabilities rather than its financial resources. One company describes this accordingly:

> Usually, you have a commercialisation strategy, and try to identify a company to take a licence based on that . . . you might have everything in place except the capacity to undertake the development of the final product and the manufacturing base . . . then you would typically look for a partner that can provide that.

Another states that:

> Our business model depends on licensing revenue for the funding of further research . . . we normally look for the company with the best financial possibilities to take a licence.

The quotes above point out two main out-licensing motives within the pharmaceutical industry. Firstly, firms license-out their patents to generate revenues (see, for example, Arora, 1997; Kline, 2003). This tends to provide an attractive way for firms to generate economic returns without carrying the investment for the development of products, and is in line with the findings of Lerner et al. (2003), who show that patent licensing provides an essential funding mechanism for DBFs. Secondly, firms license-out their patents for joint product development and commercialisation. Such decisions may relate to financial constraints as well as limited in-house manufacturing skills. Accordingly, firms sometimes license-out their patents to access a third party's knowledge base (see, for example, Gulati, 1999).

Depending on the motive for a licence, a licensing model is developed, normally consisting of upfront and milestone payments as well as royalties.

To determine the size of these payments, the potential returns the licensee can generate based on a licence are assessed by analysing the market for the product. Such calculations are conducted openly since it is necessary for the licensee to provide information about its market, on the basis of which the deal's financial aspects can be negotiated. An understanding of what can be achieved in the market is hence required by both parties in order to achieve a compromise. Moreover, milestones are determined in relation to further development of the product, if required. Milestone payments are settled accordingly. This is because licensing deals often relate to joint product development projects, which comprise the know-how of the licensor. Upfront and milestone payments are applied to cover the licensor's development costs. If a larger upfront payment is made, the licensee is taking a higher risk in terms of carrying a more substantial part of the development costs. This means that a higher upfront payment comes with lower subsequent royalties.

Moreover, licensing agreements can be of either an exclusive or a non-exclusive nature. Within the pharmaceutical industry, non-exclusive licences are generally not given, since the value decreases substantially for the licensor. Accordingly, firms look to find a partner that would take the licence exclusively. In relation to platform technologies, however, non-exclusive licences are sometimes given. For instance, if a licensee has already developed a product based on platform technology, for which it has already obtained exclusivity, a non-exclusive licence in relation to the platform technology can be given in a second step.

4.4.2.2 Patent in-licensing

Although DBFs and integrated pharmaceutical firms engage in out-licensing as well as in-licensing, pharmaceutical firms pursing a product-based business model are more focused on strengthening their product pipeline through in-licensing than DBFs. Because pharmaceutical firms generate returns mainly on the basis of commercialising products, they rely on technology markets to extend and diversify their product pipeline to meet their profitability targets. Accordingly, if a sufficient number of projects cannot be generated internally, they license-in patents from third parties to extend their pipeline based on external R&D (see, for example, Grindley and Teece, 1997), but also to secure FTO and obtain exclusivity for internal development projects being threatened by a blocking patent (see, for example, Hall and Ziedonis, 2001). The motives of patent in-licensing can be very different depending on the situation and the type of company. These are best illustrated by the following quotes from IPR management experts at three different companies:

It can be that a competitor has a research project in clinical phase II and that the only chance to reach the market with a competing medicine at about the same time is to license-in the whole project from another company.

Sometimes a company has claimed something that you think will be essential for you to obtain freedom-to-operate . . . in some cases we have licensed in patents to make sure that we do not infringe any external patents when our product reaches the market.

Research is unpredictable . . . if you close down a project you need to generate a new one . . . for us, technology licensing provides a way of making sure that we always have a sufficient number of projects in our pipeline.

This implies that firms license-in patents to reduce time-to-market, secure FTO, and extend their product pipeline. The relevance of doing so on a continuous basis is suggested by the fact that many pharmaceutical firms have established sourcing teams specialised in the identification of licensing opportunities. These attend relevant conferences and events worldwide in order to identify recent product developments of interest and approach potential partners for in-licensing. Before a licensing deal is closed, a due diligence investigation is conducted of the patents concerned by the licensee.[31] In doing so, potential patent portfolio synergies are assessed by analysing the firm's patent protection in terms of FTO and exclusivity before and after the licensing deal.

4.4.3   Portfolio Management

4.4.3.1   Portfolio reviews
When a product has been commercialised, a review of the IPR covering it is typically conducted. This involves cost–benefit analysis of each patent which needs to be re-approved by the responsible IPR manager after a certain amount of time. The importance of the cost–benefit analysis depends on the size of the firm's patent portfolio. For firms with a smaller patent portfolio, related cost–benefit analyses are not considered to be worth the effort since the relevant patents are known. Firms with relatively large patent portfolios, however, categorise their patents according to specific qualitative criteria in order to prioritise these. The firms investigated reveal that a patent may be relevant either commercially or strategically according to three criteria:

- They may cover products or platform technologies that are relevant to the firm's business model.
- They may have economic potential in terms of relating to product development projects which may be of interest to the firm's business model in the future.

- They may serve as bargaining chips if the firm is sued by a third party for infringement, and thus may be of relevance as something to fall back on.

After a portfolio review has been conducted, patents are highlighted that are important to the firm's business model in terms of exclusivity, that have economic potential and can provide a bargaining chip. Patents that do not fulfil any of these criteria are regularly abandoned. In contrast, reviews of the firm's trademark portfolios do not usually follow any formalised procedures. This is because trademarks are categorised according to products, and companies know which trademarks are relevant as soon as a trademark has been accepted by health authorities. The trademarks which are not in use will be revoked after a certain amount of time.[32]

4.4.3.2 Patent enforcement

From the moment of marketing authorisation, firms manage their IPR to defend the competitive position of their products. This includes handling third party challenges to the firm's IPR portfolio and the monitoring of relevant therapeutic areas in order to identify possible infringers. Accordingly, there is a shift in focus from securing the firm's competitive position to defending it as the product is brought to market.

To identify possible infringers, databases are used to monitor patent applications of interest. This can result in enforcement by suing for infringement or claiming invalidity over third party patents.[33] How firms proceed against infringers depends on whether it the infringer is a competitor or a non-related third party that is looking not to manufacture a competing product, but to apply the technology on another market. Since firms do not want to destroy actual or potential markets, they would rather approach non-related firms for negotiations in order to gain a share of the patent-related returns. Accordingly, they would look to settle for a licensing deal. In contrast, a competitor will be sued for infringement if the firm can make a strong case. The litigation procedure depends on the jurisdiction in which the infringement takes place. To decide how to proceed, a technical assessment is made of the third party's patent claims in order to determine whether it is a competitor or a non-related firm, and hence if the claims relate to another market.

However, it is unusual for pharmaceutical firms with competing products to infringe each other's patents, since development projects within a therapeutic area are carefully monitored in terms of FTO. As one of the respondents tells us:

> The cost of developing a new drug requires us to make constant evaluations of competitor projects . . . it is very uncommon that any patents are overseen . . . there are few surprises in terms of patent litigation before data exclusivity expires.

This means that patent infringements are more likely to happen when generic competition enters the market.

In licensing agreements too, entitlement to enforcement is an essential aspect. This can be settled in different ways. Often a waterfall structure is applied, in which the licensor has a certain number of months to proceed against the infringer. If this is not done, the licensee is then entitled to take action. However, it is also common for the licensee to have the right to proceed against the infringer initially. The licensor would generally want to have the right to enforce, because its royalties depend on the revenue the licensee generates with the product on the market. Yet, if the licensee has more substantial financial resources, it is often in a better position to enforce. Usually firms want the right to enforce when they have a significant share of the market. In contrast, enforcement rights are of less interest if the collaboration is in the research phase and the collaboration partner has all the commercialisation rights.

4.4.3.3   Trademark communication and enforcement

Before marketing authorisation, the management of trademarks is focused around the trademark generation process described above. After market launch, however, when trademark protection has been acquired, the focus shifts to strengthening the trademark through communication in different marketing activities. This is usually done by means of detailing, to enhance brand loyalty among prescribers. Accordingly, during the first part of the commercial phase, the company looks to build brand equity. The relevance of doing so is suggested not least by the fact that pharmaceutical firms spend 25 per cent of their sales on marketing (European Commission, 2009).

Secondly, when brand equity has been established, originator firms look to defend it against confusingly similar trademarks and counterfeiting. This is especially essential after data exclusivity has expired, when counterfeit products become more of a concern. To identify trademark infringements and counterfeiting, firms have established reporting tools and monitoring systems. If a conflicting trademark is found, mediation is generally initiated in a first step. In a second step, if no agreement is reached, most companies would proceed to an arbitration court. It should, however, be noted that that trademark communication and enforcement is mainly a concern of companies pursuing a product-based business model.

4.5   MANAGERIAL IMPLICATIONS

From a management perspective, the present study underlines the importance of considering IPR in relation to NPD in order for companies to generate sustainable economic returns based on the firm's innovation efforts. In doing so, IPR management not only provides a support task for R&D and product management, but is rather a prerequisite for successful NPD commercialisation. This means that firms need to manage NPD and IPR in an integrated manner. To achieve this, the integration of IPR experts into cross-functional product lifecycle teams was found to be essential. The firms investigated reveal that these consist of staff from R&D, business development and marketing, as well as their patent and trademark departments. Hence, the firm's IPR management interacts with several departments involved in the firm's lifecycle management teams; and hence provides a cross-functional activity. Since the functions of patents and trademarks are different, however, these are often managed in separate patent and trademark departments, but are aligned to the firm's products, which are coordinated through the lifecycle teams. In terms of coordination, these teams resemble what Gassmann and Von Zedtwitz (2003) refer to as centralized venture teams – that is, R&D projects are most often geographically centralised, which enables stronger cross-functional integration of the firm's IPR management (see Nadler and Tushman, 1997).

On a strategic level, these teams focus on applying the right product strategy, in terms of positioning the product in the market. Because companies want to position their products where they can achieve the strongest possible competitive advantages, the positioning of IPR needs to be aligned with the product strategy. Hence, to maximise exclusivity around the competitive advantage created, it is important for IPR experts to actively participate in the development of product strategies. This includes advising product managers on how to position the product in relation to the patent landscape to maximise exclusivity. Similarly, IPR experts support product managers in tailoring the IPR situation to the commercialisation strategy. For example, if the company looks to commercialise its invention on the technology market and has a potential buyer, the IPR situation needs to fit what that particular buyer intends to achieve with the invention on the market (see, for example, Lichtenthaler, 2006).

On an operational level, meetings of the team are regularly held to assess the current situation in terms of new product discoveries, related benefits and implications, and when the NPD will reach the market. Throughout the stage-gate process (see Cooper, 1985), the IPR situation is assessed and discussed with regard to exclusivity and FTO – especially if new discoveries have been made. In doing so, IPR experts give guidance to the R&D department concerning technology areas that remain unexplored and for which patent protection can be obtained. Moreover, scientists advise IPR experts on the essential aspects of their inventions, which ought to be claimed. Similarly, the marketing and trademark department engage in the trademark generation process to support the establishment of brand equity.

Smaller firms also have lifecycle management teams, which are responsible for specific development projects. However, their team structures tend to be more flexible in terms of team staff participating in several projects. Since their organisations are smaller in size, such structures are required. Moreover, they often rely on outsourcing substantial parts of their IPR management to external service providers – usually IPR law firms. Instead of coordination through lifecycle management teams, these firms' IPR management is conducted in collaboration between senior executives and external service providers. Typically, the objectives of the IPR management are outlined by the firm, while the operative IPR management – in terms of filing applications, prosecution as well as fee administration – is the task of the external service provider.

4.6   CONCEPTUAL FRAMEWORK AND PERFORMANCE IMPACT

The central findings of the exploratory study are summarised in Figure 4.2, describing how firms within the pharmaceutical industry conduct their IPR management throughout the NPD process.

Initially, firms' IPR management is concerned with supporting their internal R&D. This involves analyses of the technical and commercial viability of the NPD project on the basis of the patent landscape. These analyses are conducted before an NPD project is approved and throughout the stage-gate process where they are used by product managers in stop/go decisions concerning the project (Cooper, 1985). Because new discoveries are constantly being made and new patents may be filed by third parties throughout the R&D process, it is important for firms to continuously reassess the IPR situation around the NPD project. For instance, if FTO cannot be secured due to a new patent application filed by a competitor, the NPD project has to be abandoned. To prevent this, firms need to manage their IPR to be responsive to both internal and external developments. This means that the firm's IPR portfolio is used proactively, to enable them to develop technology resources of relevance for future competitive advantage. Hence, firms' IPR management supports the development of dynamic capabilities (Teece et al., 1997), in terms of

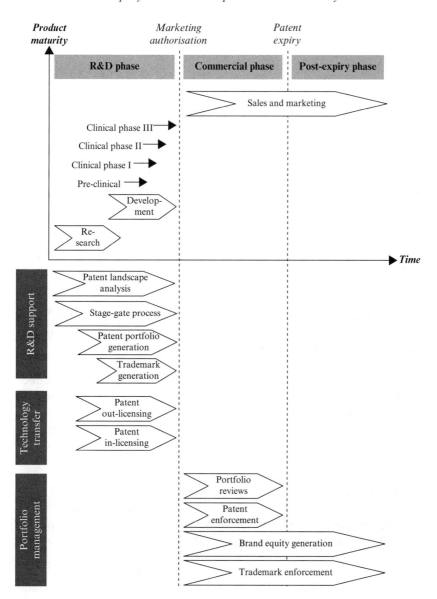

Figure 4.2   Conceptual framework of IPR management in the
pharmaceutical industry

blocking relevant technology spaces (see, for example, Granstrand, 1999), which leaves research options open and enhances the firm's responsiveness to shifts in competitive forces (see Porter, 1985).

Throughout the clinical phases, patent applications are filed as more discoveries about the capacity of the product are made – for example, additional therapeutic effects. This is essential to protect the firm's unique technology resources from imitation (see, for example, Blind et al., 2006; Cohen et al., 2002) and to achieve the objective of maximising exclusivity. To establish a monopoly position the IPR management is hence conducted reactively to the NPD process. This means that the IPR management provides a support task for NPD in order to make technology resources imperfectly imitable as they are discovered, postulated as essential to firm performance by resource-based theorists (see, for example, Barney, 1991). Moreover, nearly all firms interviewed manage their IPR both proactively and reactively in relation to the NPD process, meaning that nearly all firms' IPR management focuses on protecting their technology resources, while at the same time also trying to enhance the firm's responsiveness to environmental factors.

After marketing authorisation, portfolio management becomes essential to extend the duration of exclusivity through effective enforcement of the firm's IPR and to preserve product market shares by creating brand loyalty through trademark communication.[34] This is achieved by combining patents and trademarks throughout the lifecycle of the product. However, only firms which commercialise their technology resources on the product market combine patents and trademarks. Moreover, patents and trademarks are most often managed in separate departments. However, staff from both departments support product managers by engaging in cross-functional NPD teams, meaning that both patents and trademarks are managed according to products.

Finally, the interviews reveal several relationships between IPR management and the financial performance of firms, which are considered by product managers to enhance the firms' performance. These findings are stated below and illustrated in Figure 4.3.

Finding 1:   Firms manage their IPR to support their internal R&D, in terms of securing FTO, which enables them to commercialise new products without infringing third party patents.

Finding 2:   Firms manage their IPR to support their internal R&D, in terms of maximising exclusivity in the appropriation, and thereby increase the profitability of their R&D investments.

Finding 3:   Firms manage their IPR to support their internal R&D, in

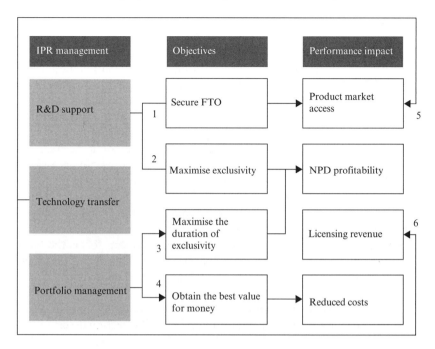

Figure 4.3   Performance impact of IPR management

terms of extending the duration of exclusivity, which contributes to the sustainability of competitive advantages created, and thus to the profitability of the firm's R&D investment.

Finding 4: Firms manage their IPR to make effective use of their R&D budgets in terms of abandoning irrelevant IPR and thereby reduce costs.

Finding 5: Firms manage their IPR to access external R&D and thereby acquire new growth potential.

Finding 6: Firms manage their IPR to commercialise their internal R&D without carrying the costs related to product development.

From a capital market perspective, pharmaceutical companies' IPR management ought to be evaluated and considered in investment analyses on the basis of how well it contributes to its financial performance. I have stated above the ways in which companies' IPR management can potentially do so. Such information can be incorporated in fundamental company analysis, and thus provide some guidance for investors.

4.7   CORPORATE IPR REPORTING

Besides examining companies' IPR management practices, I explored firms' IPR reporting decisions – that is, voluntary information disclosures made concerning their IPR, and their management of these rights. This was done to assess what drives companies' disclosure decisions and what kind of information they provide. Secondly, I looked at the IPR information being requested by financial analysts, and the incorporation of such information into their company valuations. This was done because the fact that some firms report on their IPR management does not necessarily mean that such information is considered to be relevant among investors. Hence, to assess the value-relevance of IPR management information additional exploratory interviews were conducted with financial analysts covering the pharmaceutical sector. Although financial analysts do not allocate financial capital, they provide the research that forms the basis for a wide range of investors' investment decisions. This means that their assessments ought to be relevant for how financial capital is allocated and, indeed, research shows that they are (see, for example, Francis and Soffer, 1997; Lys and Sohn, 1990). Financial analysts were therefore considered to be an appropriate target group for interviews. This section describes my findings.

4.7.1   IPR Reporting Decisions

Disclosure decisions of public firms depend on the expected commercial impact of the information, on security regulations and the guidelines of the stock exchange (see Hopt and Voigt, 2004; Healy and Palepu, 2001). Most often, security regulations require firms to disclose information about patent expiry dates, licensing agreements or litigation issues (see BaFin, 2005). This type of information was also found in most of the explored firms' annual reports. In addition, the firms investigated revealed that their investor relations (IR) department regularly approaches the firm's IPR department in order to obtain and communicate IPR information to shareholders. Such information can be complementary to disclosure requirements and is sometimes also more detailed. It is found that smaller firms – without any products on the market – are more willing to communicate information about their IPR. This is because larger firms – which often have several products on the market – generate more stable returns and have other complementary assets on which investors base their investment decisions. Smaller firms, on the contrary, may not yet generate any revenues and therefore have no cash-flows and only a few complementary assets for investors to base their assessments on. By reporting on their

IPR, they therefore look to communicate growth opportunities, with a high probability of materialising these in the future. As stated by two DBFs:

> ... our patents are our lifeblood. Without them we would not be able to tap into capital markets ... we need to communicate patent values to investors.

> Investors are not interested in patent numbers, but want to know that we can turn our patents into profits ... We actively communicate our ability of doing so beyond the requirements of disclosure regulations.

This implies that IPR reporting decisions are driven by information requested by investors. Most information disclosures, however, were conducted on the basis of the companies' own assessments, without any detailed information, enabling investors to evaluate the accuracy of companies' disclosures. This raises concerns not only about the accuracy of the disclosed IPR information, but also about its credibility among investors. Still, the respondents perceive that certain disclosures create trust in the robustness of the company's IPR protection of a product. To achieve this, they disclose information about general measures taken to reduce risks of litigation, and sometimes even information about their own FTO and exclusivity assessments. To communicate the fact that exclusivity has been obtained, firms would usually disclose information on the essential patents covering the product – that is, what they are protecting, as well as the expected dates of expiry. However, more specific information concerning the strengths and weaknesses of the firm's IPR portfolio is not disclosed. This is because firms do not want competitors to take action on the basis of such information.

Some companies also disclose more detailed information about licensing agreements than is required by disclosure regimes. In the US, for example, firms have to file an 8-K report after a licensing agreement if the deal is expected to have a significant commercial impact. When doing so, firms can make decisions concerning the detail of their disclosures. This means that some firms will provide more information than others about payment structures, in terms of settled milestone payments and royalty rates. For instance, most firms will disclose whether the royalty fee is in single or double digits, while only a few firms will disclose the exact percentage. In contrast, the terms of the licence, such as which markets it relates to as well as whether it has been given on an exclusive or non-exclusive basis, were found to be disclosed by most firms.

4.7.2   Financial Analysts' Assessments of IPR Information

Financial analysts consider firms' IPR management specifically in relation to the valuation of products – depending on the company's business model – but not as an activity in itself. This is explained by one analyst: 'When companies generate their revenues on the technology market, their IPR is considered in a licensing context . . . when companies generate their revenue through product commercialisation, IPR assessments are made in relation to its products.'

Typically, financial analysts employ either capital market-oriented or fundamental analytic valuation methods and, sometimes, even a combination of the two (DVFA, 2005). Capital market-oriented methods require the identification of peer groups – that is, comparable companies or similar deals from which financial ratios can be derived for the valuation. A general approach is to derive the price-earnings (P/E) ratio from M&A deals involving companies with similar characteristics, and employ the P/E multiple on the EBITDA of the valuation target. However, many DBFs are cash-flow negative, meaning that capital-market-oriented models fail to accurately put a price tag on these, as the multiple approach does not consider growth opportunities in a firm's product pipeline, leading to an equity value equal to zero. Furthermore, the product pipeline of these companies tends to be unique so that it is difficult to find comparable companies. For this reason, a product pipeline valuation approach is most often taken, in which future revenue streams are estimated for each product and discounted back to their NPV. This is done both for products on the market and products under development, which together constitute the company's value.[35] Upfront, a fundamental analysis is conducted, for each product, providing the basis for a discounted cash-flow (DCF) calculation (DVFA, 2005). Accordingly, the firm value is the NPV of its product pipeline and its products on the market. The financial analysts interviewed revealed this to be the most commonly used approach, especially for smaller companies with negative cash-flows.[36]

Within the pipeline valuation approach, IPR information is incorporated in several ways. This occurs during the fundamental analysis in relation to the forecasted cash-flows. Firstly, the exclusivity situation of each product is analysed to determine future revenue streams. This is done on the basis of the type of protection the firm has obtained. For example, patent protection of the chemical compound of a drug is regarded as providing better exclusivity than a formulation patent, and is thus associated with higher future revenues. In this sense, patents are valued on the basis of the premium price the company can achieve with the product. A stronger patent position, in terms of exclusivity, thus means less competition and a higher premium price. Hence, IPR information enters the valuation model implicitly, through the estimated cash-flows.

Secondly, analysts evaluate for how long the premium price can be maintained. This involves looking at the expiry dates of relevant patents. To do so, reassessments are constantly made, with a focus on two particular events – that is, marketing authorisation and the expiry of the primary patent. Typically, the first assessment is made when the development project has reached clinical phase II or III, where attrition rates decrease substantially. This is because tests with actual patients are first made in clinical phase II – making assessments about the prospects of a product less uncertain, as the probability that the information is going to materialise increases. At this point, analysts' main concern is whether the firm has or will be able to obtain exclusivity for the product. The underlying reasoning, one analyst tells us, is that: 'If a company cannot exclude competitors from the commercialisation process, it is unlikely to be able to generate sufficient income to cover development costs.' Analysing whether a firm is likely to obtain exclusivity involves assessing whether it has any pending patents or even any that have been granted. Not surprisingly, granted patents are valued higher than pending ones. Further, the geographical scope of these patents is examined to determine whether exclusivity can be obtained for the company's main markets.

Reassessments of the exclusivity situation and the expected duration of exclusivity are also made on a continuous basis. For example, although analysts do not consider formulation patents of importance in obtaining exclusivity during the development phase, they can positively contribute to a firm's value from a product lifecycle perspective. By this I mean that when a product has reached the market and the primary patent is about to expire, patents with later expiry dates are considered together with further lifecycle management measures – see, for example, new second indications and new packaging design – that may enable the firm to uphold exclusivity for some additional time. Although financial analysts models are restrictive in extending the duration of exclusivity, this can add a few years to exclusivity in terms of the point when generic competition is expected. Accordingly, patents with later expiry dates can enable the company to maintain a premium price after the primary patent has expired.

Usually, however, extensive generic competition is accounted for. Trademarks are therefore not considered to have the potential to preserve product market share or premium price at this point, unless the trademark is very well known, which can allow the firm to maintain some market share on the basis of a smaller premium price. Financial analysts therefore sometimes engage with prescribers to determine their loyalty to the brand.

This factor is then weighted in their assessments of how extensive generic competition will be at the point of patent expiry.

Furthermore, the DVFA (2005) report on analysts' valuation practices within the biotechnology industry suggests that FTO contributes more to firm value than exclusivity. Although I find that some financial analysts consider the FTO situation in their valuations, only four out of the twelve analysts interviewed actively requested and processed such information. As securing FTO was found to be an essential objective of IPR management in all firms in the study, this finding is rather surprising. Instead, I find that many analysts are unaware of the legal risks of not having secured FTO. As one analyst put it: 'I'm not familiar with the term freedom-to-operate.' After explaining its meaning and the reason why companies pursue this objective, the same analyst admitted: 'That is probably something we should consider.'

However, FTO assessments require specific knowledge about the patent system and the ability to analyse patent claim structures. Hence, DVFA (2005) recognises the difficulties attached to FTO assessments. For this reason, the analysts – those that considered FTO important – reveal that they rely on FTO assessments conducted by the company, and their reporting on this item. At the same time, no additional information is provided for analysts to verify the accuracy of the company's statement about the FTO situation. This finding is confirmed by the IPR management experts interviewed, revealing that companies do not disclose any detailed information about their FTO analysis.

Besides the IPR situation around products, financial analysts find information on companies' technology transfer activities to be value-relevant. The analysts interviewed reveal such information to be relevant in two ways. Firstly, if a technology is acquired that adds to the company's product pipeline, the technology provides a new growth opportunity. This means that information about the details of the deal, concerning the exclusivity and FTO situation, are relevant. Secondly, if the company intends to commercialise its R&D on the technology market – as opposed to the product market – this changes the context of the valuation. This is because revenues in most cases will be generated through patent licensing. Hence, the company may receive upfront and milestone payments, but share only a part of the revenue the licensing partner generates after product commercialisation, according to the settled royalty rate. This, of course, affects the profit potential of the company, and thus its value. Information on payment structures, which are outlined in licensing agreements, is therefore value-relevant.

For the reasons described above, analysts evaluate the licensing deals conducted by the firm. As one analyst explains:

> Licensing agreements provide essential forward-looking information that has already materialised ... By looking at the royalty rate and the markets for which a licence has been given, we are better able to determine the future earnings potential of that company ... if a company has been able to generate revenue from its patents in the past, there is also reason to believe that the company will be able to do so in the future.

However, analysts reveal that firms are often reluctant to disclose all the information requested. For instance, it is common for them to report on the size of upfront and milestone payments, but not when the milestones are settled and which criteria the firm needs to meet to obtain their payments. This makes it difficult to assess the probability of the milestone payments actually occurring. Moreover, as indicated by the interviewed firms' reporting practices, financial analysts find them reluctant to disclose precise information about the royalty rate.

The interpretation of the licensing data depends on whether it relates to an in- or out-licensing deal. In relation to out-licensing deals, for example, financial analysts prefer a higher royalty rate as this indicates higher future economic returns. In contrast, in relation to in-licensing, a higher royalty rate indicates higher forthcoming costs. If the company is expected to commercialise a product based on taking out a licence, the main concern of the analysts is not, however, the cost of the licence. Rather, they will want to know whether exclusivity can be obtained for the product. One analyst tells us that:

> The information we receive is not value-relevant as such, but needs to be put in its context. When a company has taken a licence to commercialise a product the most essential aspect is whether it will be able to do so exclusively. If, on the other hand, a company has licensed out a patent for revenue purposes, we need to find out how much money the company is likely to make.

Accordingly, analysts assess patent licensing information according to the objective of the deal.

4.7.3   IPR Reporting and Company Valuation

Several findings were made about firms' IPR reporting, and its potential to reduce asymmetric information on capital markets. Firstly, IPR reporting is capital market driven, meaning that pull effects provide its rationale. This implies that IPR reporting has the potential to reduce asymmetric information. On the other hand, the effectiveness of IPR reporting depends on the awareness of financial analysts and investors about the importance of IPR management. The interviews show that their

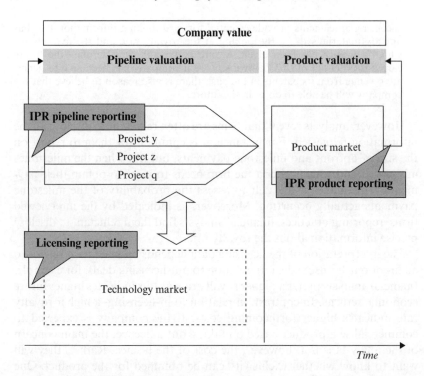

Figure 4.4   IPR reporting and company value

awareness has its limits. This is not least suggested by the finding that most analysts simply neglect the risks of not having secured FTO for a product. Furthermore, analysts do not request information about companies' IPR policies – that is, how their IPR management systematically interacts with the product development process. Rather, information requests are limited to the IPR situation around companies' products and information about its technology transfer activities.

Secondly, firms' IPR management is assessed from a product lifecycle perspective, and mainly in relation to two events, namely, product launch and patent expiry. How IPR reporting contributes to company value is illustrated in Figure 4.4, which shows the type of IPR information analysts request at different stages of the product lifecycle.

Accordingly, during the R&D phase, analysts assess the IPR situation around each product in the firm's pipeline. More specifically, they look at the exclusivity situation in terms of which type of patent protection the firm has obtained or is likely to obtain for its product. Related information is incorporated into their revenue forecast as the premium price the company can charge for its product in the future. In addition, some analysts consider the FTO situation in this context, and discount for perceived risks. Also, a company's technology transfer activities are considered in the context of the company's product pipeline. This is typically done on the basis of information disclosures about the details of relevant licensing agreements. The relevance of such information depends on the objective of the deal. For example, if the patents have been licensed-in to extend the firm's product pipeline, the analysts would mainly look at the exclusivity situation in terms of whether the licence has been obtained on an exclusive basis, and for which markets. In contrast, if a patent has been licensed-out for technology commercialisation, the financial aspects of the deal are more value-relevant. When the product has reached the market, however, the focus shifts towards measures taken to extend the duration of exclusivity beyond expiry of the primary patent. Thirdly, financial analysts mainly rely on firms' own assessments of the IPR situation. Although some analysts would sometimes search for important patents in public databases, none of them had a genuine background in assessing patent information. Moreover, the information communicated to financial analysts is not provided in detail. Hence, analysts to a large extent trust in the accuracy of companies' own assessments. Accordingly, they rely on companies' voluntary disclosures, often without being able to verify the correctness and plausibility of the information ex ante. For verification they therefore make assessments ex post. For example, if a firm claims to have secured FTO, and ends up losing an infringement lawsuit, the correctness of the information provided by the firm will be questioned in the future.

Interesting also is that financial analysts discount for firms being reluctant to disclose requested IPR information. As another analyst puts it: 'We need information to make an assessment of a company's profit potential . . . IPR information provides a part of our analysis . . . when companies are reluctant to disclose requested information about their IPR, this means additional risk . . . we discount if we don't have the information we need.' This finding implies that IPR reporting has a direct impact on the firm's share price, and thus its costs of capital.

NOTES

1. Red biotechnology refers to the use of organisms for the improvement of medical processes. This includes designing organisms to manufacture pharmaceutical products. Because of the increasing relevance of biotechnology in pharmaceutical products, firms in the field of red biotechnology were also included in the sample.
2. Before the development of penicillin only a fraction of medicines available actually cured diseases.

3. An NCE is a new compound that has not previously been approved for human use.
4. Major progress was made in fields such as cell biology, physiology, enzymology and pharmacology.
5. Biotechnology can be broadly defined as the application of biological systems and organisms to technical and industrial processes.
6. rDNA is created by combining DNA sequences to form DNA that does not exist naturally.
7. Diagnostics is a technique or branch of medical science dealing with the classification of diseases; therapeutics is a branch of medical science concerned with the treatment of diseases.
8. As the technology is embodied in a product, little tacit knowledge is required to use it.
9. For a more detailed discussion about the structure of the pharmaceutical industry within the EU, see European Commission (2009).
10. Detailing is an activity in which firms visit doctors to inform them about new medicines and their benefits.
11. It should be noted that their sample considers only the 30 largest pharmaceutical companies in the EU.
12. Occasionally they may even enter the market before patent expiry if they believe the patent is invalid or have found a way to produce the medicine without infringing third party patents.
13. In the pharmaceutical industry, the term generic can be defined from a trademark as well as a patent perspective (WTO, 2006). From a trademark perspective, medicines can have different types of names. For instance, most originator firms sell their products under their own trademarked brand names. In addition, however, each medicine has a name for the chemical substance, describing the product's molecular structure, which is not proprietary. Moreover, medicines have generic names – that is, names that provide a simpler version of the name of the chemical substance, and thus can be remembered more easily. Accordingly, medicines that are commercialised with only the generic name can be referred to as generic products from a trademark perspective, as the product is not protected by the brand name given by the firm (Hurwitz and Caves, 1988). By contrast, from a patent perspective, the term generic is used for equivalents to originator medicines, which are launched as patent protection expires. These generic products are sold under the generic name, and thus are also generic from a trademark point of view, or under another brand name. In the present study, however, generics are referred to as replica drugs that are launched on the market after patent expiry at a significantly lower price, regardless of whether they have a brand name or not. Firms selling generic products from a patent perspective are therefore referred to as generic firms.
14. Because the development of medicines is a global undertaking, recent efforts have been made to harmonise such practices. Hence, the EMEA-FDA Good Clinical Practice (GCP) Initiative aims to achieve greater convergence of the clinical research process; see Doc. Ref. General-EMEA/INS/GCP/541006/2008.
15. In clinical phase IV the product is already authorised for commercialisation. It is therefore often said that there are only three clinical phases.
16. The *attrition rate* is the percentage of failed product development projects.
17. As lined out by Directive 2001/83/EC Art. 6, further information on the particular information and documents required for the application can be found in Art. 8(3), 10, 10a, 10b or 11 of Annex I to the Directive.
18. See Note 155 of the European Commission (2009).
19. According to the EMEA: 'Two medicinal products are bioequivalent if they are pharmaceutically equivalent alternatives and if their bioavailabilities after administration in the same molar dose are similar to such degree that their effects, with respect to both efficacy and safety, will be essentially the same' (see CPMP/EWP/QWP/1401/98).
20. In the US originator products are filed for as a new drug application (NDA) in conformity with the Food, Drug, and Cosmetic Act, Sec. 505; 21 USC § 355(b)(2). Generic products are filed for as an abbreviated new drug application (ANDA).

21. Within the EU, Directive 2004/27/EC amending Directive 2001/83/EC and Regulation 726/2004 settle the rules concerning data and marketing exclusivity periods as well as related harmonisation efforts.

22. The firms pursuing this business model had annual revenues exceeding 1 billion EUR.

23. Besides patent out-licensing, DBFs can also commercialise their R&D through other types of deals such as assignments or mergers and acquisitions. However, out-licensing is most common and therefore used as a term for commercialising R&D without bringing a product to the market.

24. Firms pursuing this business model are referred to as DBFs. It should be noted that the term is used regardless of whether the products provided by these firms are based on biotechnology.

25. The firms pursuing this business model had annual revenues below 1 billion EUR.

26. Moehrle et al. (2005) provide a detailed description of how patent information can be used within R&D management.

27. Bergmann et al. (2008) show how patent information can be used to detect risks of patent infringements.

28. Biological patents are in principle no different from the types of patents described, other than that they relate to inventions in the field of biotechnology. This can be genetic material, DNA sequences as well as related methods for manufacturing and use, antibodies and other types of proteins. In contrast to chemically synthesised molecules, however, biological products are based on living material, which is more complex in structure and not fully defined.

29. For a definition of medical device patents, see European Union Medical Devices Directive 93/42/ECC, or the Federal Food, Drug and Cosmetic Act (FDCA), 21 USC § 321(h) for the US.

30. Decisions on whether to assign or license a patent relate to the type of deal and financial considerations. In general, however, the firms investigated reveal that patents are licensed rather than assigned. For this reason, this section will focus on patent licensing.

31. Although there is no licensee or licensor before a licensing agreement has been reached, these terms are used for the sake of simplicity.

32. For example, within the EU, CTMs are revoked 'if, within a continuous period of five years the trade mark has not been put into genuine use in the Community in connection with the goods or services in respect of which it is registered, and there are no proper reasons for non-use' (Art. 50(1)(a) CTMR).

33. However, infringement cases usually occur later during the commercial phase when *data exclusivity* expires and generic firms prepare for marketing authorisation; data exclusivity protects clinical test data, which is submitted to the regulatory agency to prove the safety and efficiency of a new medicine.

34. Although trademarks do not provide exclusivity, they can extend the duration for which higher economic returns can be generated.

35. For products under development, expected future revenues are multiplied by historical attrition rates for the clinical phase the product is in, to account for the risk of the company not obtaining marketing authorisation for its product.

36. For a more detailed description of the pipeline valuation approach, see DVFA (2005).

5. IPR management, corporate disclosures, and stock market valuations in the pharmaceutical industry

5.1 DESIGN OF THE EMPIRICAL STUDY

The exploratory study in Chapter 4 set out how pharmaceutical firms conduct their IPR management, and its association with their financial performance. Taking these findings, together with past research showing that IPR contribute to both firm productivity and market values (see Section 2.4), as well as research pointing to the ability of companies to reduce asymmetric information, and thereby also stock market uncertainty (see Section 2.8.3), through voluntary IPR reporting, it seems reasonable to assume that information on firms' IPR management is value-relevant – that is, under the assumption of informationally efficient stock markets, it should be reflected in share prices. In this chapter, the assumption of informational market efficiency is examined in relation to the relationships identified between IPR management and firms' financial performance (see Section 4.6). These relationships are operationalised as in Figure 5.1, and examined accordingly.

Secondly, previous studies as well as the exploratory interviews reveal that some firms report on their IPR management on a voluntary basis (see Section 4.7). Moreover, I find evidence that such information is explicitly considered by financial analysts, but often inadequately disclosed. However, empirical research on the valuation effects of IPR management disclosures is still fairly limited, especially when it comes to continuous active reporting decisions, rather than particular events. In an attempt to at least partially bridge this research gap, I examine whether IPR reporting contributes to the informational efficiency of stock markets, leading to reduced stock market uncertainty. The relationships between IPR reporting and stock market uncertainty are derived and operationalised on the basis of the findings of the exploration conducted among financial analysts (see Section 4.7.3), and are displayed in Figure 5.2.

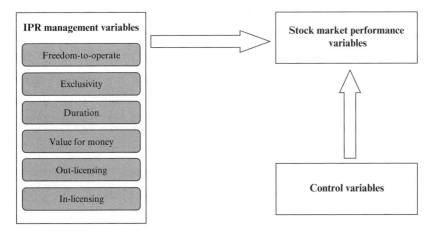

Figure 5.1   Research model – 'IPR management'

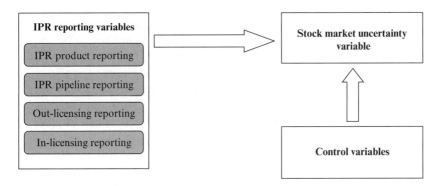

Figure 5.2   Research model – 'IPR reporting'

Accordingly, this chapter examines two main questions:

- Do share prices reflect information about firms' IPR management?
- Can firms reduce stock market uncertainty through IPR reporting?

To operationalise the derived research models, and examine the questions stated above, a questionnaire was developed, on the basis of which a survey was conducted among pharmaceutical firms listed on the stock exchange. The first part of this chapter describes this process in terms of how the data for the empirical study was gathered. Secondly, some descriptive statistics are displayed to create a better understanding of how firms manage their IPR, and which aspects they report on, but also to enhance the reader's understanding of the dataset, its benefits and its limits. I then proceed to hypothesise some relationships between firms' IPR management and their share price performance (see Figure 5.1), and examine these through a multivariate analysis. Finally, I turn to the relationship between firms' IPR reporting and stock market uncertainty (see Figure 5.2). These hypothesises are derived separately and examined accordingly, also through a multivariate analysis.

5.2   SAMPLING AND DATA COLLECTION

The quantitative empirical study was – like the exploratory study in the previous chapter – conducted within the pharmaceutical industry. As mentioned in Chapter 1, the study was restricted to the pharmaceutical industry because past research has shown that firms' IPR management practices differ fundamentally across industries, and that both patents and trademarks are important in discrete technology industries (see, for example, Arundel and Kabla, 1998; Cohen et al., 2000; Malmberg, 2005), especially in relation to pharmaceutical products (see, for example, Arora et al. 2002; Bessen and Meurer, 2008a; Lanjouw, 1998; Sandner and Block, 2011). This suggests the pharmaceutical industry to be a good starting point for examining the value-relevance of firms' IPR management.

Data collection was undertaken through a survey questionnaire – developed on the basis of insights drawn from previous studies as well as the exploratory interviews – operationalising firms' IPR management practices as well as related voluntary corporate disclosures. Besides focusing on the pharmaceutical sector, including red biotechnology, a prerequisite for participating in the survey was that the firm was listed on the stock exchange, either within the EU or in the US. This restriction was set, firstly, because the US and the EU provide the main markets for pharmaceutical products and, secondly, because IPR regimes outside the US and the EU are often considerably weaker, meaning that a firm's IPR management will have less impact – if any – on the share price if they mainly operate in other markets. To arrive at the final population I also excluded firms focusing on generics or functional foods. This was done because these firms' business models are fundamentally different, not least in terms of relying considerable less on IPR – something that was discovered through the exploratory interviews. Under these restrictions, I identified a total population of 493 firms through the Bloomberg database.[1] Some details about the population and the sample can be seen in Table 5.1.

Table 5.1   Population and sample statistics

Sample	Number
Generated population	554
Less non-relevant firms	61
Corrected population	493
No. of respondents	73
Response rate	14.8%

For each firm in the population, a contact person was identified. This was done either through the USPTO register of patent attorneys and patent agents – that is, if the firm was headquartered in the US – or through the EPO patent attorney register if the firm was headquartered in the EU. For cases in which a contact person could not be identified through these registers – perhaps because the company had no in-house patent attorney – a contact person with IPR, R&D or licensing experience was identified through the firm's homepage or various press releases.

Having generated the contact details, some of the firms were randomly contacted via email, for a pre-test of the questionnaire prior to the survey. The questionnaire was pre-tested with 12 IPR management representatives, which had four main objectives. The first objective was to ensure the understandability and consistency of the stated questions. By this I mean that respondents understood the same thing by the terminology used. Secondly, the confidentiality of the information requested was assessed. This was done in order to ensure that most of the respondents were not reluctant to answer the stated questions for confidentiality reasons. Thirdly, a major objective was to assess whether the IPR management representatives were aware of the firm's corporate disclosure practices. As indicated by the exploratory interviews, the pre-test revealed that the investor relations department is typically responsible for the communication of value-relevant information to the stock market. In relation to the firm's IPR management, however, the IPR department would be approached in relation to such information. The IPR management representative would therefore generally be aware of the company's IPR-related information disclosures. I therefore decided that the approach of asking IPR management representatives also about the firm's external IPR reporting practices seemed reasonable.

Following the pre-test, every contact person in the population received a personalised letter with a physical copy of the survey questionnaire. To increase the response rate, the letter stated the objective of the study and its potential benefits to the pharmaceutical industry. In addition, it ensured the confidential treatment of all data. Each letter also contained a link through which the survey questionnaire could be accessed and submitted online. About three weeks after the letters were posted, each contact person who had not yet responded received a reminder via email. An additional two weeks later, the remaining non-responding part of the population received an additional reminder via telephone. At all times, however, the participants had the opportunity to contact a researcher with questions about the survey.

The survey resulted in 78 forms being submitted, of which 73 were sufficiently complete to be used in the empirical analysis. Considering that the final sample represents about 15 per cent of the total population of listed pharmaceutical firms in the EU and the US, it is to be considered to be representative, although some similar studies – for example, Blind et al. (2006) – have received higher response rates. These studies, however, focused mainly on German companies, which is likely to have had a positive effect.[2] In addition, and in contrast to the studies mentioned, the present study also requested information about IPR lawsuits, which Köhler (2010) suggests is a particularly sensitive issue. Finally, it should be noted that, although the sample was not selected completely randomly, there is no bias to be expected from the sample selection process that should impose restrictions on the generalisation of the results to the population of public pharmaceutical firms.

Besides the use of survey data, secondary accounting and stock market data was gathered for the operationalisation of the dependent variables as well as some of the control variables. More specifically, data was gathered from the participating companies' income statement – for example, annual revenues and R&D expenditures – and information on firms' total assets was derived from their balance sheet. From the cash-flow statement, information about the issuance of common stock, the repurchase of common stock, and common dividends paid was gathered. Additionally, stock market data in terms of share prices, trading volumes and market capitalisation was collected. All the data was derived for the fiscal years 2007, 2008 and 2009 from Bloomberg after the survey was completed. Hence, the secondary data was matched with the survey questionnaire data in a second step.

5.3 DESCRIPTIVE STATISTICS

This section summarises the descriptive statistics from the conducted survey. It describes the sample in relation to the position of the respondents, general firm characteristics, as well as the companies' IPR management and IPR reporting practices.

5.3.1   Position of the Respondents

To complete the questionnaire, comprehensive knowledge about both the firm's IPR, in a business model context, and related information disclosures was required of the respondents. Hence, an assessment of the data quality, in terms of respondents' ability to answer the stated questions, was essential. The current position of the respondents at their respective firm was requested for this purpose. The distribution of the respondents among the predefined categories can be found in Figure 5.3. It shows that 44 per cent of the questionnaires were completed by the head of the IPR department. The second largest category was senior executives – that is, management board members – underlining the managerial relevance of IPR. The others held various senior positions such as head of legal department, head of R&D or head of business development (BD). It should also be noted that 96 per cent of the respondents were head of a department or on the management board. This suggests the collected data are of high quality.

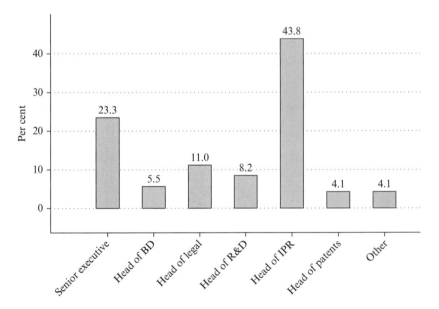

Figure 5.3   Current position of the respondents

5.3.2   Firm Characteristics

To assess the characteristics of the responding firms and create a better understanding of the sample, I decided to request data regarding firm size, firm age, R&D intensity, patent and trademark activity, and finally business model.

5.3.2.1   Firm size

Past research shows that corporate IPR management practices depend on the size of the firm (see, for example, Allegrezza and Guarda-Rauchs, 1999; Arundel and Kabla, 1998). This is something that needs to be controlled for in the multivariate analysis. At the same time, however, I want to be able to generalise the findings across firms in the pharmaceutical industry. For this reason, a sample that is representative of firms of different sizes is needed. To assess whether this is the case, firms were asked to provide information on the number of full-time employees.

Figure 5.4 shows that firms of all categories are well represented in the sample and that the largest category (25 per cent) consists of smaller firms with one to 50 employees.

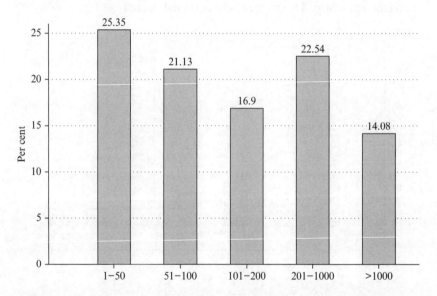

Figure 5.4   Sample according to number of full-time employees

5.3.2.2   Firm age

Capital market studies often differentiate between firms according to age (see, for example, Bittelmeyer, 2007; Pastor and Veronesi, 2003). Theoretically, this is because survival rates increase with the maturity of the firm's business model. The respondents were therefore asked to indicate the age of their company. Figure 5.5 reveals that most firms in the

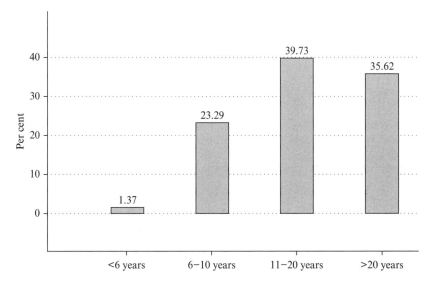

Figure 5.5   Sample according to firm age

sample had existed for at least 11 years and that only one firm had existed for less than six years. Hence, although many of the firms are relatively small, they have existed for quite some time. This is presumably due to the relatively long R&D process in the pharmaceutical industry, meaning that it takes time for firms to grow.

5.3.2.3   R&D intensity

Because the present study is mainly concerned with the valuation of technology-driven firms – that is, firms that invest in R&D – it was important to assess the R&D intensity of the firms in the sample. This is because past research shows that firms with high R&D expenditures relative to sales are more difficult to value (see, for example, Aboody and Lev, 2000; Amir et al., 1999; Chan et al., 2001). In terms of sales, most of the companies in the sample are also rather small, generating less than 50 million USD annually. However, 29 per cent of the sample also generated more than 100 million USD on a yearly basis. It is interesting that many firms spend more on R&D than they generate in revenue on an annual basis. While only about 5 per cent of the sample spend less than 2 million USD on R&D, about 22 per cent generate less than 2 million USD in annual revenue (see Table 5.2). I therefore conclude that several of the responding firms have few assets-in-place and these consist mainly of growth opportunities. Accordingly, the sample seems to serve the purpose of the present study well.

Table 5.2   Annual revenue and R&D spending in million USD

	Sample distribution in % of total firms according to revenue and R&D spending in 2009					Median	N
	<2	2 to 10	11 to 50	51 to 100	>100		
Annual revenue	21.92	15.07	21.9	12.33	28.77	11 to 50	73
Annual R&D spending	5.48	19.18	47.95	10.96	16.44	11 to 50	73

5.3.2.4   Patent and trademark activity

For IPR management to constitute a value-relevant activity, firms need to exhibit an IPR portfolio that needs to be managed. This must be controlled for in the econometric study. Examining the sample, I find that the largest category of firms had a patent portfolio consisting of 10 to 50 patent families (see Table 5.3). It should also be noted that the distribution of the firms in the sample according to the size of their patent portfolio largely resembles their distribution according to R&D spending. For trademark families, however, a different distribution is found. Most firms had a portfolio of two to 10 trademark families, and often also less than two trademarks. Arguably, this is because several firms do not have a product on the market yet, and therefore presumably rely less on trademark protection. Finally, I find that, although many of the companies are relatively small, all firms in the sample owned IPR.

Table 5.3   Number of patent and trademark families

	Sample distribution in % of total firms according to number of patent and trademark families					Median	N
	<2	2 to 10	11 to 50	51 to 100	>100		
Patents	5.48	19.18	42.47	13.70	19.18	11 to 50	73
Trademarks	17.81	49.32	20.55	1.37	10.96	2 to 10	73

5.3.2.5   Business model

As shown in the exploratory study, pharmaceutical companies pursue two main business models, generating revenues on either the technology or the product market (see Section 4.3). Because this can potentially influence the performance contribution of different IPR management tasks, it is an aspect that should be controlled for. I therefore examine the companies in

Table 5.4   Product market and licensing activity

	Sample distribution in % of total firms according to number of products and licences in 2009					Median	N
	None	1 to 2	3 to 4	5 to 10	>10		
Products on the market	32.88	34.25	4.11	2.74	26.03	1 to 2	73
Products under development	0	8.22	35.62	35.62	20.55	5 to 10	73
Patent in-licensing	28.77	31.51	16.44	10.96	12.33	1 to 2	73
Patent out-licensing	28.77	21.92	26.03	12.33	10.96	1 to 2	73

the sample according to the number of products they have on the market, the size of their product pipeline, as well as their licensing activity (see Table 5.4).

Looking at the distribution of companies according to the number of products they have on the market, I find it to be rather U-shaped. Sixty-seven per cent of respondents have fewer than two products on the market, while 26 per cent have more than ten products. Only 7 per cent have between three and ten products. In conformity with the exploratory study, this suggests that pharmaceutical firms pursue two distinct business models. They either generate their revenues on the technology market, and therefore have none or few products, or focus on product commercialisation and thus have a large number of products on the market (see, for example, Farag, 2009; Rothaermel and Deeds, 2004).

In addition, the respondents were requested to provide information about the size of their product pipeline. This was done because the valuation of a company also incorporates the valuation of its growth opportunities (see, for example, Guo et al., 2005). According to the size of their product pipeline, the sample follows more of a normal distribution. All of the respondents had at least one product under development and as many as 71 per cent had between three and ten products in the pipeline. This underlines the importance of diversification in the pharmaceutical industry.

Analogously to the provision of product data, firms were asked to submit information on their patent licensing activity. Based on the information provided, I find that most firms also engaged on the technology market in 2009, in terms of licensing patented technologies. Seventy-one per cent at some point licensed-in a patent, and the largest category (31.5 per cent) did so once or twice. Similarly, 71 per cent licensed-out a patent, and the largest category (26 per cent), did so three or four times on an annual basis. Hence, patent licensing seems to form a part of most firms' business models, not least since several firms do not have a product on the market and presumably rely on patent out-licensing for the generation of economic returns.

5.3.3   IPR Management

The following section describes the companies in the sample according to the age of their IPR department, their IPR management objectives, motives for IPR protection, and the relevance of different IPR management tasks. All items were operationalised on a five-point Likert-type scale.

5.3.3.1   IPR department
Approximately 14 per cent of the respondents did not yet have an IPR department (see Figure 5.6). This can be compared with companies in the German electronics industry, in which Pangerl (2009) finds that 70 per cent of the respondents did not have a patent department, suggesting that

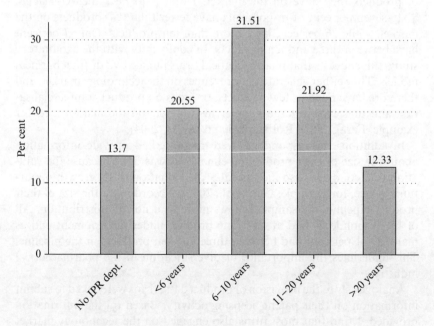

Figure 5.6   Sample distribution according to age of the IPR department

IPR management is of relatively high importance in the pharmaceutical sector. It should be noted, however, that most of the respondents' IPR departments had existed for less than ten years. This means that many firms established their IPR department years after the firm was initially formed (compare Section 5.3.2.2). There are at least two potential explanations for this finding. Firstly, IPR management is a relatively young task which has received more attention recently than only a few years ago (see, for example, Frey et al., 2008; Rivette and Kline, 2000). Secondly, it is a task that is heavily outsourced. For example, Wagner (2007) finds that firms with high fluctuations in the number of yearly patent applications tend to outsource patent filings to smooth workload fluctuations. Hence, as shown in the exploratory study, he finds that IPR management in smaller firms is often supported by external service providers.

5.3.3.2 Objectives

The exploratory interviews revealed that securing FTO, maximising exclusivity, maximising the duration of exclusivity, and obtaining the best value for money were important IPR management objectives. Table 5.5 essentially confirms these findings. In total, 85 per cent rated securing FTO as of very high importance to their company. The equivalent category was also found to be the median for the objective of maximising exclusivity, which was considered to be of very high relevance by 58 per cent of the respondents. Similarly, 53 per cent of the firms considered maximising the duration of exclusivity to be of very high importance. Finally, obtaining the best value for money was found to be the least relevant objective, although 32 per cent of the respondents considered it to be of very high relevance. These findings underline the validity of the exploratory study, showing that the IPR management objectives identified apply to a wide range of companies in the pharmaceutical industry.

Table 5.5   Objectives of firms' IPR management

	Sample distribution in % of total firms according to relevance						Median	N
	Irrelevant	Low	Medium	High	Very high	Mean		
FTO	1.37	1.37	1.37	10.96	84.93	4.77	Very high	73
Exclusivity	8.22	4.11	15.07	15.07	57.53	4.10	Very high	73
Duration	8.22	8.22	15.07	15.07	53.42	3.97	Very high	73
Value for money	1.37	8.22	24.66	34.25	31.51	3.86	High	73

5.3.3.3 Motives for IPR protection

Past research shows that firms patent for many reasons (see, for example, Blind et al., 2006; Ceccagnoli et al., 2005; Cohen et al., 2000; Pitkethly, 2001). In addition, several studies differentiate between complex and discrete technologies in the context of motives to patent (see, for example, Cohen et al., 2000; Granstrand, 1999; Reitzig, 2004b). These studies suggest that firms in discrete technology fields patent to protect products from imitation, and thus use patents as limited exclusion rights, while firms in complex technology fields rely more on patents for strategic purposes – for example, to enhance the company's competitive position. However, Blind et al. (2006) find that the use of strategic patent functions has extended across technology fields, meaning that firms in discrete technologies also rely on strategic patenting. This finding is confirmed by the present study.

Although patents are considered to be most important to protect products, various additional strategic patent functions are perceived to be almost equally important (see Table 5.6). Forty-five per cent of the respondents consider patents to be of very high relevance in prolonging protection beyond expiry of the primary patent in terms of filing secondary patent applications. As shown by the exploratory interviews, this motive is of particular relevance in the pharmaceutical industry, where the innovation process is divided into several clinical phases. Because certain therapeutic effects can only be determined in the later clinical phases, through studies with actual patients, related patent applications are filed at this

Table 5.6   Motives to patent

	Sample distribution in % of total firms according to relevance					Median	N
	Irrelevant	Low	Medium	High	Very high	Mean		
Protection	0	0	5.48	60.27	34.25	4.29	High	73
Duration	2.74	5.48	23.29	23.29	45.21	4.03	High	73
Defensive blocking	0	12.33	23.29	34.25	30.14	3.82	High	73
Offensive blocking	1.37	8.22	26.03	39.73	24.66	3.78	High	73
In-licensing	8.22	13.70	36.99	21.92	19.18	3.30	Medium	73
Out-licensing	6.85	17.81	20.55	15.07	39.73	3.63	High	73
Reputation	4.11	19.18	20.55	30.14	26.03	3.55	High	73
Signalling	2.74	23.29	27.40	23.29	23.29	3.41	Medium	73

point, while patents related to, for instance, the chemical compound are often filed even before the development phase commences. Furthermore, patents are found to be used widely for both offensive and defensive blocking purposes. For example, 64 per cent of the sample regards defensive blocking to be of high or very high importance to their firm.

Turning to patent licensing, I find that the largest category (37 per cent), consider in-licensing to be of medium relevance, while the largest category (40 per cent) of the respondents regard patent out-licensing as highly important. Presumably, this is due to the relatively high share of smaller companies, for which patent out-licensing provides an essential commercialisation strategy, but who do not rely much on in-licensing, which theoretically goes hand-in-hand with a product-based business model (see, for example, Farag, 2009).

Finally, the reputation and signalling motives are well distributed across the different categories. Forty-seven per cent of the companies consider patents of high or very high importance for signalling growth opportunities to the capital market. However, the median is found in the medium category, showing that the use of patents to attract financial capital is not among the most important motives. Similarly, 56 per cent consider patents to be of high or very high relevance in enhancing the reputation of the firm as a technology leader. The distribution of firms according to the reputation item follows the distribution of the signalling motive. Probably, firms with only a few assets-in-place consider patents to be relevant for signalling and reputation purposes, while firms which already generate stable cash-flows tend to be valued on the basis of these.

Like patents, trademarks are found, on average, to be most important as a means of protection against imitation. However, trademarks are almost equally important for communication purposes in marketing activities, but also for product identification by patients and prescribers. All trademark motives follow similar distributions, have the same median, and close means (see Table 5.7). This suggests that those firms for which trademarks are important use their trademarks for all these purposes, meaning that the protection, communication and identification motives are highly complementary.

Turning to the protection motive, the largest category (38 per cent) perceives trademark protection to be of very high importance to their firm, while an additional 22 per cent find this motive to be of high importance. In relation to trademark communication, the largest category (30 per cent) considers patents to be of high importance. Also, 32 per cent of the respondents perceived trademarks to be of very high importance for product identification purposes.

Table 5.7   Motives for trademark protection

	Sample distribution in % of total firms according to relevance						Median	N
	Irrelevant	Low	Medium	High	Very high	Mean		
Protection	6.85	10.96	21.92	21.92	38.36	3.73	High	73
Communication	9.59	5.48	27.40	30.14	27.40	3.60	High	73
Identification	10.96	13.70	16.44	27.40	31.51	3.55	High	73
Legal substitution	53.52	21.13	12.68	8.45	4.23	1.89	Irrelevant	71
Commercial substitution	51.39	20.83	12.50	12.50	2.78	1.94	Irrelevant	73
Combination exclusivity	20.55	13.70	15.07	21.92	28.77	3.25	Medium	73
Combination duration	24.66	16.44	8.22	28.77	21.92	3.07	High	73

In addition, I find that trademarks are used as complements to patents rather than as substitutes. As many as 54 per cent of respondents consider trademarks to be irrelevant as a substitute for patent protection, if a patent cannot be obtained due to patentability issues. Similarly, 51 per cent consider trademarks to be irrelevant as a substitute for patents, if patent protection was found not to be commercially viable for one reason or another. In contrast, I find that the largest category (29 per cent) consider the combination of patents and trademarks to be of very high importance to maximise exclusivity. At the same time, however, 21 per cent considered the use of trademarks for this purpose to be irrelevant. Probably these are firms without any product on the market.

Looking at the use of trademarks to extend appropriation beyond patent protection, I find a similar U-shaped distribution. Fifty-one per cent consider trademarks to be of high or very high relevance to extend appropriation beyond patent protection, although the second largest category perceives this trademark strategy to be irrelevant to their business. These results are in line with the findings of Blind et al. (2006) – that is, that trademark protection is associated with the patent protection motive – in showing that trademarks are mainly used together with patents in order to maximise exclusivity and its duration.

5.3.3.4   R&D support

As shown by the exploratory interviews (see Section 4.4.1), R&D support is an essential task for pharmaceutical firms' IPR management. To support the firm's internal R&D, regular patent searches are conducted. According to Table 5.8, 52 per cent of respondents do this at least monthly. Only 3 per cent had never conducted any patent searches, underling the importance of patent information in the context of IPR management (see, for example, Moehrle et al., 2005; Thumm, 2004).

Table 5.8   Patent search frequency

	Sample distribution in % of total firms according to frequency						Median	N
	Never	Annually	Biannu-ally	Quar-terly	Monthly	Mean		
Patent searches	2.74	8.22	10.96	26.03	52.05	4.16	Monthly	73

In terms of supporting the firm's internal R&D, two main objectives for these searches were identified (see Table 5.9).[3] The first motive relates to whether the firm will be able to secure FTO for its product development projects. This was shown to be the most important objective of pharmaceutical firms' IPR management. As many as 62.5 per cent also consider this objective to be of very high relevance to their patent searches. The second motive relates to the extraction of information to assess the latest technological developments in the firm's markets. Also, this motive is perceived to be important, although less so than the FTO assessment motive – the categories medium, high, and very high were found to be equally large (26 per cent each).

Table 5.9   Motives for patent searches

	Sample distribution in % of total firms according to relevance						Median	N
	Irrelevant	Low	Medium	High	Very high	Mean		
FTO	6.94	5.56	4.17	20.83	62.50	4.26	Very high	72
Technology develop-ments	4.11	23.61	26.39	26.39	26.39	3.33	Medium	72

Table 5.10   Patent information in project funding decisions

| | Sample distribution in % of total firms according to relevance | | | | | | | |
	Irrelevant	Low	Medium	High	Very high	Mean	Median	N
FTO	8.22	16.44	10.96	23.29	41.10	3.73	High	73
Exclusivity	8.22	15.07	30.14	20.55	26.03	3.41	Medium	73

Finally, the firm's IPR management is sometimes directly integrated in their product development process. For example, some firms explicitly use patent information to assess the commercial viability of a R&D project in terms of whether the firm will be able to obtain exclusivity and secure FTO for it. This forms part of the material on the basis of which project funding decisions are made (see Section 4.4.1.2). The high relevance of securing FTO is underlined once more in that the largest share (41 per cent) consider FTO assessments to be of very high importance in project funding decisions (see Table 5.10). Similarly, 47 per cent of the sample consider exclusivity assessments to be of very high or high relevance for such decisions. These findings, however, suggest that companies are even more concerned with assessing the risks of patent lawsuits than the potential of obtaining exclusivity, when funding their R&D projects.

5.3.3.5   Technology transfer

Besides conducting internal R&D, most firms are active on the technology market. An important IPR management task was therefore shown to be support of the firm's technology transfer activities. This involves, for example, the identification of licensing opportunities – something that is especially important for firms which pursue a licensing-based business model. The survey also shows that firms search for licensing opportunities on a regular basis (see Table 5.11). The largest category (32 per cent) screen the market for out-licensing potential on at least a monthly basis, and the second largest category does so on a quarterly basis (28 per cent). This was also found to be true in relation to in-licensing opportunities, for which most firms also search on a monthly (24 per cent) or a quarterly (25 per cent) basis.

Firms engage in patent licensing for different motives (see, for example, Lichtenthaler, 2006; Pitkethly, 2001; Section 4.4.2). Of the different in-licensing motives mentioned during the exploratory interviews, I find two motives to be of particular relevance – that is, extending the company's product pipeline and securing FTO (see Table 5.12). Fifty-three per cent

Table 5.11   Identification of licensing opportunities

	Sample distribution in % of total firms according to frequency						Median	N
	Never	Less often	Annu-ally	Quar-terly	Month-ly	Mean		
In-licensing searches	7.04	25.35	18.31	25.35	23.94	3.34	Annually	71
Out-licensing searches	8.45	14.08	16.90	28.17	32.39	3.62	Quarterly	71

Table 5.12   Motives to license-in

	Sample distribution in % of total firms according to relevance						Median	N
	Irrelevant	Low	Medium	High	Very high	Mean		
Product pipeline motive	10.96	20.55	15.07	15.07	38.36	3.49	High	73
FTO motive	6.85	10.96	21.92	26.03	34.25	3.70	High	73
R&D budget motive	21.92	28.77	27.40	12.33	9.59	3.59	Low	73
Time-to-market motive	15.07	15.07	27.40	31.51	10.96	3.08	Medium	73

considered extending the company's product pipeline to be of high or very high relevance to their firm, meaning that patents are used to facilitate technology acquisitions which may potentially lead to the commercialisation of new products. Furthermore, 60 per cent perceived the motive of securing FTO to be of high or very high relevance to their firm. Also, on average, this objective is found to be the most important in-licensing motive. Hence, firms mainly license-in patents that are potentially blocking an internal R&D project.

The motive to reduce the R&D budget is found to be of less importance. Because R&D can sometimes be conducted more efficiently externally than internally, acquiring an external technology can be more

Table 5.13   Motives to license-out

	Sample distribution in % of total firms according to relevance						Median	N
	Irrelevant	Low	Medium	High	Very high	Mean		
Revenue motive	9.59	4.11	13.70	19.18	53.42	4.03	Very high	73
Product market motive	8.22	4.11	16.44	34.25	36.99	3.88	High	73

cost-efficient than internal product development. However, 51 per cent of the respondents found the motive to reduce the R&D budget of low relevance or irrelevant, while only 9 per cent perceived in-licensing to be of very high relevance for this purpose. Similarly, undertaking an external development project can potentially reduce the firm's time-to-market, compared with the company starting a new R&D project internally from day one. However, although this objective is considered to be highly important to 32 per cent of the respondents, 30 per cent perceive it to be of low relevance or even irrelevant.

In relation to patent out-licensing, two main objectives were identified among pharmaceutical companies. Of these motives, I find the revenue motive to be especially important (see Table 5.13). As many as 53 per cent consider out-licensing for this purpose to be of very high importance, suggesting that this is how many firms generate economic returns based on their R&D investments. By contrast, the product market motive refers to firms that, besides generating revenues, license-out their patents to gain access to the product market. This could be firms without certain complementary assets, such as skills in product development, which look to bridge such internal deficits through a strategic alliance. Also this motive is considered to be of very high relevance by 37 per cent of the respondents and as highly important by an additional 32 per cent.

Firms also structure their licensing model according to what they want to achieve with the licence as well as product development-related risk assessments (see Table 5.14 and Section 4.4.2.1). If a larger upfront payment is made, the licensee is taking a higher risk in terms of carrying a more substantial part of the development costs. In that case, subsequent royalty payments will be lower. Accordingly, there is always a trade-off between upfront payments and royalties. Comparing trade-offs between

Table 5.14   Licensing model

	Sample distribution in % of total firms according to relevance						Median	N
	Irrelevant	Low	Medium	High	Very high	Mean		
Upfront/ milestone payments	1.37	10.96	13.70	32.88	41.10	4.01	High	73
Royalties	2.78	15.28	34.72	31.94	15.28	3.42	Medium	72

upfront payments and royalties, upfront payments were found to be more important. The reason for this is probably that firms need financial capital upfront to finance their innovation activities. This would, along with past research, suggest an important role for licensing in the financing of innovation (Lerner et al., 2003).

The findings described above lead me to the conclusion that patent licensing forms an important part of pharmaceutical firms' IPR management.

5.3.3.6   Portfolio management
Most firms conduct reviews of their IPR portfolio according to which they categorise and prioritise their IPR (see Section 4.4.3.1). Table 5.15 shows that such reviews are most often conducted biannually (37 per cent) or annually (44 per cent).

Table 5.15   Portfolio reviews' frequency

	Sample distribution in % of total firms according to frequency						Median	N
	Never	Every 3 yrs.	Every 2 yrs.	Annu- ally	Biannu- ally	Mean		
Portfolio reviews	5.48	6.85	6.85	43.84	36.99	4.00	Annually	73

In addition, 32 per cent of the respondents considered the categorisation of the firm's IPR portfolio according to predefined criteria to be of very high relevance (see Table 5.16). The exploratory study shows that firms do so to prioritise their IPR, and abandon irrelevant IPR to reduce costs. The abandonment of irrelevant IPR was also found to be of very high

Table 5.16   Content of portfolio reviews

	Sample distribution in % of total firms according to relevance					Median	N
	Irrelevant	Low	Medium	High	Very high	Mean		
Categori-sation	8.22	6.85	21.92	31.51	31.51	3.71	High	73
Abandon-ment	12.33	9.59	12.33	36.99	28.77	3.60	High	73

importance to 29 per cent of the respondents. I therefore conclude that many firms look to make their IPR management as cost-effective as possible, giving some support to the finding that they manage their IPR to obtain the best value for money.

Besides categorising and prioritising the company's IPR, firms also manage their IPR portfolio to defend their competitive position (see Section 4.4.3.2). This involves the enforcement of their IPR portfolio. The conducted survey shows that 71 per cent of the sample perceive patent enforcement to be of very high or high importance (see Table 5.17). Hence, the vast majority of pharmaceutical firms seem to enforce their IPR, although many of them are relatively small. However, several IPR management experts in smaller companies revealed that they often have a larger collaboration partner which could take action against an infringer if necessary. Trademark enforcement, on the other hand, is found to be of less relevance to most firms. The largest category (25 per cent) is found to be medium relevance, while the categories low, high and very high are almost equally large.

The perceived importance of patent and trademark enforcement should, however, also be considered in relation to the likelihood of infringements. Taking this into consideration, I find that most firms do not engage in any litigation on a yearly basis. About 63 per cent of the firms in the sample did not face any patent lawsuits in 2009, and as many as 74 per cent did not file any patent lawsuits (see Table 5.18). Equally, more than 90 per cent of all firms did not face any trademark lawsuits, while 89 per cent did not file any. Hence, overall IPR lawsuits are rather uncommon in the pharmaceutical industry.

The above findings are also consistent with those of the exploratory study, suggesting that the pharmaceutical industry in general exhibits only a few lawsuits. According to the firms in the survey, this is due to provisions providing exemptions from patent infringements for research purposes.

Table 5.17   IPR enforcement

	Sample distribution in % of total firms according to relevance						Median	N
	Irrelevant	Low	Medium	High	Very high	Mean		
Patent enforce-ment	6.85	8.22	13.70	34.25	36.99	3.86	High	73
Trademark enforce-ment	13.70	21.92	24.66	20.55	19.18	3.10	Medium	73

Table 5.18   IPR lawsuits

	Sample distribution in % of total firms according to number of IPR lawsuits in 2009					Median	N
	None	1 to 2	3 to 4	5 to 10	>10		
Patent lawsuits (defendant)	63.01	23.29	8.22	4.11	1.37	None	73
Patent lawsuits (plaintiff)	73.97	17.81	4.11	1.37	2.74	None	73
Trademark lawsuits (defendant)	91.55	5.63	1.41	1.41	0	None	71
Trademark lawsuits (plaintiff)	88.57	4.29	4.29	2.86	0	None	70

Furthermore, data exclusivity prevents the commercialisation of competing products for some time, and FTO assessments are relatively easy to make in discrete technology fields. IPR lawsuits are therefore mostly limited to situations where generic competitors enter the market. It should, however, be noted that, although IPR lawsuits do not occur frequently, pharmaceutical firms consider IPR enforcement to be an important task.

5.3.4   IPR Reporting

An essential part of the survey was to assess firms' IPR reporting practices. As suggested by the exploratory study, I find that many firms report on at

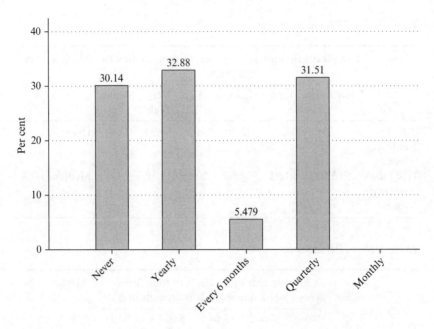

Figure 5.7   Frequency of IPR reporting

least some aspects of their IPR management, although 30 per cent did not disclose any IPR management information at all. Of the companies committed to IPR reporting, about 33 per cent of the respondents reported on an annual basis and another 32 per cent quarterly (see Figure 5.7). This finding indicates that most firms' IPR reporting takes place through their annual and quarterly reports.

5.3.4.1   Reporting channels

The relevance of annual and quarterly reports for the disclosure of IPR-related information is also suggested by Table 5.19. Accordingly, 43 per cent of the respondents find annual and quarterly reports to be of very high importance for IPR reporting purposes. Press releases too seem to provide a relevant reporting channel, with 50 per cent finding them to be of very high or high relevance. By contrast, I find that firms do not rely much on conference calls or their homepage to report on their IPR. Thirty-three per cent of respondents find conference calls to be irrelevant for IPR reporting purposes, while only 8 per cent consider them to be of very high relevance. Similarly, 31 per cent find publications on the firm's homepage to be an irrelevant reporting channel, while only 8 per cent view them as of very high relevance. The main IPR reporting channels hence seem to be

Table 5.19   IPR reporting channels

	Sample distribution in % of total firms according to relevance							
	Irrelevant	Low	Medium	High	Very high	Mean	Median	N
Financial reports	0	5.88	17.65	33.33	43.14	4.14	High	51
Press releases	14.00	12.00	24.00	26.00	24.00	3.34	High	50
Conference calls	34.00	28.00	18.00	12.00	8.00	2.32	Low	50
Homepage	30.61	26.53	22.45	12.24	8.16	2.41	Low	49

annual and quarterly reports, as well as press releases. Research on firms' IPR reporting should therefore address these two reporting channels in order to capture the larger share of IPR-related information disclosures.

5.3.4.2   IPR pipeline reporting

Turning to the content of firms' IPR reporting, I first look at firms reporting on the IPR situation around its product pipeline. This includes aspects related to FTO, exclusivity, the duration of exclusivity, the geographical scope of patent protection, and the geographical scope of trademark protection. As shown by the exploratory study, exclusivity reporting concerns the types of patents covering the pipeline, while the duration relates to secondary patent applications with the potential to add to the duration of exclusivity.

I find that firms tend not to disclose information about the FTO situation in relation to their product pipeline (see Table 5.20). As many as 82 per cent never reported on the FTO situation. Nor did the vast majority of respondents report on the type of patents covering their product developments, although this was found to be more common. Sixty-one per cent revealed that they never reported on this item, but 20 per cent did so annually, and an additional 15 per cent did so on a quarterly basis. Reporting on secondary patents was found to be less common. Seventy-six per cent did not update the stock market on secondary patent applications and their potential to extend the duration of exclusivity. However, it should be noted that the economic benefits of such patents do not materialise until the end of the product lifecycle – which may be 20 years ahead – while the potential sales effect of the type of patent protection will materialise when the product is launched. The relative importance of exclusivity reporting at this point – compared with reporting on the duration of exclusivity – is

Table 5.20   IPR pipeline reporting

	Sample distribution in % of total firms according to frequency							
	Never	Annu- ally	Biannu- ally	Quar- terly	Month- ly	Mean	Median	N
FTO situation	81.94	12.50	1.39	4.17	0	1.28	Never	72
Type of patent	60.56	19.72	4.23	15.49	0	1.75	Never	71
Secondary patents	76.39	15.28	2.78	5.56	0	1.38	Never	72
Patent scope	59.72	27.78	4.17	8.33	0	1.61	Never	72
Trademark scope	87.32	9.86	0	2.82	0	1.18	Never	71

also suggested by the fact that comparatively many (40 per cent) report on the geographical scope of patent protection in relation to their pipeline. Trademarks, on the other hand, seem to be of less concern, with only 13 per cent of the sample reporting on the geographical scope of trademark protection.

5.3.4.3   IPR product reporting

In the exploratory study I find that firms report on the IPR situation in relation to their products on the market (see Section 4.7). However, at the same time, I find IPR reporting to be rather rare (see Table 5.21). For example, 20 per cent of respondents choose to report on the FTO situation. About 41 per cent disclose information about the type of patent covering the product. Relatively many (49 per cent) report on secondary patents. This can be compared with the equivalent IPR pipeline reporting item, where 76 per cent did not disclose any information. Finally, reporting on the geographical scope of patent protection seems to remain fairly constant throughout the product lifecycle. Although more firms are found to report on the geographical scope of trademark protection in relation to products on the market, 75 per cent did not.

5.3.4.4   Out-licensing reporting

The survey confirms that some firms report on their out-licensing activities, but shows that many do not (see Table 5.22). For example, 47 per cent never disclose any information on the objective of the deal, implying that it is often difficult for investors to assess how out-licensing deals fit into

Table 5.21   IPR product reporting

	Sample distribution in % of total firms according to frequency							
	Never	Annu-ally	Biannu-ally	Quar-terly	Month-ly	Mean	Median	N
FTO situation	79.59	8.16	4.08	8.16	0	1.41	Never	49
Type of patent	59.18	14.29	2.04	22.45	2.04	1.30	Never	49
Secondary patents	51.02	18.37	6.12	22.45	2.04	2.06	Never	49
Patent scope	57.14	22.45	4.08	14.29	2.04	1.82	Never	49
Trademark scope	75.00	18.75	0	4.17	2.08	1.40	Never	48

Table 5.22   Out-licensing reporting

	Sample distribution in % of total firms according to frequency							
	Never	Rarely	Some-times	Often	Always	Mean	Median	N
Objective of the licence	47.06	7.84	17.65	9.80	17.65	2.43	Rarely	51
Upfront payments	47.06	7.84	21.57	15.69	7.84	2.29	Rarely	51
Royalty rate	52.94	7.84	17.65	15.69	5.88	2.14	Never	51
Duration of the licence	52.94	9.80	15.69	11.76	9.80	2.16	Never	51
Market coverage	41.18	11.76	5.88	13.73	27.45	2.75	Rarely	51
Exclusivity details	41.18	9.80	9.80	13.73	25.49	2.73	Rarely	51

the company's business model. About 18 per cent of the sample, however, always reported on this item.

Reporting on the deal's financial aspects was rather uncommon. Forty-seven per cent are found never to report on planned upfront and milestone payments and 53 per cent never report on the royalty rate. Also disclosure about the duration of the licence is relatively rare. Looking at the two extremes, 53 per cent never did so, while only 9 per cent revealed that they always do so. More firms are found to report on the non-financial terms of the deal. Twenty-seven per cent revealed that they always report on the markets for which the licence was given, and 25 per cent would report on whether the licence was given on an exclusive or non-exclusive basis.

5.3.4.5   In-licensing reporting

Firms reporting on their in-licensing deals follow a similar pattern. What is notable, however, is that they report less on a deal's financial aspects. Sixty per cent are found never to report on settled upfront and milestone payments (see Table 5.23). In addition, 63 per cent reveal that they never report on the royalty rate item. On average, firms also report less on the markets covered by the licence and whether it has been given on an exclusive basis, than they do on equivalent items for out-licensing deals. On the contrary, relatively many firms report on the duration aspect of in-licensing deals. Presumably, these firms follow a product-based business model. Hence, they look to commercialise a product based on the licence taken, in which the duration of the licence plays an important role.

Table 5.23   In-licensing reporting

	Sample distribution in % of total firms according to frequency							
	Never	Rarely	Some-times	Often	Always	Mean	Median	N
Objective of the licence	50.94	18.87	11.32	9.43	9.43	2.08	Never	53
Upfront payments	60.38	20.75	9.43	7.55	1.89	1.70	Never	53
Royalty rate	62.26	16.98	11.32	9.43	0	1.68	Never	53
Duration of the licence	45.28	15.09	13.21	7.55	18.87	2.40	Rarely	53
Market coverage	50.94	13.21	7.55	13.21	15.09	2.28	Never	53
Exclusivity details	41.51	11.32	7.55	18.87	20.75	2.66	Rarely	53

5.4   THE STOCK MARKET'S VALUATION OF FIRMS' IPR MANAGEMENT: A MULTIVARIATE ANALYSIS

In efficient stock markets, share prices reflect firms' IPR management. This implies that investors have rational expectations – that is, they are forward-looking and consider all available value-relevant information (see, for example, Greenhalgh and Rogers, 2010). Accordingly, on average, investors price shares correctly, with only minor random errors and without any systematic mispricing (see, for example, Hall et al., 2005). On this assumption, firms committed to IPR management should systematically outperform others as investors incorporate related future economic benefits in their valuations. This is suggested by past research showing that investors recognise the future economic benefits of both patents and trademarks, but also distinguish valuable IPR from lemons (see, for example, Neuhäusler et al., 2011; Sandner and Block, 2011). To see if stock markets also correctly recognise the future economic benefits of IPR management, this study investigates whether several IPR management indicators are reflected in share prices. In doing so, it assesses the informational efficiency of stock markets.

5.4.1   Hypothesis and Operationalisation

5.4.1.1   Dependent variable

Efficient stock markets impound the value of firms' IPR, meaning there should be no association between IPR and future stock market returns. This is because the firms' IPR stock is already reflected in its share price. Hence, share price increases only occur as a consequence of new events' associated economic benefits – see, for example, new IPR applications – which accumulate to the firm's market value. Past research has therefore focused on the relationship between IPR portfolios and Tobin's q – that is, the firm's market value relative to the replacement value of its assets (see, for example, Neuhäusler et al., 2011; Sandner and Block, 2011). This measurement provides a snapshot of the firm's market value at a given point in time. IPR management, however, is a continuous task. This means that related economic benefits do not occur as a result of particular events, such as new IPR applications, but rather as a result of systematic approaches. Moreover, financial reporting standards do not require companies to disclose most information of this kind. This suggests that share prices do not fully reflect the value of their IPR management. Rather, it is expected to be associated with long-term economic returns, as firms committed to IPR management will systematically outperform its competitors.

For this reason, stock market buy-and-hold returns (BHR) enter the model as the dependent variable.

Buy–hold provides a long-term investment strategy, where the investor is not concerned with daily security prices, but rather seeks a good rate of return over a longer period of time. A strong argument for this strategy is the EMH, which implies that securities' prices reflect the fundamental value of the security at all times, meaning that there is no point in trading. This variable has also been used in several past studies on the valuation consequences of the intangible economy (see, for example, Barth et al., 1998; Chan et al., 2001; Lev and Zarowin, 1999).

The BHR was calculated as the absolute return on each firm's share. The calculation was conducted for a time-frame of two years, from the first trading day in January 2008, for each firm in the sample. This was done because pharmaceutical firms' share price is highly volatile, not least because of high attrition rates and regulatory unpredictability. By taking a two-year perspective, particular events and related volatility average out a bit, which better enables the long-term financial benefits of firms' IPR management to be assessed. Finally, it should be noted that the dependent variable was standardised around the average. Hence, stock market returns are considered in relative terms.

5.4.1.2   Independent variables

The operationalisation of the independent variables was conducted on the basis of the findings from the review of the literature as well as the exploratory study of pharmaceutical firms' IPR management. The theoretical foundation of the derived hypothesis can be found in Section 4.6, conceptualising the relationship between pharmaceutical firms' IPR management and their financial performance. This theoretical construct describes the firm's IPR management in relation to FTO, exclusivity, the duration of exclusivity, value for money, out-licensing and in-licensing. Indicators operationalising these aspects of firms' IPR management are therefore expected be value-relevant. It should also be noted that all the derived indicators can be influenced by managerial action and were measured on a five-point Likert-type scale.

Freedom-to-operate   Past research shows that firms manage their IPR to secure FTO (Grindley and Teece, 1997; Lichtenthaler, 2006). They do so to reduce the risk of infringing third party patents when commercialising their products (see, for example, Blind et al., 2006; Cohen et al., 2002; European Commission, 2009). This finding was also confirmed by the exploratory study, which revealed that securing FTO was a major objective of pharmaceutical firms' IPR management and was seen as essential to reduce legal costs related to patent infringements (see Section 4.3). For this reason, in informationally efficient stock markets, measures taken to secure FTO should contribute to firms' share price performance. Hence, the following hypothesis is derived:

H1:   The more firms are committed to the management of their IPR to secure FTO, the higher stock market returns they will yield.

To secure FTO, firms conduct regular patent searches and FTO analysis. For example, Thumm (2004) finds that a major task of firms' IPR management is to evaluate the patent landscape to reduce risks of legal conflicts. Similarly, the firms in the study reveal that they conduct patent searches on the basis of which they assess the FTO situation of their product development projects throughout the R&D phase. According to these analyses, they proactively position patent applications to secure FTO, and thereby defensively block competitors. This enables them to react to shifts in competition and preserve their technological edge in future markets or technological fields without being restricted in their product development efforts due to inadequate patent protection (see, for example, Blind et al., 2006; Pitkethly, 2001). Finally, the exploratory study shows that some firms also explicitly consider the FTO situation in their project funding decisions to reduce the risk of conducting additional research and product development for which FTO cannot be obtained. On the basis of these findings, securing FTO is operationalised as shown in Table 5.24.

Table 5.24   Operationalisation of 'FTO'

Independent variables	Description	Mean	SD	Min.	Median	Max.
FTO analysis	We conduct regular FTO analysis	4.264	1.210	1	5	5
Defensive blocking	We use patents to defensively block competitors	3.822	1.005	2	4	5
FTO funding	We base our project funding decisions on the FTO situation	3.726	1.367	1	4	5

Exclusivity   Within resource-based models, technological knowledge has gained recognition as a resource in itself (see, for example, Grant, 1996), essential to the development of new competitive technology-based products. From a resource-based view, IPR is therefore important to enable firms to establish competitive advantages in making technology resources imperfectly imitable (see, for example, Barney, 1991), by raising the costs of imitation (Levin et al., 1987; Mansfield et al., 1981). In doing so, IPR provide important isolation mechanisms, postulated as crucial to firm performance by resource-based theorists (see, for example, Grant, 1991; Wernerfelt, 1984). The investigation reveals that firms in the pharmaceutical industry manage their IPR from a resource-based view in order to maximise exclusivity in the appropriation of economic returns. This finding suggests that measures taken to maximise exclusivity are associated with future economic benefits. Hence:

H2:   The more firms are committed to the management of their IPR to maximise exclusivity, the higher stock market returns they will yield.

To obtain the objective of maximising exclusivity, firms rely on both patents and trademarks. Empirical research shows that firms manage their patents to protect products and technologies from imitation and obtain exclusivity in the appropriation of the economic returns from their R&D investments (see, for example, Blind, 2006; Pitkethly, 2001). Moreover, studies have shown that those patents which are used to protect products from imitation are the most valuable (see, for example, Blind et al., 2009a). This should be true not least of the pharmaceutical industry, where product development costs have increased substantially in recent years (Lehman, 2003). Hence, pharmaceutical firms heavily rely on patents to support their product market strategy in safeguarding their market share (Arundel and Kabla, 1998; European Commission, 2009). Moreover, firms also rely on trademark protection to appropriate investments in technological innovation (Allegrezza and Guarda-Rauchs, 1999). For example, Malmberg (2005) shows that trademarks in the pharmaceutical industry are associated with new product launches. In addition, Sandner and Block (2011) find that trademarks are comparatively valuable in the pharmaceutical industry, suggesting that they are important instruments for the appropriation of economic returns. Finally, the interviews conducted show that some firms consider whether exclusivity can be obtained in their project funding decisions to ensure that their R&D investments are commercially viable. Accordingly, the indicators in Table 5.25 were derived for exclusivity.

Table 5.25   Operationalisation of 'Exclusivity'

Independent variables	Description	Mean	SD	Min.	Median	Max.
Patent protection	We use patents to protect our products from imitation	4.288	0.565	3	4	5
TM protection	We use trademarks to protect our products from imitation	3.740	1.270	1	4	5
Exclusivity funding	We base our project funding decisions on the exclusivity situation	3.411	1.256	1	3	5

Duration of exclusivity   The profitability of firms' R&D investments depends on the duration for which exclusivity can be obtained. This is suggested by both past research and the exploratory interviews carried out in the study. In the strategic management literature, the sustainability of firms' competitive advantages has been widely emphasised as key to the financial performance of firms (see, for example, Barney, 1991; Porter, 1985; Rumelt, 1984). From an IPR management perspective, this means that firms' IPR need to support the sustainability of their competitive advantages by making their products imperfectly imitable throughout the product lifecycle. Hence, pharmaceutical firms rely heavily on IPR (Arundel and Kabla, 1998) to support their product market strategy in safeguarding their market share throughout the lifecycle of their products (European Commission, 2009). This implies that IPR management measures to extend the duration of exclusivity are associated with future economic benefits. Taking the above arguments together, the following hypothesis is derived:

H3:   The more firms are committed to the management of their IPR to extend the duration of exclusivity, the higher stock market returns they will yield.

To maximise the duration of exclusivity, firms manage their IPR proactively. They file additional patent applications during the later stages of the development phase, and thus with later expiry dates than that of the primary patent (see, for example, European Commission, 2009). Some firms also rely on trademarks to support their branding strategies, aimed at creating brand loyalty (see, for example, Aaker, 1995), enabling them to charge premium prices (Dall'Olmo et al., 1997; Reichheld, 1996). This is especially important when generic competition enters the market. For

Table 5.26   Operationalisation of 'Duration'

Independent variables	Description	Mean	SD	Min.	Median	Max.
Secondary patents	We use patents to prolong the protection of our products	4.027	1.080	1	4	5
TM commu-nication	We use trademarks to prolong the protection of our products	3.603	1.222	1	4	5
IPR combina-tion	We use both patents and trademarks to prolong the protection of our products	3.068	1.531	1	4	5

example, Mendonca et al. (2004) argue that the primary motive for firms to use trademarks is to extend appropriation beyond patent protection. Accordingly, Jennewein (2005) shows how firms combine patents and trademarks, building brand equity in the process. On the basis of these findings, the indicators in Table 5.26 were derived.

Value for money   IPR protection is expensive not only to obtain, but also to maintain (European Commission, 2007). This means that firms ought to be concerned about the costs of their IPR portfolio, especially since an extensive IPR portfolio is not necessarily associated with higher financial performance. For example, Reitzig (2004b) finds that patent fences in discrete technologies are only value enhancing if substitute technologies are easy to obtain. Furthermore, Grindley and Teece (1997) show that the value of firms' patents depends on their alignment with technology fields where the firm possesses particular strengths. Otherwise, an extensive patent portfolio mainly increases costs rather than enhances the firm's financial performance. This was also suggested by the exploratory inter-views, which showed that smaller firms in particular are concerned with obtaining the best value for money in terms of making effective use of their R&D budget. From a capital market perspective, this should signal more effective use of their invested financial resources, leading to higher returns on their investments. This leads us to the following hypothesis:

H4:   The more firms are committed to the management of their IPR to obtain the best value for money, the higher stock market returns they will yield.

To achieve this objective, firms systematically abandon non-core IPR, and thus reduce the costs of their IPR portfolio. For example, the explora-

Table 5.27   Operationalisation of 'Value for money'

Independent variables	Description	Mean	SD	Min.	Median	Max.
Portfolio reviews	We conduct regular IPR portfolio reviews	4.000	1.106	1	4	5
IPR abandonment	We abandon irrelevant IPR	3.603	1.331	1	4	5

tory study shows that firms conduct regular reviews of their IPR portfolio. On the basis of these reviews, irrelevant IPR are identified and abandoned (see Section 4.4.3.1). Following these findings, value for money was operationalised on the basis of the indicators in Table 5.27.

Patent out-licensing   Due to the increasing specialisation in different stages of the R&D process, firms collaborate in technology-based product development (Rothaermel and Deeds, 2004). This is true not least of the pharmaceutical industry, where the integration of biotechnology into the development of pharmaceutical products has led to the formation of specialised DBFs, focusing on early stage product development. Because these firms rely on collaboration partners in order to finance their research activities, patent licensing provides an integral part of their business models (Farag, 2009; Lerner et al., 2003). Gassmann et al. (2010) accordingly argue that their competitive advantage depends on them having relevant IPR for out-licensing purposes. Following these arguments, I derive the hypothesis below:

H5:   The more firms are committed to patent out-licensing, the higher stock market returns they will yield.

Patents may be out-licensed for monetary or product-related purposes (see Section 4.4.2.1). For example, Sheehan et al. (2004) find that the generation of licensing revenue is an important reason for firms to patent, enabling them to generate economic returns on the technology market without product commercialisation. Hence, firms file for patent protection without having any intention of making internal use of the patent (see, for example, Davis and Harrison, 2001; Ernst, 1996).

In addition, patents are out-licensed to gain access to another firm's technological knowledge or product development skills (see, for example, Lichtenthaler, 2006). Accordingly, the firms in the study reveal that, without IPR, they would not be able to gain access to external technologies

Table 5.28   Operationalisation of 'Patent out-licensing'

Independent variables	Description	Mean	SD	Min.	Median	Max.
Out-licensing activity	Number of annual out-licensing deals	2.548	1.323	1	2	5
Revenue motive	We license-out patents to generate revenue	4.027	1.312	1	5	5
Product market motive	We license-out patents for joint product development	3.877	1.201	1	4	5

in the long run, as monetary compensation is not a sustainable substitute for IPR in strategic partnerships. Firms therefore find IPR to be the only way of gaining access to the technological knowledge of third parties.

Patent out-licensing is accordingly operationalised by the number of out-licensed patents, indicating the commitment of firms to this activity. The additional indicators operationalise the motive behind their licenses (see Table 5.28).

Patent in-licensing   According to Chesbrough and Teece (1996), only a few firms can afford to develop all the technologies that might provide a competitive advantage internally. This implies a need for firms to acquire external proprietary technology resources to maintain their technological edge, and is suggested by research showing a demand among established pharmaceutical firms for access to external technology resources. For example, the pharmaceutical industry exhibits the highest share of firms perceiving patent in-licensing to have become increasingly important (Sheehan et al., 2004). In particular, pharmaceutical firms with relatively thin product pipelines are found to be more likely to license-in proprietary external technologies to bridge internal weaknesses as well as build new strengths through the accumulation of external technology resources (Higgins and Rodriguez, 2006). This means that in-licensing provides future economic benefits to the firm, and thus should also be reflected in its share price, leading us to the following hypothesis:

H6:   The more firms are committed to patent in-licensing, the higher stock market returns they will yield.

The investigation conducted here reveals that firms license-in patents to improve their financial performance in several ways. Firstly, in addition to

Table 5.29   Operationalisation of 'Patent in-licensing'

Independent variables	Description	Mean	SD	Min.	Median	Max.
In-licensing activity	Number of in-licensing deals in 2009	2.466	1.345	1	2	5
Pipeline motive	We license-in patents to extend our product pipeline	3.493	1.454	1	4	5
FTO motive	We license-in patents to secure FTO	3.699	1.244	1	4	5

supporting research in order to find solutions to a problem (March, 1991), external sources of technological knowledge can be important to product development (Leonard-Barton, 1995). Past research has also suggested that, due to shortening product lifecycles, the acquisition of external technologies has become a requirement for firms to keep up with the pace of technological change (see, for example, Levinthal, 1998; Lichtenthaler, 2006). The integration of such technologies is supported by the acquisition of related patents (Bader, 2008; Lichtenthaler, 2006). Accordingly, I find that firms license-in patents in order to extend their product pipeline. Secondly, patents are licensed-in to secure FTO in relation to the firm's internal development projects, and thus to enable product commercialisation (see, for example, Lichtenthaler, 2006; Pitkethly, 2001). This leads us to the indicators in Table 5.29.

5.4.1.3   Control variables

In the empirical research model, I control for internal environmental factors which do not directly relate to firms' IPR management, but are expected to have an influence on their financial performance. A summary of the control variables is provided in Table 5.30.

Firstly, I control for firm size measured by annual revenue, which was derived from the respective firms' income statements. In conformity with Sandner and Block (2011), I also control for R&D spending, the number of patents and number of trademarks, which I divided by the firm's annual revenue to obtain the intensity of these variables and consider the use of IPR and R&D spending in relation to the size of the firm.[4] Further, like Guo et al. (2005), I control for the number of products the company has on the market, from which revenues are generated, but also its growth potential, in terms of the size of its product pipeline. Both of these variables were operationalised on a five-point Likert-type scale. Moreover, as in Lev and Zarowin (1999), sales growth is controlled for and calculated

Table 5.30 Control variables – summary statistics

Control variables	Description	Mean	SD	Min.	Median	Max.
Firm size	Annual revenue in million USD	1627.540	7411.001	0.551	24.000	45000.000
Revenue growth	Annual percentage change in revenue	0.834	3.074	−0.960	0.230	24.500
R&D intensity	Average R&D/revenue	5.781	16.505	0.0229	0.700	120.933
Patent intensity	Average patents/revenue	7.559	24.892	0.000	1.071	200.000
Trademark intensity	Average trademarks/revenue	1.430	2.529	0.000	0.179	11.000
Products on the market	Number of products on the market	2.545	1.599	1.000	2.000	5.000
Firm age	Years since firm formation	4.096	0.802	2.000	4.000	5.000
Market-to-book	Average book value/market cap.	3.141	2.721	0.550	2.040	12.950
Trading volume	Average daily trading volume	536136.0	1493223.0	1535.880	120496.5	9125343.0
Region	Dummy	0.370	0.486	0.000	0.000	1.000

for each firm over the two-year period for which the BHR were derived. Finally, I control for dividends as well as the net issue of shares – that is, measures that directly influence companies' share price. In theory, the share price decreases on the ex-dividend day, as holding the share no longer gives the shareholder the right to that dividend (see, for example, Kalay, 1984). The issue of new shares, on the other hand, dilutes the price of existing shares, as these are normally issued at a lower price. This has also been confirmed by empirical evidence showing that share prices fall by approximately 3 per cent after the announcement of an equity issue (Asquith and Mullins, 1986). In contrast, share buy-backs tend to increase the share price as the supply is being reduced. For example, Zhang (2005) shows that share prices increase with stock repurchases, at least in the short term. I therefore calculate the net issue to be the issue of new shares less any share buy-backs. As with the dividends variable, the net issue variable was derived from the respective firms' cash flow statement. The annual numbers were added together into one observation and divided by two, to obtain the average share flows for the two-year period concerned. Both variables were considered in relation to the average total market capitalisation over the period. This was done because, if a net issue doubles the outstanding value of the shares, the dilution will theoretically be larger than if the value increases by a lesser amount.

Besides internal environmental factors, I also control for external ones using a regional dummy, taking value 1 for the US and 0 for the EU. This addresses macroeconomic factors and regulatory differences that may potentially influence share prices. Finally, it should be noted that all financial figures were converted into USD, using the exchange rate converter of the European Commission. The exchange rate for the last day of the year was taken to ensure the comparability of all observations.

5.4.2 Estimation Methods

Given the characteristics of the dependent variable, linear regression analyses with ordinary least squares (OLS) estimations were applied. This well-established estimation method will not be described in detail. However, it is worth mentioning explicitly how some specifics of the OLS properties were assessed.

Firstly, OLS estimations assume that there is no non-linear relationship between the dependent and any of the independent variables. To assess this assumption, various scatter-plot matrices were used to display these relationships graphically. From this I found no evidence suggesting that there might be any non-linear relationships.

Furthermore, OLS estimations assume homoscedasticity – that is, that the error term has a constant variance. Heteroscedasticity would violate this assumption and often occurs as a consequence of the distribution of the dependent variable not being symmetric. To deal with potential heteroscedasticity, I transformed the dependent variable into its logarithm (see Wooldridge, 2005).

In addition to the multivariate OLS estimations, bivariate correlations were conducted to assess the consistency of the explanatory variables, but also to address the potential for multicollinearity in the models. Because several variables were often used to describe similar aspects of companies' IPR management, this measure was essential. Moreover, the variance inflation factor (VIF) was examined for each model. In all models, the VIF was found to be well below its critical value of ten (see STATA, 2011). Exactly the same procedures were taken in the models examining the relationship between IPR reporting and volatility (see Section 5.5.2).

5.4.3 Empirical Findings

In this section I present the results of the econometric analyses. This includes both bivariate and multivariate analyses, although the emphasis is on the multivariate regressions. However, the bivariate analysis provides some complementary insights concerning the consistency of the relationships being examined. Tables showing the results from the bivariate analysis are displayed in the Appendix.

5.4.3.1 Freedom-to-operate

The basic model (M0), including only the control variables, reveals some interesting results (see Table 5.31). Firstly, and as expected, I find that the sales growth and the number of products variables both have a positive and significant impact on the dependent variable. Accordingly, sales growth as well as more products on the market contribute to higher stock market returns. Also, as expected, dividends have a significantly negative impact on the dependent variable. More surprising is the strong negative impact of the regional dummy, revealing that European firms on average outperform US ones. Presumably, this is an effect of the macroeconomic and regulatory environment.

Net issue and firm size both have a negative but not significant impact on stock market returns. Surprisingly, this is also the case for the size of the firm's product pipeline, suggesting that investors systematically discount firms' growth potential, in terms of technological innovations which have not yet reached the market. The low significance of this relationship suggests that it does not apply to every pipeline product. Most likely,

Table 5.31 Multivariate analysis of 'FTO'

DV = BHR	M0		M1a		M1b		M1c		M1d	
	Coef.	SE	Coef.	SE	Coef.	SE	Coef.	SE	Coef.	SE
Firm size	-0.145	0.103	-0.159	0.105	-0.154	0.105	-0.143	0.104	-0.164	0.107
Revenue growth	0.361***	0.101	0.356***	0.102	0.359***	0.102	0.372***	0.105	0.370***	0.107
R&D intensity	-0.011	0.256	-0.009	0.259	-0.025	0.258	-0.009	0.257	-0.012	0.265
Patent intensity	0.218	0.225	0.213	0.227	0.234	0.228	0.210	0.228	0.211	0.233
Trademark intensity	-0.060	0.132	-0.057	0.141	-0.066	0.133	-0.053	0.134	-0.059	0.142
Products on the market	0.337***	0.075	0.355***	0.079	0.332***	0.076	0.341***	0.077	0.353***	0.080
Product pipeline	-0.213*	0.124	-0.193	0.128	-0.207	0.125	-0.222*	0.127	-0.200	0.131
Net issue of shares	-0.182	0.126	-0.183	0.129	-0.157	0.133	-0.192	0.129	-0.173	0.136
Dividends	-0.239**	0.101	-0.248**	0.102	-0.230**	0.102	-0.240**	0.101	-0.242**	0.104
Region dummy	-0.417*	0.217	-0.363	0.223	-0.411*	0.218	-0.407*	0.220	-0.348	0.227
Patent searches			-0.001	0.087					-0.016	0.099
Defensive blocking					-0.070	0.103			-0.015	0.108
FTO funding							0.031	0.077	0.047	0.087
F	4.95***		4.54***		4.50***		4.45***		3.79***	
N	73		72		73		73		72	
R^2	0.444		0.454		0.448		0.445		0.459	

Note: Significance Level * $p<0.10$, ** $p<0.05$, *** $p<0.01$.

innovations that are closer to reaching the market are undervalued less, as opacity and attrition rates decrease.

Finally, neither R&D nor trademarks really contribute to shareholder returns, while patents do, although not significantly. A potential explanation for the weak insignificant impact of the R&D intensity variable could be that investors do not have any particular knowledge about R&D expenditures and therefore do not explicitly consider these (see, for example, Ughetto, 2007). A more refined explanation stems from past research, which shows that financial analysts find technology-driven firms difficult to value (see, for example, Amir et al., 1999). Also, in conformity with accounting standards, R&D investments are, at least partly, instantaneous costs (see Section 2.8.1). This means that R&D spending reduces profits. It could therefore well be that the positive and negative effects that are reflected in the R&D indicator balance out, resulting in a nonsignificant effect.

The trademark intensity variable turns out to be insignificant, although Sandner and Block (2011) show that trademarks are highly valuable in the pharmaceutical industry. However, my sample contains a relatively high number of young firms, focusing on the early stages of the product lifecycle. Presumably, these companies pursue a licensing-based business model, for which trademarks are less important. Although I control for this through the number of products the firm has on the market, it is likely to have contributed to the insignificant effect.

A possible explanation for the relatively strong but insignificant impact of the patent intensity variable would be that patents do not automatically contribute to firms' share price performance, but do so if they are related to an important product, or if firms report on them. Indeed, past research shows that an extensive patent portfolio does not automatically contribute to companies' financial performance (Reitzig, 2004b). For example, Blind et al. (2009a) find that patents which are used for protection motives tend to be relatively valuable. Similarly, Austin (1993) finds that patents which were linked to products, and which had received more substantial publicity, also received higher valuation by the stock market.

Turning to the FTO variables, – that is, the variables that describe proactive measures to secure FTO – I look at FTO analysis, defensive blocking and FTO funding (see Table 5.24). The bivariate analysis does not reveal any significant correlation between any of the independent variables and the dependent variable (see Table 5.A1). Interesting, however, is the negative and significant correlation between FTO funding and sales growth. Possibly this correlation occurs as firms which restrict their R&D investments to products for which FTO can be obtained do not pursue certain profitable projects. This raises the question of whether FTO funding actually contributes to firm performance. But companies do not seek to secure FTO in order to increase sales. They do so to reduce the risks of patent lawsuits. In addition, I therefore look at the relationship between patent lawsuits against the firm and the FTO funding variable, and find a negative significant correlation between the two (see Table 5.A2). Hence, firms that base their funding decisions on the FTO situation may on the one hand miss NPV positive R&D investments, but at the same time reduce the risks of patent lawsuits.

The findings of the multiple regression analysis are consistent with those of the bivariate analysis. Although the model explains a substantial part of the variance in the dependent variable, measures to secure FTO do not have any significant impact on stock market returns. There is accordingly no evidence for H1. It shall, however, be noted that proactive measures to secure FTO are not necessarily related to future economic benefits. In contrast, I find a negative correlation between the FTO funding variable and sales growth. Rather, the FTO variables indicate a reduced risk of patent lawsuits, and thus a lower probability of negative financial consequences for the firm. In that sense, securing FTO is to be seen as an insurance against patent lawsuits. My findings suggest that stock markets do not price this kind of insurance – the effects of the independent variables are both weak and insignificant – although it should be emphasised that these insignificant effects ought not be over-interpreted.

5.4.3.2 Exclusivity

For the operationalisation of exclusivity, I rely on three variables – that is, patent protection, trademark protection, exclusivity funding (see Table 5.25). The bivariate analysis shows a strong positive and significant correlation between patent protection and the dependent variable (see Table 5.A3). Furthermore, I find that exclusivity funding is significantly negatively correlated with the dependent variable. However, in contrast to the FTO funding variable (see previous section), exclusivity funding is not negatively correlated with sales growth. An explanation for this would be that firms that do not pursue R&D projects, for which exclusivity cannot be obtained, do not actually miss any growth opportunities. This view implies that projects for which exclusivity cannot be obtained are not profitable, while projects for which FTO cannot be obtained may well be, despite the risk of patent lawsuits. However, regardless of the profit potential of a project, stock markets seem to discount for companies having implemented IPR policies according to which they base their project funding decisions on the exclusivity situation – presumably due to more restrictive policies leading to the cancellation of a larger share of their R&D projects. This is not least indicated by the strong negative correlation between the

Table 5.32 Multivariate analysis of 'Exclusivity'

DV = BHR	M0		M2a		M2b		M2c		M2d	
	Coef.	SE	Coef.	SE	Coef.	SE	Coef.	SE	Coef.	SE
Firm size	−0.145	0.103	−0.123	0.102	−0.115	0.101	−0.055	0.107	−0.029	0.104
Revenue growth	0.361***	0.101	0.316***	0.103	0.356***	0.098	0.374***	0.098	0.327***	0.098
R&D intensity	−0.011	0.256	−0.036	0.252	−0.100	0.252	0.020	0.247	−0.081	0.243
Patent intensity	0.218	0.225	0.221	0.222	0.266	0.220	0.223	0.217	0.264	0.212
Trademark intensity	−0.060	0.132	−0.009	0.133	0.035	0.135	−0.093	0.128	0.036	0.135
Products on the market	0.337***	0.075	0.314***	0.075	0.429***	0.084	0.279***	0.077	0.344***	0.088
Product pipeline	−0.213*	0.124	−0.159	0.125	−0.294**	0.126	−0.227*	0.120	−0.243*	0.125
Net issue of shares	−0.182	0.126	−0.123	0.129	−0.190	0.123	−0.150	0.123	−0.108	0.123
Dividends	−0.239**	0.101	−0.224**	0.099	−0.272***	0.099	−0.267***	0.098	−0.275***	0.096
Region dummy	−0.417*	0.217	−0.403*	0.213	−0.351	0.213	−0.456**	0.210	−0.382*	0.206
Patent protection			0.355*	0.200					0.319*	0.190
Trademark protection					−0.193**	0.089			−0.156*	0.087
Exclusivity funding							−0.202**	0.085	−0.161*	0.084
F	4.95***		4.94***		5.19***		5.35***		5.30***	
N	73		73		73		73		73	
R^2	0.444		0.471		0.484		0.491		0.539	

Note: Significance Level * p<0.10, ** p<0.05, *** p<0.01.

exclusivity funding and the number of products the company has on the market. It therefore seems that investors discount for firms bringing fewer products to the market, regardless of the exclusivity situation.

The multiple regression analysis confirms the findings of the bivariate analysis. Patent protection has a significantly positive impact on the dependent variable, also in the full model, suggesting a high degree of consistency. Its modest significance could imply that the perceived relevance of patent protection, among investors, depends on the commercial relevance of the product it relates to, or the level of attention the patent has received among corporate outsiders (see Austin, 1993).

The exclusivity funding variable has a negatively significant impact on the dependent variable, also when controlling for the number of products on the market amongst others. Accordingly, it seems likely that the cancellation of product development projects in general sends a negative signal to the stock market, rather than the positive expected signal that the firm only pursues commercially viable R&D projects. This view finds support in the exploratory study, in which IPR management experts reveal that there is always pressure on pharmaceutical companies to have a sufficient number of products in their pipeline to meet future profitability targets. In essence, this means that the abandonment of one project puts pressure on the company to replace it with a new one. Presumably, this is also the view of stock markets. It shall be noted that this argument implies that stock markets do not explicitly value the exclusivity funding variable as an IPR management indicator, but the abandonment of R&D projects.

Interestingly, it is also the trademark protection variable that exhibits a significantly negative impact on the dependent variable. As argued above, it could be that investments in trademark protection are not seen as valuable early in the product lifecycle, but rather reduce profits. Because many firms in the sample do not yet have a product on the market, this seems likely. However, the weak and insignificant pairwise correlation of the trademark protection variable with the BHR variable raises concerns about its consistency. Some caution should therefore be taken in interpreting this finding. I conclude that there is only evidence in support of H2 in relation to patent protection.

5.4.3.3 Duration of exclusivity

In this section I look at proactive measures to extend the duration of exclusivity, and more specifically secondary patents, trademark communication and IPR combination (see Table 5.26).

Looking first at the pairwise correlations, I find that secondary patents are significantly negatively correlated with the dependent variable, while the variables trademark communication and IPR combination do not exhibit

Table 5.33 Multivariate analysis of 'Duration'

DV = BHR	M0		M3a		M3b		M3c		M3d	
	Coef.	SE	Coef.	SE	Coef.	SE	Coef.	SE	Coef.	SE
Firm size	-0.145	0.103	-0.133	0.104	-0.128	0.106	-0.122	0.103	-0.111	0.105
Revenue growth	0.361***	0.101	0.375***	0.102	0.380***	0.104	0.389***	0.101	0.402***	0.104
R&D intensity	-0.011	0.256	0.005	0.256	-0.042	0.259	0.020	0.253	0.021	0.261
Patent intensity	0.218	0.225	0.218	0.225	0.262	0.232	0.213	0.223	0.224	0.232
Trademark intensity	-0.060	0.132	-0.067	0.132	-0.051	0.133	-0.042	0.131	-0.048	0.132
Products on the market	0.337***	0.075	0.308***	0.080	0.363***	0.082	0.393***	0.082	0.368***	0.090
Product pipeline	-0.213*	0.124	-0.219*	0.124	-0.237*	0.128	-0.275**	0.128	-0.279**	0.130
Net issue of shares	-0.1823	0.126	-0.187	0.126	-0.167	0.128	-0.192	0.125	-0.191	0.128
Dividends	-0.239**	0.101	-0.236**	0.100	-0.244**	0.101	-0.218**	0.100	-0.220**	0.102
Region dummy	-0.417**	0.217	-0.426**	0.217	-0.411*	0.217	-0.442**	0.215	-0.445***	0.217
Patent prolong	-0.108	0.097	-0.108	0.097					-0.091	0.097
TM communication					-0.075	0.090			-0.019	0.099
IPR combination							-0.116	0.072	-0.102	0.081
F	4.63***		4.54***		4.54***		4.85***		4.10***	
N	73		73		73		73		73	
R²	0.455		0.450		0.450		0.467		0.475	

Note: Significance Level * p<0.10, ** p<0.05, *** p<0.01.

any significant correlation with stock market returns (see Table 5.A4). An interesting side-note, revealed by the bivariate analysis, is also that trademark communication and IPR combination are positively correlated with the number of products a company has on the market. This underlines the finding of the exploratory study that, for firms pursuing a product-based business model, trademarks are of relatively high importance. In contrast, companies with relatively few products on the market seem to rely more on patents, among other things to prolong exclusivity. This is suggested by the significantly negative correlation between the patent prolong variable and the number of products the firm has on the market. It could well be that companies pursuing a licensing-based business model rely more on patents for this purpose. This is not least because additional secondary patents provide a way of generating royalties over a longer time-frame.

The findings of the multiple regression analysis are largely consistent with the findings of the correlation analysis, except that the secondary patents variable turns out to be insignificant. Hence, all variables that describe proactive measures to extend the duration of exclusivity do not have any significant impact on the dependent variable, and even the pair-wise correlations turn out to be rather weak. The weak and inconsistent effects suggest that proactive measures taken to extend the duration of exclusivity are not reflected in companies' share price. However, while the present study does only consider stock returns over a two-year period, the potential economic benefits of such measures often lie many years ahead. Possibly, capital market participants do not forecast far enough ahead to capture the economic effects of such measures. Indeed, some of the financial analysts interviewed were reluctant to add to the duration of exclusivity beyond the expiry of the primary patent, especially when conducting early valuations of products under development. Perhaps an analysis over a longer period of time would reveal a different picture. My findings, however, reveal no evidence for H3.

5.4.3.4 Value for money

To obtain the best value for money, firms conduct regular reviews of their IPR portfolio and abandon irrelevant IPR (see Table 5.27). Not surprisingly, the bivariate analysis reveals that the IPR abandonment variable has a negative correlation with the firm's patent and trademark intensity, meaning that these firms generate the same revenues with less IPR (Table 5.A5). Accordingly, it was hypothesised that because such measures reduce the costs of companies' IPR portfolios, they ought to signal a company's commitment to making effective use of its R&D budget. However, I find a significant correlation only between the portfolio reviews variable and the dependent variable, which is surprisingly negative. Turning to the

Table 5.34 Multivariate analysis of 'Value for money'

DV = BHR	M0		M4a		M4b		M4c	
	Coef.	SE	Coef.	SE	Coef.	SE	Coef.	SE
Firm size	−0.145	0.103	−0.141	0.104	−0.133	0.104	−0.133	0.104
Revenue growth	0.361***	0.101	0.364***	0.102	0.341***	0.102	0.3456**	0.104
R&D intensity	−0.011	0.256	0.032	0.261	−0.034	0.256	−0.009	0.266
Patent intensity	0.218	0.225	0.178	0.231	0.212	0.225	0.192	0.232
Trademark intensity	−0.060	0.132	−0.067	0.132	−0.116	0.140	−0.110	0.142
Products on the market	0.337***	0.075	0.315***	0.080	0.327***	0.076	0.317***	0.080
Product pipeline	−0.213*	0.124	−0.193	0.126	−0.210*	0.124	−0.200	0.127
Net issue of shares	−0.182	0.126	−0.202	0.129	−0.158	0.128	−0.171	0.133
Dividends	−0.239**	0.101	−0.231**	0.101	−0.206*	0.104	−0.207*	0.105
Region dummy	−0.417*	0.217	−0.406*	0.218	−0.363	0.221	−0.366	0.223
Portfolio reviews			−0.080	0.095			−0.041	0.104
IPR abandonment					−0.100	0.086	−0.084	0.096
F	4.63***		4.54***		4.64***		4.21***	
N	73		73		73		73	
R^2	0.455		0.450		0.456		0.457	

Note: Significance Level * $p < 0.10$, ** $p < 0.05$, *** $p < 0.01$.

184

multivariate analysis, even this variable turns out to be insignificant. Here, too, the combination of the weak and insignificant effects of the independent variables suggests that cost-efficiency-related IPR management measures are not reflected in the firm's share price. Or, more precisely, there is no evidence for H4. It may be that the cost side of companies' IPR management is considered to be less relevant than the income side among investors.

5.4.3.5   Out-licensing

For the operationalisation of patent out-licensing, I look at firms' out-licensing activity and two related motives – that is, revenue generation and product market access (see Table 5.28). Surprisingly, I find a significant but negative pairwise correlation between patent out-licensing activity and stock market returns (see Table 5.A6). Even more surprising is that the same relationship is also true for the revenue motive variable, while the product motive variable turns out to have a positively significant impact on the dependent variable. Besides, the bivariate analysis shows that both licensing motives are negatively correlated with the number of products the firm has on the market, while no such relationship is found for the number of out-licensing deals. This implies that companies with fewer products on the market are not necessarily more active in out-licensing, but that licensing is more important to these companies – something that was suggested by the exploratory study.

The findings of the bivariate analysis are also confirmed by the multivariate analysis. Both the out-licensing activity variable and the revenue motive variable are found to have a negative impact on the dependent variable, while a positive impact is found for the product motive variable, providing a mixed picture concerning H5. The findings clearly show that the stock market discounts out-licensing activity, the related revenue motive, but not the product motive. A plausible theoretical explanation for this finding would be that the stock market prefers firms to generate their revenue on the product market rather than on the technology market. At first sight, this seems to contradict past findings showing that stock markets value royalty income higher than other income (Gu and Lev, 2004). However, Gu and Lev (2004) also show that companies most often do not disclose such information in the public domain. It is therefore possible that stock markets simply have access to too little information to properly value companies' licensing deals. In addition, royalties first occur on the firm's income statement ex post to revenue generation. Hence, as a licensing deal is closed, investors depend on companies disclosing related information for ex ante valuations. As shown by the exploratory study, the lack of such information may lead capital market participants to discount for related uncertainty.

Table 5.35 Multivariate analysis of 'Out-licensing'

DV = BHR	M0		M5a		M5b		M5c		M5d	
	Coef.	SE	Coef.	SE	Coef.	SE	Coef.	SE	Coef.	SE
Firm size	−0.145	0.103	−0.110	0.099	−0.177*	0.102	−0.092	0.098	−0.086	0.086
Revenue growth	0.361***	0.101	0.361***	0.096	0.334***	0.100	0.341***	0.095	0.294***	0.082
R&D intensity	−0.011	0.256	0.002	0.243	0.023	0.250	−0.115	0.240	−0.107	0.206
Patent intensity	0.218	0.225	0.184	0.215	0.203	0.220	0.295	0.211	0.284	0.181
Trademark intensity	−0.060	0.132	−0.072	0.126	−0.119	0.132	−0.035	0.123	−0.119	0.108
Products on the market	0.337***	0.075	0.330***	0.072	0.284***	0.078	0.384***	0.072	0.324***	0.065
Product pipeline	−0.213*	0.124	−0.155	0.120	−0.148	0.125	−0.240**	0.116	−0.116	0.103
Net issue of shares	−0.182	0.126	−0.182	0.120	−0.152	0.124	−0.161	0.118	−0.106	0.102
Dividends	−0.239**	0.101	−0.282***	0.097	−0.297***	0.102	−0.192**	0.095	−0.288***	0.084
Region dummy	−0.417*	0.217	−0.508***	0.209	−0.459***	0.213	−0.377*	0.202	−0.490***	0.175
Out-licensing activity			−0.198***	0.073					−0.155**	0.069
Revenue motive					−0.166**	0.082			−0.239***	0.082
Product market motive							0.257***	0.079	0.382***	0.074
F	4.63***		5.64***		5.09***		6.15***		8.93***	
N	73		73		73		73		73	
R²	0.455		0.504		0.478		0.526		0.6631	

Note: Significance Level * p<0.10, ** p<0.05, *** p<0.01.

Despite stock markets generally discounting for patent out-licensing activity, the product motive turns out to be positively significant. There are at least three potential explanations for this finding. Firstly, firms which license-out their patents for product motives are more likely to participate in the development process, and to receive upfront and milestone payments which have a more immediate revenue effect, and thus appear sooner in companies' income statements, than potential future royalties associated with the revenue motive. Furthermore, if a company engages in collaboration, more detailed information is likely to have been made publicly available, and presumably such deals also receive more attention in the media. Finally, it could be that the potential future benefits of products are higher than the economic benefits that can be realised on the technology market, as the value added – in terms of product development – will contribute to higher margins. Hence, at the same time that out-licensing may be a way of generating revenue, firms can potentially earn more through product commercialisation. Because licensing deals for product motives tend to take place during the later clinical phases, the value of these deals may also be relatively high. However, relatively few out-licensing deals can be of product motive nature, as investors seem to discount for patent out-licensing activity in general.

5.4.3.6 In-licensing

I find stock markets' valuations of patent in-licensing deals to be rather different from their valuation of out-licensing deals. As with patent out-licensing, I look at firms' in-licensing activity and the two main motives for licensing-in patents, being either to extend the firm's product pipeline or to secure FTO (see Table 5.29).

The bivariate analysis reveals a relatively strong and positively significant correlation between firms' in-licensing activity and the dependent variable (see Table 5.A7). Similarly, a significantly positive correlation of BHR with the pipeline motive is found, but not with the FTO motive. In addition, I find a positive correlation for both patent in-licensing deals and the pipeline motive with the number of products the firm has on the market, indicating that these variables are associated with a product-based business model.

The findings of the bivariate analysis are also consistent throughout the multivariate analysis, in which both in-licensing activity and pipeline motive indicators show positive and significant effects on the dependent variable, in the full model also, while no significant effects for the FTO motive variable were found. Accordingly, firms which license-in patents in general, and with the motive of extending their product pipeline in particular, exhibit higher stock market returns. This finding, however, somewhat

Table 5.36 Multivariate analysis of 'In-licensing'

DV = BHR	M0		M6a		M6b		M6c		M6d	
	Coef.	SE	Coef.	SE	Coef.	SE	Coef.	SE	Coef.	SE
Firm size	−0.145	0.103	−0.209**	0.100	−0.181*	0.098	−0.145	0.104	−0.221**	0.096
Revenue growth	0.361***	0.101	0.307***	0.098	0.318***	0.096	0.367***	0.103	0.300***	0.094
R&D intensity	−0.011	0.256	0.008	0.242	0.171	0.247	−0.037	0.262	0.097	0.242
Patent intensity	0.218	0.225	0.211	0.213	0.114	0.214	0.245	0.232	0.1900	0.211
Trademark intensity	−0.060	0.132	−0.047	0.125	−0.136	0.126	−0.070	0.134	−0.142	0.125
Products on the market	0.337***	0.075	0.245***	0.078	0.301***	0.072	0.339***	0.076	0.246***	0.075
Product pipeline	−0.213*	0.124	−0.249**	0.118	−0.228**	0.116	−0.202	0.126	−0.224*	0.115
Net issue of shares	−0.182	0.126	−0.155	0.120	−0.160	0.119	−0.166	0.131	−0.100	0.120
Dividends	−0.239**	0.101	−0.150	0.100	−0.215**	0.095	−0.234**	0.102	−0.146	0.097
Region dummy	−0.417*	0.217	−0.425**	0.205	−0.314	0.206	−0.415*	0.218	−0.327	0.201
In-licensing activity			0.251***	0.087					0.176**	0.090
Product pipeline motive					0.214***	0.069			0.188**	0.074
FTO motive							−0.043	0.082	−0.110	0.077
F	4.63***		5.77***		5.98***		4.47***		5.84***	
N	73		73		73		73		73	
R^2	0.455		0.510		0.519		0.446		0.563	

Note: Significance Level * $p < 0.10$, ** $p < 0.05$, *** $p < 0.01$.

contradicts the negative impact of the product pipeline size variable on BHR. While the size of companies' product pipeline is negatively associated with stock returns, in-licensing deals to extend their pipeline exhibit a positive impact on the dependent variable. Presumably this is because investors view related outcomes as highly uncertain, but see in-licensing deals as additional proof of commercial potential, exhibiting higher chances of commercial success.[5] Moreover, it is likely that that these deals relate to later clinical phases, where attrition rates decrease substantially, while the pipeline size variable may describe a higher share of early stage projects.

5.5   IPR REPORTING AND STOCK MARKET UNCERTAINTY: A MULTIVARIATE ANALYSIS

Although past research has shown that IPR are reflected in firms' market values (see, for example, Neuhäusler et al., 2011; Sandner and Block, 2011), strands of the literature find that additional IPR-related information disclosures reduce asymmetric information in stock markets (see, for example, Gu and Lev, 2004; Seethamraju, 2003). In this section I examine whether additional IPR reporting can help reduce asymmetric information related to technology-driven firms, but also which kinds of IPR information are potentially associated with reduced stock market uncertainty.

To bridge informational deficits companies can, besides making mandatory information disclosures, also engage in voluntary reporting. A review of the literature on voluntary information disclosures shows that this can reduce stock market uncertainty, as well as firms' costs of capital (Brown et al., 2004; Coller and Yohn, 1997; Healy and Palepu, 2001; Verrecchia, 2001). Because mandatory IPR-related information disclosures are relatively few, and rather restrictive (see Section 2.8), I decided to look at voluntary IPR reporting.

Past studies have used several proxies for voluntary information disclosures, including management forecasts (see, for example, Miller and Piotroski, 2000), qualitative metrics based on Association for Investment Management and Research (AIMR) data[6] (see, for example, Healy et al., 1999; Lang and Lundholm, 1993; 2000), but also self-constructed variables (see, for example, Botosan, 1997; Miller, 2002). All these approaches have their limits. The present study, however, takes the approach of self-constructed variables, some implications of which ought to be considered. Firstly, this involves judgements made by the researcher on which measurements are important in terms of their value-relevance. To mitigate potential biases on the part of the researcher, I conducted interviews with both IPR management experts and financial analysts to assess which kinds of indicator are requested by the stock market, and what type of information is disclosed. Secondly, as my variables describe general IPR reporting practices and not particular events, they may provide noisy measurements of disclosure. At the same time, this approach has the advantage of capturing all sorts of reporting channels – that is, annual reports, press releases, analyst meetings, conference calls and a variety of other publications. This means that no reporting channels have been omitted from the analysis, which is essential, not least since my study reveals that firms also report on their IPR through various press releases. Finally, like any survey with self-constructed measurements, the approach adopted has the disadvantage that its results are difficult to replicate.

However, the approach has some important benefits. Firstly, it enables me to consider IPR reporting in connection with how firms manage their IPR, but also how financial analysts evaluate their IPR management. By this I mean that the indicators for companies' IPR reporting were derived on the basis of exploratory interviews conducted upfront with financial analysts and IPR management experts. Hence, I considered how firms use their IPR, but also how financial analysts value related information when deriving indicators. Secondly, as I examine several IPR reporting items, I am able to compare the relevance of reporting on different items and thus identify areas where additional information disclosure may be especially relevant. Finally, self-constructed measurements can be used for any company without being restricted to pre-selected companies, chosen by a data service provider, which tend to be skewed towards larger companies (Francis et al., 2008). As my main focus is on smaller technology-driven companies, this approach suits the present study well.

5.5.1 Hypothesis and Operationalisation

5.5.1.1 Dependent variable
Past research suggests a link between the deterioration in the value-relevance of information provided by financial statements, and increased stock market volatility. For example, accounting bodies, and perhaps most notably the Jenkins Committee, contend that financial statements have lost in value-relevance due to the transition of the US economy from being industrially oriented towards becoming more intangible. Accordingly, Kothari (2001) suggests that the recent increase in stock market volatility is in part a consequence of financial reporting practices failing to adapt. Meanwhile, research scholars have argued that enhanced disclosure and improved quality of financial reporting would help mitigate information asymmetries about companies' performance and thereby

reduce the volatility of stock prices (Diamond and Verrecchia, 1991; Healy et al., 1999). Similarly, a link between stock return volatility and the asymmetric information component of companies' costs of capital has been conceptualised (Froot et al., 1992; Leuz and Verrecchia, 2000). Finally, Easley and O'Hara (2004) hypothesise that financial reporting quality has an impact on volatility and thus companies' costs of capital.

Stock market volatility has also been previously used as a proxy for uncertainty at the firm level in empirical studies (see, for example, Bloom et al., 2007; Leahy and Whited, 1996). Moreover, prior studies have used the volatility of security returns as a proxy for asymmetric information (see, for example, Lang and Lundholm, 1993; Lobo and Mahmoud, 1989). This approach is also taken by Chan et al. (2001) when investigating the relationship between R&D intensity and stock market uncertainty, which they argue stems from asymmetric information regarding intangibles.

To examine whether IPR reporting mitigates asymmetric information and thereby reduces firms' costs of capital, return volatility enters the model as a dependent variable. Return volatility is calculated as the standard deviation of the monthly returns over 24 months (cf. Chan et al., 2001), from January 2008 onwards. It should also be noted that the dependent variable was standardised around the average. Accordingly, return volatility is considered in relative terms.

5.5.1.2 Independent variables

The independent variables were operationalised on a five-point Likert-type scale to measure the frequency of IPR reporting on various items. This is because increases in the rate at which investors learn about firm fundamentals reduce stock market uncertainty (Rogers et al., 2009). Hence, more frequent disclosures are likely to lower return volatility as there will be fewer surprises. Drawing upon insights from past findings together with exploratory interviews, I identify two main areas – that is, product-related IPR reporting and licensing-related IPR reporting – in which more frequent information disclosures are likely benefit the informational efficiency of stock markets.

Product-related IPR reporting   Past research has pointed to the valuation difficulties associated with intangible assets. For example, Chung et al. (2005) show that investors discount for the uncertainty attached to intangible assets, arguing that this is due to insufficient information disclosures about their value. Moreover, Guo et al. (2005) investigate whether product-related indicators, such as the share of patent protected products, have an impact on the valuation of 122 biotech IPOs. They also find that the ratio of patented products has a negative impact on the

BHR of firms' shares, suggesting that investors discount even proprietary intangible assets. In contrast, however, Austin (1993) finds that patents within the biotechnology industry which are linked to key products receive higher valuations than non-linked patents. Taking these findings together, it seems that patents covering products are undervalued, but less so than patents which are used for other purposes. In addition, Austin (1993) finds that patents which receive attention in the media also exhibit higher valuations. This implies that reporting on patents provides value-relevant information to stock markets, and is presumably most important in the context of the valuation of the company's products. Furthermore, I find that financial analysts consider IPR not as such, but in relation to the product lifecycle (see Section 4.7.3). If requested information concerning the IPR situation around a product is not disclosed, analysts reveal that they will discount for the resulting uncertainty in their valuations. Taking these findings together, I derive the following hypothesis:

H7a: The more firms are committed to reporting on the IPR situation around their products, the lower their return volatility.

My findings show that analysts make assessments of the IPR situation not only for products on the market, but also in relation to products under development. This implies that information about the IPR situation is also value-relevant in relation to the firm's product pipeline. I therefore take the same arguments as above, and hypothesise that:

H7b: The more firms are committed to reporting on the IPR situation around their product pipeline, the lower their return volatility.

Turning to the operationalisation of the indicators, the financial analysts interviewed reveal that a major concern is whether the company will be able to obtain exclusivity on the basis of the IPR covering the product and, if so, for what time-frame (see Section 4.7.3). To assess this, they look at the type of patent protection the firm has obtained. For example, in relation to NCE products, analysts want to know whether the firm has a patent covering the chemical compound or only for a certain field of medical use. This information provides a basis for assessing if the product can be commercialised exclusively. In addition, although financial analysts are restrictive in extending the duration of exclusivity in their valuation models, secondary patent applications can add a few years to exclusivity in terms of the point when generic competition is expected. Usually, extensive generic competition is accounted for. Trademarks are therefore typically not considered to have the potential to preserve market share

Table 5.37   Operationalisation of 'IPR product reporting'

Independent variables	Description	Mean	SD	Min.	Median	Max.
Product exclusivity	We report on the type of patents protecting our products	1.746	1.105	1	1	4
Product duration	We report on the duration of secondary patents protecting our products	1.375	0.795	1	1	4
Product FTO	We report on the FTO situation related to our products	1.278	0.697	1	1	4

Table 5.38   Operationalisation of 'IPR pipeline reporting'

Independent variables	Description	Mean	SD	Min.	Median	Max.
Pdev exclusivity	We report on the type of patents protecting our product pipeline	1.939	1.314	1	1	5
Pdev duration	We report on the duration of secondary patents protecting our product pipeline	2.061	1.298	1	1	5
Pdev FTO	We report on the FTO situation related to our product pipeline	1.408	0.911	1	1	4

at this point. Finally, some financial analysts also consider the relevance of patents for securing FTO. This is, however, secondary to exclusivity assessments, but could potentially reduce uncertainty among investors. Based on these findings, the indicators in Table 5.37 were derived for IPR product reporting.

The same indicators were derived in relation to firms' IPR product pipeline reporting, but operationalised separately in the questionnaire (see Table 5.38).

Licensing-related IPR reporting   Gu and Lev (2004) examine the stock market's valuation of royalty income compared with other earnings. They find that the multiple assigned by investors to royalty income is approximately three times larger than the multiple for other earnings. In addition, they show that royalty income reporting signals the ability of companies to materialise their intangible investments, leading to higher valuations of subsequent R&D expenditure. However, despite the evident value-relevance of royalty income, they show that a substantial number of companies engaged in patent licensing chose not to report this item. Overall, approximately half of the firms provided quantitative information on their royalty income. The remaining firms only provided a general discussion on patent licensing in their annual report, but without any figures on royalty income.

Seethamraju (2003) takes a different approach in examining information disclosures conducted when the actual deal is announced, as opposed to reporting on realised benefits. In doing so, he looks at the stock market's valuation of IPR acquisitions, and more precisely trademark acquisitions. He finds that additional voluntary information disclosures, both of quantitative and qualitative nature, are associated with higher stock market returns, which, he argues, come as a consequence of reduced uncertainty associated with future profits related to the trademark. This is found to be especially true for quantitative information disclosures about the size of the market the trademark covers, its growth potential and the price at which the trademark was acquired.

Accordingly, past research shows that the stock market values information both about IPR being commercialised on the technology market, in terms of subsequent royalty income, but also about IPR acquisitions, implying new growth opportunities. Similarly, I find that financial analysts in the pharmaceutical industry assess value potential in relation to patent out-licensing and in-licensing deals (see Section 4.7.2).[7] Hence, they value firms' patent licensing when the actual deal has been closed, and not only ex post, when economic benefits have been realised. This leads us to the following hypotheses:

H8a: The more firms are committed to reporting on their patent out-licensing deals, the lower their return volatility.

H8b: The more firms are committed to reporting on their patent in-licensing deals, the lower their return volatility.

Taking the approach of examining information disclosures about actual licensing deals has the advantage that this kind of information can be obtained earlier, as the deal is closed – that is, before revenues are actually generated. Moreover, additional qualitative forward-looking information is sometimes disclosed in this context. I therefore decided to focus on reporting on licensing deals instead of generated royalty income.

Table 5.39   Operationalisation of 'Out-licensing reporting'

Independent variables	Description	Mean	SD	Min.	Median	Max.
L-out financials	We report on the royalty fee in relation to patent out-licensing deals	2.137	1.371	1	1	5
L-out exclusivity	We report on whether the licence has been given exclusivity	2.725	1.698	1	2	5

Table 5.40   Operationalisation of 'In-licensing reporting'

Independent variables	Description	Mean	SD	Min.	Median	Max.
L-in financials	We report on the royalty fee in relation to patent in-licensing deals	1.679	1.015	1	1	4
L-in exclusivity	We report on whether the licence has been given exclusivity	2.660	1.652	1	2	5

The exploratory interviews show that licensing deals are valued on the basis of the financial terms of the contract. For example, from an out-licensing perspective, a high royalty rate indicates future economic benefits to come. Accordingly, the financial analysts interviewed reveal that reporting on the royalty rate in a licensing agreement substantially reduces uncertainty about the potential revenue from the deal. Following this finding, reporting on the royalty rate enters the model as an independent variable. Moreover, the analysts reveal the exclusivity terms of the licence to be another source of uncertainty. This is not least because these terms set the boundaries for further revenue potentially being generated from the patent. For instance, if the licence has been given exclusively, the licensor will not be able to generate further revenues from it through additional licensing deals. This restricts the profit potential of the patent. Hence, the exclusivity terms of the deal enters the model (see Table 5.39).

From an in-licensing perspective, uncertainty in financial analysts' valuation models also relates to the indicators described above, although their interpretation is rather different as a high royalty reduces the future profit potential of the licence taken. Moreover, in relation to in-licensing deals, analysts perceive higher potential future benefits of exclusivity, as this also indicates exclusivity in the commercialisation of the technology based on the licence taken. The indicators exclusivity and financials are therefore operationalised separately in relation to in-licensing deals (see Table 5.40).

5.5.1.3   Control variables

Past research has categorised the determinants of stock market volatility into macroeconomic, industry-specific and firm-specific factors. I control for macroeconomic factors using a regional dummy, taking 0 for Europe, and 1 for the US. Further, to control for industry-specific factors, I decided to focus on the pharmaceutical industry, for reasons mentioned above.

Turning to firm-specific factors, past research has shown that smaller firms experience relatively high return volatility (see, for example, Pastor and Veronesi, 2003). Hence, I control for firm size measured by annual revenue. Moreover, previous studies reveal a relationship between R&D intensity and return volatility (see, for example, Chan et al., 2001). Because both patents and trademarks are associated with R&D expenditures to which past research has attached asymmetric information, I also decided to control for patent and trademark intensity, as potential sources of uncertainty. For all the variables described above, I use averages of the years 2008 and 2009 – that is, the time-frame of the analysis.

Furthermore, as in the previous research model (see Section 5.4.1.3), and in conformity with Guo et al. (2005), I control for the number of products a company has on the market. Although I am not aware of this variable having been used in previous studies on stock market volatility, there are good theoretical reasons for its inclusion – not least because products potentially signal the ability of firms to materialise their R&D investments, as shown by Gu and Lev (2004) in relation to royalty income. Moreover, products provide assets-in-place from which continuous cash-flows can be generated – something that should reduce the risk of more severe valuation errors. Also, like Rajgopal and Venkatachalam (2011) and Chan et al. (2001), I include firms' average market-to-book ratio in my model.[8] The theoretical reasoning behind this is that firms with a larger share of growth opportunities, relative to assets-in-place, are likely to be subject to more substantial valuation errors and therefore to experience greater stock return volatility. In addition, I control for sales growth. This is because past research has shown that various growth measurements are associated with stock market volatility (see, for example, Bloom, 2009). Finally, trading volume enters the model, as several studies have shown that volatility is lower in more liquid markets (see, for example, Brock and Lebaron, 1996; Karpoff, 1987; Lee and Rui, 2002).

Table 5.41 Control variables – summary statistics

Control variables	Description	Mean	SD	Min.	Median	Max.
Firm size	Annual revenue in million USD	1627.540	7411.001	0.551	24.000	45000.000
Revenue growth	Annual percentage change in revenue	0.834	3.074	−0.960	0.230	24.500
R&D intensity	Average R&D/revenue	5.781	16.505	0.0229	0.700	120.933
Patent intensity	Average patents/revenue	7.559	24.892	0.000	1.071	200.000
Trademark intensity	Average trademarks/revenue	1.430	2.529	0.000	0.179	11.000
Products on the market	Number of products on the market	2.545	1.599	1.000	2.000	5.000
Firm age	Years since firm formation	4.096	0.802	2.000	4.000	5.000
Market-to-book	Average book value/market cap.	3.141	2.721	0.550	2.040	12.950
Trading volume	Average daily trading volume	536136.0	1493223.0	1535.880	120496.5	9125343.0
Region	Dummy	0.370	0.486	0.000	0.000	1.000

It shall be noted that all financial figures were converted into USD, using the exchange rate converter of the European Commission. The exchange rate for the last trading day of the year was taken to ensure the comparability of all observations. A summary of the control variables is provided in Table 5.41.

5.5.2   Empirical Findings

In this section I present the results of the econometric analysis. This includes both a bivariate and a multivariate analysis, although the emphasis is on the multivariate regressions. As for the research model examining the contribution of companies' IPR management to their stock market performance, the bivariate analysis provides some complementary insights concerning the consistency of the relationships examined. The tables showing the results of the bivariate analyses are displayed in the Appendix. As for the estimation methods, the same procedures were used as in the previous research models (see Section 5.4.2).

5.5.2.1   IPR pipeline reporting

Turning first to the basic model (M7a) in Table 5.42, I find that the patent intensity variable significantly contributes to share price volatility, while R&D intensity does not. In addition, I find that companies' market-to-book ratio is negatively associated with return volatility. Both these findings contradict Chan et al. (2001), who find R&D intensity and companies' market-to-book ratio to be associated with higher share price volatility. However, the study by Chan et al. (2001) is conducted across industries. It may well be that, although the economic benefits from R&D investments in the pharmaceutical industry are indeed uncertain, investors view these as an important way for companies to maintain their competitiveness. Moreover, Chan et al. (2001) do not control for patent intensity. Looking at the pairwise correlations, I find that R&D, trademarks and patents are all associated with higher return volatility (see Table 5.A8). However, when controlling for all three, my findings show that stock market uncertainty is attached to patents rather than R&D or trademarks. At first sight this finding seems unlikely because patents tend to be regarded as productive outputs of the innovation process, while R&D investments provide more uncertain inputs. The finding that investors are deprived by assessing companies' patents, rather than their R&D, therefore has little theoretical support. However, the increasing pace of strategic patenting, leading to a high share of lemon patents, will undoubtedly have made it more difficult for investors to value companies' patents, not least where insufficient information is provided for them to do

Table 5.42 Multivariate analysis of 'IPR pipeline reporting'

DV = Volatility	M7a		M7b		M7c		M7d		M7e	
	Coef.	SE	Coef.	SE	Coef.	SE	Coef.	SE	Coef.	SE
Firm size	0.020	0.130	−0.000	0.124	0.007	0.129	0.022	0.128	0.004	0.124
Revenue growth	0.166*	0.098	0.125	0.094	0.156	0.097	0.191*	0.098	0.147	0.096
R&D intensity	−0.034	0.226	−0.023	0.214	−0.050	0.224	−0.010	0.222	−0.008	0.216
Patent intensity	0.410**	0.202	0.386**	0.192	0.425**	0.200	0.390*	0.199	0.376*	0.193
Trademark intensity	0.038	0.125	−0.019	0.120	0.038	0.124	0.015	0.124	−0.029	0.122
Products on the market	−0.153**	0.072	−0.151**	0.070	−0.137*	0.073	−0.167**	0.073	−0.165**	0.072
Firm age	−0.222*	0.129	−0.131	0.126	−0.198	0.129	−0.252*	0.129	−0.164	0.129
Market-to-book	−0.192*	0.098	−0.160*	0.093	−0.193*	0.097	−0.224**	0.098	−0.183*	0.096
Trading volume	−0.130	0.131	−0.182	0.125	−0.149	0.130	−0.143	0.129	−0.182	0.126
Region dummy	0.443**	0.215	0.610***	0.217	0.499**	0.220	0.451**	0.217	0.580**	0.220
Pdev exclusivity reporting			−0.267***	0.087					−0.238***	0.107
Pdev duration reporting					−0.202*	0.116			0.013	0.138
Pdev FTO reporting							−0.272*	0.138	−0.169	0.144
F	5.86***		6.68***		5.65***		5.80***		5.70***	
N	73		71		72		72		71	
R²	0.486		0.555		0.509		0.515		0.565	

Note: Significance Level: * p<0.10, ** p<0.05, *** p<0.01.

so. It is therefore entirely plausible that investors perceive a high degree of uncertainty about the economic value of companies' patents, in terms of whether they will enable them to appropriate economic returns more effectively. In addition, patents come with legal uncertainty (see, for example, Lemley and Shapiro, 2005). Possibly, the legal boundaries of the patent and the risks of infringements create additional uncertainty among investors. What can be said is that it seems that stock market volatility stems from the patent situation rather than from uncertainty about companies' R&D investments, at least in the pharmaceutical industry. Still, the question of whether this uncertainty relates to the validity of the patents, the likelihood of lawsuits, or simply to firms' ability to secure exclusivity, is left unanswered. It seems, however, that the main source of uncertainty is not whether the company is able to create valuable intangible assets, but rather whether it can appropriate the related economic benefits effectively.

Turning to the reduction of asymmetric information about the IPR covering the company's product pipeline, I look at reporting on three essential aspects of the IPR situation – namely FTO, exclusivity and the duration of exclusivity (see Table 5.38). As has been shown, these objectives are essential to firms' IPR management (see Section 4.3), which are also of concern to financial analysts (see Section 4.7.2).

The multivariate analysis of the IPR pipeline reporting variables reveals some interesting findings (see Table 5.42). In the bivariate analysis, only the exclusivity variable turns out to be significant (see Table 5.A8). The other reporting variables do not exhibit any substantial pairwise correlation with the dependent variable, nor are these relationships significant. This finding is also consistent throughout the multivariate analysis, implying that the main source of uncertainty about the IPR situation around a company's product pipeline is whether the company will be able to obtain exclusivity for its product before marketing authorisation. Interestingly, the FTO and the duration variables also turn out to be significant in the multivariate analysis – although not in the full model. The low pairwise correlations of these variables with BHR and their insignificant impact in the full model, however, suggest that they are inconsistent estimators. This leads me to conclude that only reporting on the exclusivity item is associated with lower return volatility. Theoretically, the duration with respect to secondary patent filings should also be of less concern at this point, not least since any potential related economic effects may lie 20 years ahead, when the primary patent expires. As for the FTO variable, the exploratory study reveals that relatively many analysts do not price FTO risks. That the FTO reporting variable does not exhibit any consistent impact on the dependent variable is therefore not necessarily surprising. H7b is accordingly accepted, but only as far as exclusivity reporting is concerned.

5.5.2.2   IPR product reporting

Turning to IPR reporting in relation to products on the market, it should be noted that the sample differs from that of the previous section. This is because all firms without a product on the market were excluded from the analysis, leaving me with 49 observations. Hence, the findings also differ in certain respects. Firstly, I find that R&D intensity is even negatively associated with return volatility. Presumably this is because all firms in the sample already have a product on the market, and thus a proven record of materialising their R&D investments. This argument is in line with the findings of Gu and Lev (2004), who show that royalty income signals the ability of firms to generate returns based on their R&D investments, making subsequent R&D spending outcomes less uncertain. In the same way, it is likely that a product on the market also signals the ability of a firm to turn future R&D investments into profits. In contrast to the previous model, I do not find any significant impact of the patent intensity variable. This suggests that patent uncertainty decreases when a product has been commercialised and revenues are being generated. Presumably, this is because there is less uncertainty about the economic value of the patents covering the products when revenues can be derived for their valuation.

The reporting variables, also in this model, relate to reporting on FTO, exclusivity and the duration of exclusivity, but this time with regard to products on the market (see Table 5.37). Looking first at the bivariate analysis, I find that both the exclusivity and the duration variables exhibit a significant negative correlation with the volatility variable (see Table 5.A9). This indicates that reporting on the duration of exclusivity becomes more of a concern to stock markets when the product is on the market and revenues are being generated. This finding is in line with those of the exploratory study among financial analysts, showing them to be more concerned about the duration of exclusivity when the product has reached the market. The reason for this is that, when revenues are already being generated, the crucial question is for how long the company can sustain its revenue generation. For example, the descriptive statistics show that firms are keener to report on secondary patents in relation to their products when they have reached the market. This finding is also consistent throughout the bivariate and multivariate analyses. In contrast, the exclusivity variable turns out to be insignificant in the multivariate analysis. Accordingly, while exclusivity reporting seems to be most important in relation to products under development, to reduce volatility, reporting on the duration of exclusivity seems more crucial when the product has reached the market. FTO reporting, however, is found to be consistently of less relevance throughout the product lifecycle – showing both weak

Table 5.43 Multivariate analysis of 'IPR product reporting'

DV = Volatility	M8a		M8b		M8c		M8d		M8e	
	Coef.	SE	Coef.	SE	Coef.	SE	Coef.	SE	Coef.	SE
Firm size	−0.013	0.112	−0.017	0.114	−0.059	0.109	−0.022	0.116	−0.055	0.113
Revenue growth	0.356	0.301	0.349	0.304	0.222	0.294	0.352	0.305	0.212	0.302
R&D intensity	−0.940*	0.481	−0.871*	0.505	−0.700	0.473	−0.913*	0.493	−0.743	0.493
Patent intensity	0.758	0.684	0.653	0.722	0.456	0.668	0.787	0.697	0.462	0.728
Trademark intensity	0.459	0.366	0.439	0.371	0.332	0.354	0.437	0.375	0.349	0.365
Products on the market	−0.122	0.086	−0.131	0.089	−0.140*	0.082	−0.122	0.087	−0.135	0.086
Firm age	−0.420***	0.146	−0.398**	0.154	−0.397***	0.140	−0.419***	0.148	−0.410***	0.150
Market-to-book	−0.528***	0.182	−0.493***	0.196	−0.391**	0.185	−0.518***	0.186	−0.408**	0.194
Trading volume	−0.048	0.114	−0.036	0.118	−0.031	0.110	−0.038	0.120	−0.048	0.116
Region dummy	0.181	0.259	0.179	0.261	0.197	0.247	0.186	0.262	0.196	0.254
Prod exclusivity reporting			−0.043	0.086					0.031	0.096
Prod duration reporting					−0.168**	0.078			−0.191**	0.091
Prod FTO reporting							−0.040	0.115	0.039	0.124
F	3.17**		2.84**		3.58***		2.82**		2.91**	
N	49		49		49		49		49	
R²	0.454		0.458		0.515		0.456		0.519	

Note: Significance Level: * $p<0.10$, ** $p<0.05$, *** $p<0.01$.

and insignificant effects. H7a is accepted, but only when it comes to reporting on the duration of exclusivity.

5.5.2.3 Out-licensing reporting

In relation to companies' reporting on out-licensing deals, I looked at two indicators – reporting the financial aspects of the deal and the exclusivity conditions (see Table 5.39). In the model, I exclude all companies which did not report any out-licensing activity in 2009, leaving me with 51 observations. This was done in order to control for potential distortions arising from firms that are keen to report on their out-licensing deals, but have not been active in out-licensing lately.

Turning to the results, the bivariate analysis shows a significant negative correlation between the financials variable and stock market volatility (see Table 5.A10). In contrast, the exclusivity variable turns out to be insignificant. The multivariate analysis confirms this finding. The financials variable exhibits a strong and significant impact on the dependent variable, while no significant impact is found for the exclusivity variable.

The financials variable remains negatively significant throughout the multivariate analysis, suggesting a high degree of consistency. What is striking is that the exclusivity variable also turns out to be significant in the multivariate analysis, but loses its significance in the full model. Further, the exclusivity variable explains relatively little of the variance in the dependent variable, compared to the financials variable. This leads me to conclude that pharmaceutical firms can reduce return volatility by reporting on the deal's financial aspects, but cannot necessarily do so through exclusivity reporting. Hence, along with past findings (see, for example, Gu and Lev, 2004), reporting on licensing revenue seems to signal the ability of companies to materialise their R&D investments, which reduces uncertainty among investors. Theoretically, reporting on licensing deal financials will accordingly lead to less underpricing, and thus to reduced costs of capital for firms that do so, giving some support to H8a.

5.5.2.4 In-licensing reporting

When examining the effects of patent in-licensing reporting – for similar reasons as for the last model – firms that did not have any in-licensing activity in 2009 were excluded from the sample, leaving me with 53 companies. As with out-licensing reporting, I consider two variables – that is, the deal's financial aspects and the exclusivity terms (see Table 5.40).

In the bivariate analysis, none of the in-licensing reporting variables exhibit a significant correlation with the volatility variable, suggesting that reporting on licensing deals does not reduce stock market uncertainty (see Table 5.A11). However, in the multivariate analysis, the exclusivity

Table 5.44 Multivariate analysis of 'Out-licensing reporting'

DV = Volatility	M9a		M9b		M9c		M9d	
	Coef.	SE	Coef.	SE	Coef.	SE	Coef.	SE
Firm size	−0.039	0.196	−0.104	0.182	−0.072	0.198	−0.106	0.185
Revenue growth	0.179	0.111	0.126	0.102	0.165	0.110	0.126	0.104
R&D intensity	−0.171	0.342	−0.116	0.315	0.093	0.374	−0.083	0.354
Patent intensity	0.171	0.368	0.119	0.334	0.086	0.367	0.109	0.341
Trademark intensity	0.055	0.210	−0.155	0.204	−0.060	0.221	−0.162	0.209
Products on the market	−0.181*	0.098	−0.290***	0.095	−0.221**	0.100	−0.291***	0.097
Firm age	−0.231	0.174	−0.148	0.160	−0.134	0.181	−0.138	0.169
Market-to-book	−0.209	0.141	−0.197	0.128	−0.171	0.141	−0.192	0.132
Trading volume	−0.053	0.255	−0.033	0.237	−0.069	0.258	−0.035	0.240
Region dummy	0.327	0.300	0.248	0.275	0.355	0.298	0.255	0.280
L-out financials			−0.305***	0.094			−0.293**	0.110
L-out exclusivity					−0.144*	0.085	−0.020	0.092
F	2.46**		3.67**		2.55**		3.28**	
N	52		51		51		51	
R²	0.374		0.508		0.418		0.509	

Note: Significance Level: * $p<0.10$, ** $p<0.05$, *** $p<0.01$.

Table 5.45 Multivariate analysis of 'In-licensing reporting'

DV = Volatility	M10a		M10b		M10c		M10d	
	Coef.	SE	Coef.	SE	Coef.	SE	Coef.	SE
Firm size	−0.002	0.142	−0.002	0.141	−0.003	0.134	−0.003	0.136
Revenue growth	0.208*	0.110	0.220*	0.109	0.199*	0.103	0.204*	0.105
R&D intensity	−0.278	0.460	−0.228	0.458	0.121	0.464	0.106	0.470
Patent intensity	−0.002	0.359	−0.039	0.357	−0.047	0.339	−0.056	0.343
Trademark intensity	0.2787	0.265	0.239	0.264	0.135	0.257	0.132	0.260
Products on the market	−0.189*	0.097	−0.210**	0.098	−0.200**	0.092	−0.206**	0.094
Firm age	−0.171	0.173	−0.158	0.172	−0.118	0.165	−0.117	0.166
Market-to-book	−0.240	0.167	−0.276	0.167	−0.275*	0.158	−0.285*	0.161
Trading volume	−0.101	0.145	−0.120	0.144	−0.123	0.137	−0.129	0.139
Region dummy	0.279	0.302	0.349	0.304	0.378	0.288	0.395	0.293
L-in financials			−0.167	0.125			−0.059	0.132
L-in exclusivity					−0.185**	0.075	−0.170**	0.083
F	2.74**		2.70**		3.34***		3.02**	
N	52		52		52		52	
R^2	0.401		0.426		0.479		0.481	

Note: Significance Level: * $p<0.10$, ** $p<0.05$, *** $p<0.01$.

variable turns out to be significant, and remains so in the full model. This implies that the main source of stock market uncertainty related to in-licensing deals is not the financial aspects, but rather whether exclusivity has been obtained. Presumably, this is only true for in-licensing deals where the firm looks to commercialise a product based on the licence taken. This would also explain the relatively low significance of the exclusivity variable, and perhaps also its inconsistency between the bivariate and multivariate analysis. This argument is consistent with the findings of the exploratory study (see Section 4.7). I therefore conclude that firms are likely only to reduce return volatility by reporting on the exclusivity item if the deal concerns a technology acquisition.

5.6   SUMMARY AND DISCUSSION

Most effects of the IPR management indicators turn out to be weak and insignificant. Turning first to the FTO variables, none of these had any substantial and significant impact on the dependent variable. It should be noted that this is although I find them to be associated with a lower probability of patent lawsuits filed against the company. In contrast, the patent protection motive – that is, the use of patents to obtain exclusivity – is found to have a positively consistent and significant impact on the dependent variable. The use of trademarks for the same purpose, however, did not show any significant effect. Hence, it seems that only patents which are directly linked to products are comprehensively reflected in share prices.

Furthermore, the variables describing companies' IPR policies require separate attention. Firstly, I find no evidence that firms restricting funding to R&D projects for which FTO can to be obtained outperform their counterparts on the stock market. More peculiar is the finding that companies which only fund projects for which exclusivity can be obtained underperformed others. This means that even though these projects are likely not to be commercially viable, their cancellation seems to signal bad news to stock markets. This finding implies that investors do not differentiate between R&D projects according to the exclusivity situation early in the R&D process – something that could potentially lead to severe misvaluations.

Turning to the duration of exclusivity, I find that neither the use of patents nor the use of trademarks to prolong protection had any significant impact on the BHR variable. All independent variables describing proactive measures to extend the duration of exclusivity turned out to be insignificant. A theoretical explanation for this finding would be that the economic benefits of proactive measures to prolong protection lay far ahead. As forecasts over a longer period of time tend to be more uncertain, it is likely that investors do not forecast that far. For example, some of the financial analysts interviewed were reluctant to add to the duration of exclusivity beyond the expiry of the primary patent, especially when conducting early valuations of products that were still under development.

Another finding was that the variables describing measures to obtain the best value for money with the company's IPR portfolio did not exhibit any significant impact on the dependent variable. A possible explanation is that investors do not explicitly consider the cost-effectiveness of companies' IPR management. One reason may be that investors looking for growth opportunities are generally more concerned with the revenue side. Furthermore, IPR costs are likely to provide a relatively small share of firms' R&D budgets.

Patent licensing activities, on the other hand, are found to be reflected in share prices – although in an unexpected manner when it comes to patent out-licensing. Surprisingly, the patent out-licensing activity variable exhibits a significantly negative impact on BHR, showing that the stock market discounts for firms being committed to patent out-licensing. The motives for patent out-licensing, however, are valued differently. While stock markets discount for the revenue motive, the product motive contributes to stock returns. This suggests that stock markets value patent out-licensing negatively in general, but not as a way of gaining access to the product market. Furthermore, the stock market is found to value patent in-licensing activity positively, but only for the product pipeline motive. These findings lead me to conclude that the stock market prefers firms to pursue a product-based business model.

The effects of the IPR management indicators are summarised in Table 5.46. The effects are summarised for the bivariate analysis and the multivariate analysis, including the full model in which all independent variables were included.

There are probably several reasons for the insignificant effects of many of the IPR management indicators are. Although one should be cautious in interpreting these results, the combination of both weak and insignificant effects could suggest that these indicators are not reflected in a company's share price. Indeed, some of the indicators even had a negative impact on the dependent variable, implying that the stock markets discount for companies being committed to IPR management. The findings of the exploratory study, showing that investors discount for lacking information, offer one possible explanation. Indeed, the METI (2004) has also argued that stock markets discount for companies' IPR management due to asymmetric information. The findings of the present study,

Table 5.46   Summary of findings – IPR management and stock market performance

Hypothesis	Variable	Bivariate	Multivariate	Full Model
FTO	FTO analysis	–	–	–
	Defensive blocking	N*	–	–
	FTO funding	–	–	–
Exclusivity	Patent protection	P***	P*	P*
	TM protection	–	N**	N*
	Exclusivity funding	N**	N**	N*
Duration	Secondary patents	N*	–	–
	TM communication	–	–	–
	IPR combination	–	–	–
Value for money	Portfolio reviews	N*	–	–
	IPR abandonment	–	–	–
Out-licensing	Out-licensing activity	N*	N***	N**
	Revenue motive	N**	N**	N***
	Product market motive	P*	P***	P***
In-licensing	In-licensing activity	P***	P***	P*
	Pipeline motive	P***	P***	P**
	FTO motive	–	–	–

Notes:
Significance Level: * $p<0.10$, ** $p<0.05$, *** $p<0.01$.
'N' stands for negative impact, 'P' for positive impact and '–' for no significant impact.

showing that companies can actually reduce stock market uncertainty by means of IPR reporting, give additional support to their statement.

A limit to the findings described above is that they do not tell us if information concerning the IPR management indicators examined had been disclosed, and thus was available to be processed by investors. This leaves us with the possibility that some of the indicators did not exhibit any significant impact on the dependent variable, either because investors did not perceive them to be value-relevant or simply because related information was not published. In a second step, complementary to the analysis of the stock market's valuation of pharmaceutical firms' IPR management, I therefore examined the stock market's reaction to companies' IPR reporting – that is, information disclosures in the public domain about the firm's IPR.

Turning to reporting about the IPR situation around the firm's product pipeline, I find that exclusively reporting significantly reduces return volatility. Taking this together with the finding that the use of patents for the protection of products has a positively significant impact on stock market returns, there are strong reasons to believe that such information is explicitly considered by investors. Secondly, it seems that investors also perceive information about certain proactive IPR management measures to be value-relevant, if expected benefits are not too far ahead. This is indicated by the secondary patent reporting variable, which in relation to products on the market exhibits a negative and significant impact on return volatility, but not in relation to products under development. Similarly, Urbig et al. (2011) argue that in the early clinical phases investors are likely to inadequately rely on information regarding the firm's ability to commercially benefit from an NPD project in the future, but do so increasingly as the event the information concerns gradually becomes nearer in time.

In addition, I find that investors generally discount for firms pursuing a licensing-based business model, but that reporting on firms' licensing activities is relatively limited, suggesting that this could be due to asymmetric information. The finding that reporting on the financial aspects of an out-licensing deal has a significant negative impact on return volatility gives support to this argument. Accordingly, a reduction in asymmetric information concerning firms pursuing a licensing-based business model should enable them to obtain funding at a lower cost and thereby reduce the costs of technological innovation. Similarly, companies can reduce uncertainty regarding their in-licensing deals by reporting on their exclusivity terms. Although the stock market is found to positively value in-licensing deals, additional reporting on this item seems to enhance the informational efficiency of stock markets. The effects of the IPR reporting indicators are summarised in Table 5.47.

Table 5.47   Summary of findings – IPR reporting and return volatility

Hypothesis	Variable	Bivariate	Multivariate	Full Model
Pipeline	Pdev exclusivity reporting	N**	N***	N**
reporting	Pdev duration reporting	–	N*	–
	Pdev FTO reporting	–	N*	–
Product	Prod exclusivity reporting	N*	–	–
reporting	Prod duration reporting	N**	N**	N**
	Prod FTO reporting	–	–	–
Out-	L-out financials	N*	N***	N**
licensing	L-out exclusivity	–	N*	–
reporting				
In-licensing	L-in financials	–	–	–
reporting	L-in exclusivity	–	N**	N**

Notes:
Significance Level: * p<0.10, ** p<0.05, *** p<0.01.
'N' stands for negative impact, 'P' for positive impact and '–' for no significant impact.

Taking the findings together, I conclude that there is asymmetric information regarding pharmaceutical firms' IPR management, which can at least partially be reduced by means of IPR reporting. On the whole, these findings provide a case for semi-strong stock market efficiency, meaning that prices adjust to reflect new IPR information made available in the public domain. However, there is no case for strong market efficiency, where prices also incorporate all information that is privately held (see, for example, Fama, 1970).

5.7   LIMITATIONS OF THE STUDY

Some limitations of the present study ought to be emphasised. The first is methodological. Like comparable studies, such as Lichtenthaler (2006) and Pangerl (2009), I rely on IPR management experts' rating of different Likert-type scale items for the operationalisation of the independent variables. Hence, my study is partly based on qualitative perceptions rather than hard numbers. This approach, however, was taken as the exploratory study revealed that most firms do not have any internal performance measurements for their IPR management. In economic terms, it was therefore not possible to draw conclusions on how much their IPR management contributes to stock market returns, nor how much IPR reporting reduces return volatility – leaving room for further research on this subject.

Secondly, throughout the literature on external reporting, the expectations of the stock market are problematic to assess. By this, I mean that it is difficult to know if reporting on an item provides positive or negative information as this depends on investors' expectations, which are often already priced based on speculation ex ante to the disclosure. As a way of dealing with this, I decided to examine whether regular disclosures reduce stock market uncertainty. This approach, however, did not enable me to distinguish between positive and negative valuation effects.

Thirdly, to conceptualise the different relationships between IPR reporting and stock market uncertainty, interviews were conducted with financial analysts. Analysts, however, only provide investment recommendations, and therefore only have an indirect impact on stock market valuations, since they do not allocate financial capital. Especially with the democratisation and complexity of capital markets, it was difficult to identify a suitable and representative group of interview partners. I decided to interview financial analysts because they could easily be identified through corporate reports and because empirical research shows that they contribute to the informational efficiency of capital markets. For example, empirical studies show that analysts' earnings forecasts and recommendations both have an impact on stock market valuations (see, for example, Francis and Soffer, 1997; Lys and Sohn, 1990). Taking the approach of interviewing financial analysts in order to operationalise the indicators used in this chapter therefore seemed reasonable.

Fourthly, it would have been preferable to conduct a panel regression analysis, not least because it would have enabled me to examine the potential of lagged valuation effects. This was, however, not possible for two main reasons. Firstly, many of the firms in my sample are rather young and had only been listed on the stock exchange for a few years. Hence, the examination of long-term valuation effects would not have been possible without excluding younger companies from the sample. As one of the main objectives of the present study was to investigate the access to capital markets of younger technology-driven firms – with potential financing constraints – this trade-off was considered to be necessary. In addition, in the absence of secondary data regarding companies' IPR management and reporting practices, I was unable to construct a panel dataset for the independent variables.

Finally, it should be noted that the results of the present study are not to be generalised beyond the pharmaceutical industry. This leaves room for plenty of further research on this subject.

NOTES

1. Bloomberg L.P. is a provider of financial services and financial markets data.
2. For example, in a similar study, Lichtenthaler (2006) finds that the response rate from German firms was relatively high.
3. Further objectives of patent searches, such as the identification of licensing opportunities and third party infringers, do not relate to R&D support and are described in the following sections.
4. The data for the respective years were added together into one observation, and divided by two, to obtain the average for 2008 and 2009.
5. Not least as the exploratory study reveals that all active licensing companies conduct a due diligence investigation of the patents before a deal is closed.
6. AIMR data is based on an annual survey on the basis of which analysts rate and rank firms according to their disclosure activities.
7. The findings of Seethamraju (2003) on trademark acquisitions thus also seem to apply to patents.
8. I use the average of the years 2008 and 2009.

APPENDIX

Table 5.A1   Bivariate analysis – 'FTO'

	(1)	(2)	(3)	(4)	(5)	(6)	(7)	(8)	(9)	(10)	(11)	(12)	(13)	(14)
BHR (1)	1.000													
Firm size (2)	0.000	1.000												
Revenue growth (3)	0.304**	−0.043	1.000											
R&D intensity (4)	−0.116	−0.075	−0.146	1.000										
Patent intensity (5)	−0.016	−0.067	−0.115	0.883***	1.000									
Trademark intensity (6)	−0.229*	−0.112	−0.190	0.592***	0.440***	1.000								
Products on the market (7)	0.396***	0.322**	−0.110	−0.287**	−0.240**	−0.335**	1.000							
Product pipeline (8)	−0.013	0.299**	−0.122	−0.044	0.013	−0.118	0.413***	1.000						
Net issue of shares (9)	−0.286**	−0.105	−0.134	0.416***	0.186	0.509***	−0.303**	−0.292**	1.000					
Dividends (10)	−0.100	−0.029	−0.055	−0.083	−0.073	−0.123	0.258**	0.187	−0.112	1.000				
Region dummy (11)	−0.150	−0.125	0.257**	0.093	0.091	−0.078	−0.282**	−0.111	−0.028	−0.184	1.000			
Patent searches (12)	−0.105	−0.103	−0.056	0.104	0.078	−0.131	−0.131	0.096	0.097	0.048	0.027	1.000		
Defensive blocking (13)	−0.199*	−0.183	−0.043	0.129	0.104	0.109	−0.180	−0.079	0.298**	0.073	0.051	0.252**	1.000	
FTO funding (14)	−0.114	−0.030	−0.304**	0.185	0.182	0.092	−0.064	0.133	0.181	0.049	−0.138	0.476***	0.207*	1.000

Note: Significance Level: * $p < 0.10$, ** $p < 0.05$, *** $p < 0.01$.

Table 5.A2   Bivariate analysis – 'FTO and patent lawsuits'

	(1)	(2)	(3)	(4)
Patent lawsuits (1)	1.000			
Patent searches (2)	−0.277**	1.000		
Defensive blocking (3)	−0.190	0.252**	1.000	
FTO funding (4)	−0.362**	0.476***	0.207*	1.000

Note: Significance Level: * $p<0.10$, ** $p<0.05$, *** $p<0.01$.

Table 5.A3 Bivariate analysis – 'Exclusivity'

	(1)	(2)	(3)	(4)	(5)	(6)	(7)	(8)	(9)	(10)	(11)	(12)	(13)	(14)
BHR (1)	1.000													
Firm size (2)	0.000	1.000												
Revenue growth (3)	0.304**	-0.043	1.000											
R&D intensity (4)	-0.116	-0.075	-0.146	1.000										
Patent intensity (5)	-0.016	-0.067	-0.115	0.883***	1.000									
Trademark intensity (6)	-0.229*	-0.112	-0.190	0.592***	0.440***	1.000								
Products on the market (7)	0.396***	0.322**	-0.110	-0.287**	-0.240**	-0.335**	1.000							
Product pipeline (8)	-0.013	0.299**	-0.122	-0.044	0.013	-0.118	0.413***	1.000						
Net issue of shares (9)	-0.286**	-0.105	-0.134	0.416***	0.186	0.509***	-0.303**	-0.292**	1.000					
Dividends (10)	-0.100	-0.029	-0.055	-0.083	-0.073	-0.123	0.258**	0.187	-0.112	1.000				
Region dummy (11)	-0.150	-0.125	0.257**	0.093	0.091	-0.078	-0.282*	-0.111	-0.028	-0.184	1.000			
Patent protection (12)	0.423***	-0.074	0.304**	-0.226*	-0.135	-0.390***	0.161	-0.120	-0.374**	-0.016	0.062	1.000		
Trademark protection (13)	0.023	0.188	-0.053	-0.114	-0.092	0.077	0.379***	-0.073	-0.037	-0.093	-0.044	0.028	1.000	
Exclusivity funding (14)	-0.314**	0.221**	0.056	0.192	0.153	0.114	-0.321	-0.142	0.213*	-0.224*	0.043	-0.149	0.051	1.000

Note: Significance Level: * $p<0.10$, ** $p<0.05$, *** $p<0.01$.

Table 5.A4 Bivariate analysis – 'Duration'

	(1)	(2)	(3)	(4)	(5)	(6)	(7)	(8)	(9)	(10)	(11)	(12)	(13)	(14)
BHR (1)	1.000													
Firm size (2)	0.000	1.000												
Revenue growth (3)	0.304**	-0.043	1.000											
R&D intensity (4)	-0.116	-0.075	-0.146	1.000										
Patent intensity (5)	-0.016	-0.067	-0.115	0.883***	1.000									
Trademark intensity (6)	-0.229*	-0.112	-0.190	0.592***	0.440***	1.000								
Products on the market (7)	0.396***	0.322**	-0.110	-0.287**	-0.240**	-0.335**	1.000							
Product pipeline (8)	-0.013	0.299**	-0.122	-0.044	0.013	-0.118	0.413***	1.000						
Net issue of shares (9)	-0.286*	-0.105	-0.134	0.416***	0.186	0.509***	-0.303**	-0.292**	1.000					
Dividends (10)	-0.100	-0.029	-0.055	-0.083	-0.073	-0.123	0.258**	0.187	-0.112	1.000				
Region dummy (11)	-0.150	-0.125	0.257**	0.093	0.091	-0.078	-0.282**	-0.111	-0.028	-0.184	1.000			
Patent prolong (12)	-0.200*	-0.042	0.156	0.164	0.150	0.101	-0.387***	-0.178	0.091	-0.090	0.113	1.000		
TM communication (13)	0.135	0.211*	0.141	0.052	0.107	0.017	0.262**	-0.078	0.062	-0.045	-0.030	-0.034	1.000	
IPR combination (14)	0.091	0.174	0.076	0.006	-0.008	-0.018	0.382***	-0.065	-0.039	0.167	-0.165	-0.018	0.520***	1.000

Note: Significance Level: * $p<0.10$, ** $p<0.05$, *** $p<0.01$.

Table 5.A5   Bivariate analysis – 'Value for money'

	(1)	(2)	(3)	(4)	(5)	(6)	(7)	(8)	(9)	(10)	(11)	(12)	(13)
BHR (1)	1.000												
Firm size (2)	0.000	1.000											
Revenue growth (3)	0.304**	−0.043	1.000										
R&D intensity (4)	−0.116	−0.075	−0.146	1.000									
Patent intensity (5)	−0.016	−0.067	−0.115	0.883***	1.000								
Trademark intensity (6)	−0.229*	−0.112	−0.190	0.592***	0.440***	1.000							
Products on the market (7)	0.396***	0.322**	−0.110	−0.287**	−0.240**	−0.335**	1.000						
Product pipeline (8)	−0.013	0.299**	−0.122	−0.044	0.013	−0.118	0.413***	1.000					
Net issue of shares (9)	−0.286*	−0.105	−0.134	0.416***	0.186	0.509***	−0.303***	−0.292**	1.000				
Dividends (10)	−0.100	−0.029	−0.055	−0.083	−0.073	−0.123	0.258**	0.187	−0.112	1.000			
Region dummy (11)	−0.150	−0.125	0.257**	0.093	0.091	−0.078	−0.282**	−0.111	−0.028	−0.184	1.000		
Portfolio reviews (12)	−0.213*	−0.008	0.086	0.045	−0.009	−0.013	−0.244**	0.098	−0.091	0.027	0.155	1.000	
IPR abandonment (13)	−0.176	0.069	−0.016	−0.343**	−0.314**	−0.436***	0.078	0.033	−0.097	0.232**	0.144	0.349**	1.000

Note: Significance Level: * p<0.10, ** p<0.05, *** p<0.01.

216

Table 5.A6   Bivariate analysis – 'Out-licensing'

	(1)	(2)	(3)	(4)	(5)	(6)	(7)	(8)	(9)	(10)	(11)	(12)	(13)	(14)
BHR (1)	1.000													
Firm size (2)	0.000	1.000												
Revenue growth (3)	0.304**	−0.043	1.000											
R&D intensity (4)	−0.116	−0.075	−0.146	1.000										
Patent intensity (5)	−0.016	−0.067	−0.115	0.883***	1.000									
Trademark intensity (6)	−0.229*	−0.112	−0.190	0.592***	0.440***	1.000								
Products on the market (7)	0.396***	0.322**	−0.110	−0.287**	−0.240**	−0.335**	1.000							
Product pipeline (8)	−0.013	0.299**	−0.122	−0.044	0.013	−0.118	0.413***	1.000						
Net issue of shares (9)	−0.286**	−0.105	−0.134	0.416***	0.186	0.509***	−0.303**	−0.292**	1.000					
Dividends (10)	−0.100	−0.029	−0.055	−0.083	−0.073	−0.123	0.258**	0.187	−0.112	1.000				
Region dummy (11)	−0.150	−0.125	0.257**	0.093	0.091	−0.078	−0.282**	−0.111	−0.028	−0.184	1.000			
Out-licensing activity (12)	−0.201*	0.212*	−0.041	−0.102	−0.108	−0.066	0.119	0.206*	−0.061	−0.100	−0.168	1.000		
Revenue motive (13)	−0.308**	−0.162	−0.095	0.132	0.104	0.039	−0.338**	0.019	0.158	−0.282**	0.049	0.399***	1.000	
Product market motive (14)	0.216*	−0.209*	0.085	0.117	0.069	0.077	−0.282**	−0.088	0.062	−0.177	0.079	0.122	0.469***	1.000

Note: Significance Level: * $p<0.10$, ** $p<0.05$, *** $p<0.01$.

Table 5.A7 Bivariate analysis – 'In-licensing'

	(1)	(2)	(3)	(4)	(5)	(6)	(7)	(8)	(9)	(10)	(11)	(12)	(13)	(14)
BHR (1)	1.000													
Firm size (2)	0.000	1.000												
Revenue growth (3)	0.304**	−0.043	1.000											
R&D intensity (4)	−0.116	−0.075	−0.146	1.000										
Patent intensity (5)	−0.016	−0.067	−0.115	0.883***	1.000									
Trademark intensity (6)	−0.229**	−0.112	−0.190	0.592***	0.440***	1.000								
Products on the market (7)	0.396***	0.322**	−0.110	−0.287**	−0.240**	−0.335**	1.000							
Product pipeline (8)	−0.013	0.299**	−0.122	−0.044	0.013	−0.118	0.413***	1.000						
Net issue of shares (9)	−0.286**	−0.105	−0.134	0.416***	0.186	0.509***	−0.303**	−0.292**	1.000					
Dividends (10)	−0.100	−0.029	−0.055	−0.083	−0.073	−0.123	0.258**	0.187	−0.112	1.000				
Region dummy (11)	−0.150	−0.125	0.257**	0.093	0.091	−0.078	−0.282**	−0.111	−0.028	−0.184	1.000			
In-licensing activity (12)	0.481***	0.375***	0.134	−0.239**	−0.1751	−0.284**	0.500***	0.297**	−0.296**	−0.129	−0.055	1.000		
Product pipeline motive (13)	0.414***	0.206*	0.080	−0.265**	−0.163	−0.075	0.276**	0.164	−0.215*	0.001	−0.222*	0.463***	1.000	
FTO motive (14)	−0.005	0.056	0.084	−0.060	0.027	−0.159	0.119	0.163	0.019	0.107	0.003	0.135	0.252***	1.000

Note: Significance Level: * $p<0.10$, ** $p<0.05$, *** $p<0.01$.

Table 5.A8   Bivariate analysis – 'IPR pipeline reporting'

	(1)	(2)	(3)	(4)	(5)	(6)	(7)	(8)	(9)	(10)	(11)	(12)	(13)	(14)
Volatility (1)	1.000													
Firm size (2)	-0.236**	1.000												
Revenue growth (3)	0.241**	-0.043	1.000											
R&D intensity (4)	0.412***	-0.075	-0.146	1.000										
Patent intensity (5)	0.431***	-0.067	-0.115	0.883***	1.000									
Trademark intensity (6)	0.241**	-0.112	-0.190	0.592***	0.440***	1.000								
Products on the market (7)	-0.457***	0.322**	-0.110	-0.287**	-0.240**	-0.335**	1.000							
Firm age (8)	-0.328**	0.244**	-0.151	-0.066	0.005	-0.207*	0.381***	1.000						
Market-to-book (9)	-0.028	-0.090	-0.066	0.105	0.126	0.197*	-0.317**	-0.154	1.000					
Trading volume (10)	-0.205*	0.679***	-0.027	-0.042	-0.014	-0.101	0.244**	0.269**	-0.050	1.000				
Region dummy (11)	0.357**	-0.125	0.257**	0.093	0.091	-0.078	-0.282**	-0.128	0.045	0.010	1.000			
Pdev exclusivity reporting (12)	-0.261**	-0.134	-0.059	-0.081	-0.057	-0.183	-0.021	0.169	0.062	-0.106	0.202*	1.000		
Pdev duration reporting (13)	-0.161	-0.090	-0.033	-0.025	0.005	-0.058	0.057	0.083	-0.032	-0.079	0.046	0.564***	1.000	
Pdev FTO reporting (14)	-0.028	-0.086	0.204*	-0.019	-0.044	-0.066	-0.157	-0.194	-0.132	-0.110	0.074	0.241**	0.292**	1.000

Note: Significance Level: * p<0.10, ** p<0.05, *** p<0.01.

Table 5.A9 Bivariate analysis – 'IPR product reporting'

	(1)	(2)	(3)	(4)	(5)	(6)	(7)	(8)	(9)	(10)	(11)	(12)	(13)	(14)
Volatility (1)	1.000													
Firm size (2)	-0.236**	1.000												
Revenue growth (3)	0.241**	-0.043	1.000											
R&D intensity (4)	0.412***	-0.075	-0.146	1.000										
Patent intensity (5)	0.431***	-0.067	-0.115	0.883***	1.000									
Trademark intensity (6)	0.241**	-0.112	-0.190	0.592***	0.440***	1.000								
Products on the market (7)	-0.457***	0.322**	-0.110	-0.287**	-0.240**	-0.335**	1.000							
Firm age (8)	-0.328**	0.244**	-0.151	-0.066	0.005	-0.207*	0.381***	1.000						
Market-to-book (9)	-0.028	-0.090	-0.066	0.105	0.126	0.197*	-0.317**	-0.154	1.000					
Trading volume (10)	-0.205*	0.679***	-0.027	-0.042	-0.014	-0.101	0.244**	0.269**	-0.050	1.000				
Region dummy (11)	0.357**	-0.125	0.257**	0.093	0.091	-0.078	-0.282**	-0.128	0.045	0.010	1.000			
Prod exclusivity reporting (12)	-0.242*	0.106	0.132	0.043	-0.127	-0.075	-0.123	0.158	0.245*	0.267*	0.133	1.000		
Prod duration reporting (13)	-0.296**	-0.177	-0.023	0.042	-0.072	-0.064	-0.145	-0.076	0.242*	-0.025	0.099	0.491***	1.000	
Prod FTO reporting (14)	-0.070	-0.067	0.077	0.055	0.147	-0.020	-0.146	-0.014	0.215	0.180	0.193	0.439**	0.401**	1.000

Note: Significance Level: * p<0.10, ** p<0.05, *** p<0.01.

Table 5.A10   Bivariate analysis – 'Out-licensing reporting'

	(1)	(2)	(3)	(4)	(5)	(6)	(7)	(8)	(9)	(10)	(11)	(12)	(13)
Volatility (1)	1.000												
Firm size (2)	-0.236**	1.000											
Revenue growth (3)	0.241**	-0.043	1.000										
R&D intensity (4)	0.412***	-0.075	-0.146	1.000									
Patent intensity (5)	0.431***	-0.067	-0.115	0.883***	1.000								
Trademark intensity (6)	0.241**	-0.112	-0.190	0.592***	0.440***	1.000							
Products on the market (7)	-0.457***	0.322**	-0.110	-0.287**	-0.240**	-0.335**	1.000						
Firm age (8)	-0.328**	0.244**	-0.151	-0.066	0.005	-0.207*	0.381***	1.000					
Market-to-book (9)	-0.028	-0.090	-0.066	0.105	0.126	0.197*	-0.317**	-0.154	1.000				
Trading volume (10)	-0.205*	0.679***	-0.027	-0.042	-0.014	-0.101	0.244**	0.269**	-0.050	1.000			
Region dummy (11)	0.357***	-0.125	0.257**	0.093	0.091	-0.078	-0.282**	-0.128	0.045	0.010	1.000		
Lout financials (12)	-0.250*	-0.196	-0.059	-0.162	-0.073	-0.289**	-0.275*	0.006	0.158	-0.144	0.082	1.000	
Lout exclusivity (13)	-0.146	-0.243*	-0.071	0.249*	0.104	0.016	-0.289**	0.078	0.224	-0.192	0.066	0.540***	1.000

Note: Significance Level: * p<0.10, ** p<0.05, *** p<0.01.

221

Table 5.A11 Bivariate analysis – 'In-licensing reporting'

	(1)	(2)	(3)	(4)	(5)	(6)	(7)	(8)	(9)	(10)	(11)	(12)	(13)
Volatility (1)	1.000												
Firm size (2)	−0.236**	1.000											
Revenue growth (3)	0.241**	−0.043	1.000										
R&D intensity (4)	0.412***	−0.075	−0.146	1.000									
Patent intensity (5)	0.431***	−0.067	−0.115	0.883***	1.000								
Trademark intensity (6)	0.241**	−0.112	−0.190	0.592***	0.440***	1.000							
Products on the market (7)	−0.457***	0.322**	−0.110	−0.287**	−0.240**	−0.335**	1.000						
Firm age (8)	−0.328**	0.244**	−0.151	−0.066	0.005	−0.207*	0.381***	1.000					
Market-to-book (9)	−0.028	−0.090	−0.066	0.105	0.126	0.197*	−0.317**	−0.154	1.000				
Trading volume (10)	−0.205*	0.679***	−0.027	−0.042	−0.014	−0.101	0.244**	0.269**	−0.050	1.000			
Region dummy (11)	0.357**	−0.125	0.257**	0.093	0.091	−0.078	−0.282**	−0.128	0.045	0.010	1.000		
Lin financials (12)	0.034	−0.146	0.198	−0.057	−0.123	−0.180	−0.227	−0.017	−0.160	−0.126	0.258*	1.000	
Lin exclusivity (13)	−0.204	−0.071	−0.007	0.236*	0.068	−0.009	−0.140	0.131	−0.144	−0.027	0.074	0.439***	1.000

Note: Significance Level: * $p<0.10$, ** $p<0.05$, *** $p<0.01$.

6. Towards forward-looking financial reporting

This chapter reviews the phenomenon of the intangible economy, and its implications. In doing so, it summarises the main findings of the present study, aiming to link the managerial aspects of intangibles to their capital market implications. Finally, I make some policy recommendations in the context of financial reporting, aimed at enhancing the informational efficiency of capital markets and reducing the costs of financing technological innovation.

6.1 THE IMPLICATIONS OF AN INTANGIBLE ECONOMY

> Today, we are witnessing a broad shift from an industrial economy to a more service based one; a shift from bricks and mortar to technology and knowledge. This has important ramifications for our disclosure and financial reporting models. (Jeffrey Garten, quoted in Upton, 2003, p. 483)

The present study has examined the implications of the shift from an industrial economy towards an intangible economy, from a capital market perspective. It has done so against a background of past research showing this shift to have contributed to the deterioration of the value-relevance of financial statements. Over the past decades, technological innovation has driven change in various industries – such as electronics, communications, pharmaceuticals, biotechnology, and so on. For example, Lev and Zarowin (1999) find US firms to have experienced an increasing pace of business change over the past 20 years – a trend which is found to be associated with increasing R&D intensity. In addition, they find that the decreasing informativeness of earnings releases is related to both business change and R&D intensity. They conclude that change-drivers, such as technological innovation, also provide drivers for the declining usefulness of financial information. Chang (1998) also finds that the decline in the value-relevance of financial statements is explained by a surge in innovation. Still, IAS require companies to expense all investments in research, and the US GAAP advocates that firms expense both research and development outlays immediately, regardless of their economic benefits – with an exemption for software R&D after technological feasibility (see Section 2.8.1). Accordingly, research scholars have argued that corporate annual reports do not provide sufficient quantitative or qualitative information on intangible assets to the public domain (see, for example, Nakanishi, 2007).

This has consequences for the informational efficiency of capital markets. For example, Aboody and Lev (2000) find that gains from insider trading are comparatively higher in technology-driven firms. They argue that this is due to asymmetric information regarding firms' R&D, meaning that public information fails to directly capture the productivity and value of intangible investments. This information problem has several implications. Firstly, as noted by Lev (2001), lacking information about intangible assets makes technology-driven companies more difficult to value. Hence, the information problem is associated with a valuation problem. Secondly, Chan et al. (2001) find that stock markets perceive additional uncertainty related to R&D-intensive firms. They argue that this is a result of stock markets having insufficient information for the valuation of these companies, which in turn creates uncertainty. This, according to Chung et al. (2005), could lead to higher costs of capital for technology-driven companies, as investors price protect for uncertainty. Indeed, research has also shown that R&D-intensive companies are systematically undervalued, meaning that they face relatively high costs of equity (see, for example, Eberhardt et al., 2004). Consequently, the financing of technological innovation will be relatively expensive.

Although a substantial amount of research has pointed at the value-relevance of patent, trademark as well as R&D-related information, and its potential to bridge the uncertainty regarding the economic value of intangible assets, this information is disclosed in a highly dispersed manner. R&D investments are sometimes expensed and sometimes capitalised, depending on the financial reporting regime and the precise nature of the investment (see Section 2.8.1). This means that these investments are sometimes found on the balance sheet, and sometimes appear as costs in the income statement. Patent and trademark information, on the other hand, is mainly available in public search databases, which require certain skills to use. In addition, the assessment of the obtainable information also requires specific knowledge not only of the technology field to be able to understand its content, but also about the IPR system.

Moreover, the increasing pace of strategic patenting, leading to an ever increasing share of lemon patents, has implications for the use of patent information in a valuation context. Because the vast amount of patent applications are of relatively low value, this is likely to create a distorted picture of the value of companies. However, although low value patents do not much contribute to firm productivity, they can be of strategic relevance in safeguarding a company's competitive position. For example, patents may be used to increase a firm's bargaining power in relation to a third party, or simply to secure FTO. For this reason, IPR needs to be considered within the context of companies' business models, rather than as a separately instrument. Assessing IPR in a managerial context may require access to private information, as there are no mandatory disclosure requirements for companies to report on most related items. The present study has, however, argued that inadequate financial reporting forms only part of the problem. While the measurement constraints of the intangible economy have been widely acknowledged, the main focus has been on the inadequacy of information provided in financial statements. But the lack of conceptual frameworks for how profits are generated from technological innovation seems to be just as notable. For example, the link between tangible assets and firm value is relatively intuitive and well established in the literature. Comparatively little is known about how technology-driven companies materialise their R&D investments. The result is a situation not only in which insufficient information is provided in the public domain, but where capital market participants also have inadequate instruments to assess the economic value of companies' growth opportunities. The latter is evident from research conducted by Amir et al. (1999), who find that technology-driven firms are covered by comparatively many financial analysts, suggesting that they are more difficult to value, together with findings showing that capital market participants do not even consider intangible assets as meaningful determinants in their investment decisions (see, for example, Ughetto, 2007).

Asymmetric information and the lack of conceptual frameworks to assess firm performance, stemming from an increasingly intangible economy, have left investors deprived when assessing the value of these firms, implying a need for new measurements to enable them to assess the future financial performance of technology-driven firms and to allocate financial capital productively (see, for example, Lev, 2001). In line with this reasoning, the present study has argued that there are two sides of the coin to enhancing the allocation of financial capital towards technological innovation. Firstly, a better understanding is needed of both value creation and value appropriation in an intangible economy, in order to provide capital market participants with a framework for assessing companies' financial performance, especially in terms of their ability to generate future economic returns based on their intangible investments. Secondly, it is essential for investors to be able to communicate related information. This, however, requires that investors know which kinds of indicators to look for, and sums up the scientific objective of this study, which has been to link the managerial implications of the intangible economy to the capital market implications, in order to (a) enhance the understanding of firms' systematic use of IPR – commercially and strategically – to gain and sustain technology-based competitive advantages, referred to as IPR management; and (b) suggest venues for communication of such information to corporate outsiders.

In Chapter 2, I identify two avenues for communicating IPR information to the capital market, which have received almost no or very little attention among research scholars. Firstly, the concept of screening is well established in the literature as a mean of reducing asymmetric information. To facilitate the screening process in public capital markets, information intermediaries, such as CRAs, have been established. These gather information that is filtered down to a rating on the creditworthiness of a company. Moreover, CRAs have access to certain private information when making these assessments, suggesting they have a potentially important function in contributing to the informational efficiency of capital markets. In the present study, I therefore examined whether corporate credit ratings incorporate, and thus communicate, patent value (Chapter 3). The objective was hereby to assess the contribution of CRAs to the informational efficiency of capital markets in an intangible economy. To my knowledge, this was also the first study to examine patent value indicators from a debt market perspective.

Secondly, following extensive research on how relevant it is for companies to signal their type to the capital market, I look at the potential for companies to do so through voluntary information disclosures. This was examined in two steps where I first looked at how technology-driven firms in the pharmaceutical industry use their IPR to support their business model (Chapter 4), in order to develop a conceptual framework describing how they generate future economic returns from their intangible investments. Based on these findings, I examined whether companies' IPR management is reflected in stock markets' valuations, and if the disclosure of such information contributes to the informational efficiency of stock markets in a second step (Chapter 5). This approach enabled me to investigate whether firms signalling commitment to IPR management reduces stock market uncertainty. The reason why I decided to look at voluntary disclosure is that disclosure regimes were found to be relatively restrictive in what they require firms to report on in relation to their IPR. My main findings are described in the following section.

6.2 MAIN FINDINGS OF THE PRESENT STUDY

Firstly, in Chapter 3, I examined the valuation of patents by CRAs. This was done to shed light on the role of patent valuation within the context of CRA credit risk assessments. On the basis of extensive past research on the stock market's valuation of patents, and their contribution to productivity gains, it was hypothesised that a larger patent output and a more valuable patent portfolio – in terms of a higher average number of forward citations and a large average family size – is associated with lower credit risk, and thus with higher corporate credit ratings. This was tested based on a panel dataset, including 191 US firms, receiving credit ratings from 1990 to 2001, using the DTI Scoreboard. Data on patents and corporate credit ratings were added from the EPO Worldwide Statistical Database (PATSTAT) and Standard & Poor's COMPUSTAT North America database.

The results show that patents are valued differently in CRA credit risk assessments than by stock markets. Patent flows had a substantial impact on corporate credit rating, while patent family size had only a marginal effect. In addition, forward citations had a negative impact on firms' rating. It was argued that the negative impact of the forward citations variable is due to its association with a higher risk of patent lawsuits. I conclude that CRAs consider patents as insurance against lawsuits rather than in terms of innovation output. This finding suggests that CRAs do not contribute to informational efficiency as expected, in terms of communicating patent value as growth opportunities to investors.

Chapter 4 explored how pharmaceutical firms manage their IPR, their external IPR reporting practices, and the perceived value-relevance of IPR information among financial analysts. The objective was to create a better understanding of how technology-driven companies generate economic returns on their intangible investments, by providing a conceptual framework on the basis of which indicators of their profit potential could be derived, but also to examine the potential of IPR reporting to reduce their costs of capital. In a first step, exploratory interviews were conducted with 21 IPR management experts in the industry, at 19 different firms. As past research has suggested that IPR management is an industry-specific task, I decided to limit my study to the pharmaceutical industry, where past research has shown that both patents (see, for example, Arundel and Kabla, 1998; Bessen and Meurer, 2008a; Lanjouw, 1998) and trademarks (see, for example, Malmberg, 2005; Sandner and Block, 2011) are of relatively high importance to the financial performance of firms, suggesting it to be a good starting point.

The study revealed some interesting findings, in terms of both how pharmaceutical companies manage their IPR and how IPR management as a task contributes to their financial performance. Notably, I find IPR management to be attached to the product lifecycle. Hence, IPR management is not to be seen as a standalone task, but is rather to be considered within the framework of product management. Moreover, the IPR management experts revealed several ways in which a company's IPR management could contribute to its financial performance. From a capital market perspective, related information ought to be value-relevant. Within investment analysis, the use of IPR management information should therefore relate to how companies' IPR management contributes to firm performance, which is described below.

Firstly, I find that firms manage their IPR to support their internal R&D, in terms of securing FTO, which enables them to commercialise new products without infringing third party patents. This finding is in line with past research showing FTO to be an important motive to patent (see, for example, Grindley and Teece, 1997; Lichtenthaler, 2006) for companies to reduce the risk of infringing third party patents by the event of product commercialisation (see, for example, Blind et al., 2006; Cohen et al., 2002; European Commission, 2009). Because patent lawsuits impose a risk also on investors, information on corporate policies and measures to secure FTO ought to be value-relevant.

Secondly, companies manage their IPR to support their internal R&D, in terms of maximising exclusivity in the appropriation process, and thereby increase the profitability of their R&D investments. From a resource-based point of view, IPR are therefore important to enable firms to establish competitive advantages in making technology resources imperfectly imitable (see, for example, Barney, 1991), by raising the costs of imitation (Levin et al., 1987; Mansfield et al., 1981). In doing so, IPR provide important isolation mechanisms, postulated as crucial to firm performance by resource-based theorists (see, for example, Grant, 1991; Wernerfelt, 1984). Hence, the protection of products and technologies from imitation is the most important motive for companies that patent (see, for example, Blind et al., 2006). From a capital market perspective, related information could help investors determine the potential profitability of a company's investments.

Thirdly, firms manage their IPR to extend the duration of exclusivity, contributing to the sustainability of the competitive advantages created, and thus to the profitability of their R&D investments. In the strategic management literature, the sustainability of firms' competitive advantages has been widely emphasised as key to the financial performance of firms (see, for example, Barney, 1991; Porter, 1985; Rumelt, 1984). From an IPR management perspective, this means that a firm's IPR must support the sustainability of its competitive advantages by making its products imperfectly imitable throughout the product lifecycle. Empirical studies have accordingly shown that pharmaceutical firms heavily rely on IPR (Arundel and Kabla, 1998) to support their product market strategy of safeguarding their product market shares (European Commission, 2009). Like the use of IPR to obtain exclusivity in the first place, measures to extend its duration will make an untimely contribution to the profitability of the company. Related information should therefore be value-relevant, especially to value-investors looking for long-term returns.

Fourthly, firms manage their IPR to make effective use of their R&D budget, in terms of abandoning irrelevant IPR, thereby reducing costs. Studies have shown that IPR protection is expensive to obtain, but also to maintain (European Commission, 2007). This means that firms ought to be concerned about the costs related to their IPR portfolio, especially since an extensive IPR portfolio is not necessarily associated with better financial performance. For example, Reitzig (2004b) finds that patent fences in discrete technologies are only value enhancing if substitute technologies are easily accessible. It has accordingly been argued that firm performance depends on the use of fewer patents, linked to the firm's overall strategy, while patents that are not essentially provide cost-drivers (Bhatia and Carey, 2007). Findings by Grindley and Teece (1997) support this view by showing that the value of a firm's patents depends on their alignment with technology fields where the firm possesses particular strengths. Accordingly, investors ought to be concerned about the cost side of companies' IPR portfolios – not least because firms which are committed to making more effective use of their financial resources will also likely provide better investment targets.

Fifthly, companies manage their IPR to access external R&D, and to acquire new growth potential. This is in line with Chesbrough and Teece (1996), who argue that only a few firms can afford to develop all the technologies that might provide a competitive advantage internally, and therefore need to acquire external proprietary technology resources to maintain their technological edge. Moreover, research shows that the pharmaceutical industry exhibits the highest share of firms that perceive patent in-licensing as increasingly important (Sheehan et al., 2004). In particular, pharmaceutical firms with relatively thin product pipelines are found to be more likely to license-in proprietary external technologies to bridge internal weaknesses as well as build new strengths in terms of the accumulation of external technology resources (Higgins and Rodriguez, 2006). By bridging internal weaknesses and building new strengths, or acquiring growth opportunities, companies are likely to become more profitable in the future. Related information should therefore signal future returns to investors.

Finally, firms manage their IPR to commercialise their internal R&D, without carrying the costs of product development. Due to increasing specialisation in different stages of the R&D process, firms collaborate in technology-based product development (Rothaermel and Deeds, 2004). This is true not least of the pharmaceutical industry, where the integration of biotechnology into the development of pharmaceutical products has led to the formation of specialised DBFs, focusing on early stage product development. Because these firms rely on collaboration partners to finance their research activities, patent licensing provides an integral part of their business model (Farag, 2009). Gassmann et al. (2010) accordingly argue that the competitive advantage of DBFs depends on having IPR for out-licensing purposes. Because out-licensing is associated with future cash-flows, related information should be value-relevant.

The relationships described above between firms' IPR management and their financial performance suggested some ways to derive new measurements to assess the ability of a company to generate economic returns based on its R&D investments. In a second step, the perceived value-relevance of these among capital market participants was therefore examined through additional exploratory interviews, this time with 12 financial analysts. This was done also to address the possibility of IPR management information being neglected due to a lack of awareness of its value-relevance.

Interestingly, I find that analysts do not consider IPR as such. Rather they do so in relation to products, throughout their respective lifecycles. More specifically, they analyse the IPR situation upfront to two specific events – that is, marketing authorisation and expiry of the primary patent. These analyses mainly concern whether sufficient patent protection has been obtained for product commercialisation and whether any lifecycle management measures have been taken to prolong appropriation beyond the expiration of the primary patent.

Furthermore, analysts consider technology flows, in terms of patent in- and out-licensing deals. Turning to patent licensing, the interviews show that licensing deals are valued on the basis of their financial terms. For example, from an out-licensing perspective, a high royalty rate indicates future economic benefits to come. Accordingly, the financial analysts interviewed reveal that reporting on the royalty rate in a licensing agreement substantially reduces uncertainty about the potential economic benefits of the deal, especially if the company follows a licensing-based business model.

Overall, however, it can be said that financial analysts are more concerned with the results of companies' IPR management than with detailed information about their practices. For example, information on companies' IPR policies was not requested by analysts. Moreover, in many cases, the analysts' knowledge of certain IPR management tasks was found to be relatively limited. In particular, FTO was found to be of concern to only a few analysts, and the risks related to not having secured FTO were neither well-known nor much considered, although this was on average named as the most important objective of the interviewed firms' IPR management. This suggests some obstacles in communication between companies and financial analysts when it comes to IPR management.

Notable also is the consequence of firms failing to provide such information, making analysts discount for related uncertainty. As analysts mainly rely on voluntary information disclosures for their assessments, this indeed suggests that IPR reporting has an impact on companies' costs of capital. Accordingly, it is even more important that IPR management information is provided in a systematic, accurate and comprehensive manner. By this I mean that companies regularly disclose not only good news or half-truths, and that the information provided enables capital market participants to form an opinion about the company's future profit potential. This is crucial not least since the firms interviewed reveal that they do not provide any detailed information about their IPR which capital market participants could use to make their own assessments. Instead, capital markets rely on internal assessments made by the company, and accurate related reporting. Ensuring that companies' IPR reporting is systematic, accurate, and sufficiently comprehensive should therefore be a major priority for policy makers.

Chapter 5 went on to examine the informational efficiency of stock markets in terms of how well they reflect companies' IPR management, and the ability of companies to reduce uncertainty through IPR reporting. The objective was to assess whether investors recognise the future economic benefits of companies' IPR management, and whether additional IPR reporting can help reduce asymmetric information related to technology-driven firms. Accordingly, the chapter examined two main questions:

- Do share prices reflect information on firms' IPR management?
- Can firms reduce stock market uncertainty through IPR reporting?

To answer the first question, a set of IPR management indicators was derived, based on the exploratory interviews described in Chapter 4, and examined in terms of their impact on the buy–hold return (BHR) of pharmaceutical companies' shares. It should be noted that this study was conducted on the assumption that the derived IPR management indicators provide value-relevant information. This assumption, however, is based on evidence from the exploratory study, which provides its theoretical foundation. Furthermore, several studies have previously found IPR information to be value-relevant (see Section 2.4), giving this assumption some additional support.

My findings suggest that most IPR management indicators are not reflected in companies' share price, although some are. At first sight, it was difficult to find a common denominator for the indicators that exhibited a significant impact on the dependent variable – that is, companies' BHR. The general pattern, however, seems to be that indicators with a significant impact are those for which related information had presumably been communicated more extensively to the stock market, probably upon request. For example, I find that the use of patents to protect products has a significant impact on companies' share price, while the strategic use of patents has not. I argue that this is because patents which are linked to a product are likely to have received more public attention. This argument is in line with the findings of Austin (1993), who shows that patents linked to products, and which have received attention in *The Wall Street Journal*, receive relatively high valuations. However, the conducted exploration showed that only a few companies report on the strategic aspects of their IPR. Hence, information on the relevance of specific patents within a strategic context is only rarely available in the public domain. Moreover, financial analysts were found to be less interested in strategic patenting than in the use of IPR to protect products. This is likely to be why companies report less on the strategic use of patents. Although strategic patents have no direct revenue effect, as they tend to provide insurance against patent lawsuits, neglecting strategic patenting could prove a source of stock market volatility, leading to unexpected losses being imposed on investors in the event of a lawsuit.

I also find that the variables describing IPR policies, such as integration of IPR information in project funding decisions, have peculiar effects on the dependent variable. While no significant effects were found for the FTO funding variable, the exclusivity funding variable had a significant but negative impact. I argue that this is because the abandonment of R&D projects is bad news for the stock market regardless of the commercial viability of the project. This implies that investors do not explicitly consider companies' IPR policies. Most likely, capital market participants are not concerned with IPR management policies as such, but rather with related results, as suggested by the financial analysts interviewed. The relatively low demand for such information is also most likely associated with the limited supply of it. This underlines the importance of creating awareness about firms' IPR management among capital market participants so that they request such information.

Patent licensing is, however, found to be reflected in share prices. Both in- and out-licensing deals had an impact on stock returns, although in different ways. While in-licensing deals seem to signal growth opportunities, and thus contribute to stock market returns – at least if used to extend the firm's product pipeline – I find that out-licensing is negatively associated with stock market returns. In relation to patent in-licensing, both a company's in-licensing activity as well as the motive of extending the firm's product pipeline, based on external R&D, was found to contribute to shareholder returns. In contrast, in-licensing for the purpose of securing FTO did not materialise in companies' share price. Presumably this is because a larger product pipeline implies additional growth opportunities, while licences taken to secure FTO do not necessarily do so. Moreover, technology acquisitions are associated with a product-based business model, which stock markets seem to prefer. This is suggested not least by the fact that firms' out-licensing activity as well as the perceived relevance of out-licensing for revenue purposes were found to have a significant but negative impact on the dependent variable. Hence, the stock market systematically discounts for companies pursuing a licensing-based business model. I therefore conclude that companies generating their revenues through product sales face comparatively lower costs of capital.

Finally, I find no significant impact for any of the trademark-related variables. One reason for this could be the high share in my sample of firms focused on early stage product development – for which trademarks are likely to be of less relevance. Furthermore, it could be that investors do not perceive trademarks, in general, to be of any substantial relevance in safeguarding product market shares – a finding that is in line with the exploratory study showing that financial analysts generally do not account for the potential of brand equity in extending the appropriation of economic returns. Rather, they make more conservative valuations in terms of accounting for substantial generic competition beyond the expiry of the primary patent. However, Sandner and Block (2011) show that trademarks in the pharmaceutical industry are indeed value-relevant. It is therefore likely that the insignificant effect of the trademark variables is due to a relatively large number of firms in my sample not having a product on the market.

While some of my findings do suggest that there is asymmetric information concerning companies' IPR management, at the same time I find that at least some of these problems can be reduced through IPR reporting. This is especially true in relation to products and patent licensing deals. Firstly, I find that reporting on the type of patent protection in the firm's product pipeline is associated with reduced return volatility. The same is true of reporting on secondary patent filings with later expiry dates in connection with products on the market. This suggests that, during the R&D phase, uncertainty relates to whether the company will be able to obtain exclusivity for its product, while, when the product is already on the market, the concern is rather for how long the company can maintain its competitive position.

In addition, some of the variables describing information disclosures on licensing deals significantly reduced return volatility. In relation to out-licensing deals, reporting on the financial aspects of the deal was found to have a negatively significant effect on the dependent variable, while reporting on the exclusivity terms did not exhibit any significant effect in the full model. On the contrary, in relation to in-licensing deals, I find that reporting on the exclusivity terms reduces uncertainty, while reporting on the financial aspects did not. Hence, companies in the pharmaceutical industry can reduce stock market uncertainty through IPR reporting, if they report on the right items.

6.3   CONCLUSIONS AND POLICY IMPLICATIONS

Although it is widely accepted that intangible assets are reflected in share prices, this does not mean that such information is adequately incorporated (see, for example, Hand and Lev, 2003). In fact, the findings of the present study show that it is not – especially when it comes to the ability of companies to systematically materialise their R&D investments. Many of my IPR management indicators had a weak and insignificant impact on the dependent variable, and several indicators even exhibited a negative impact. A possible explanation for this is revealed by the exploratory study's finding that financial analysts discount for informational deficits, even regarding companies' IPR. Even more importantly, I find that voluntary IPR reporting can reduce stock market uncertainty. This shows that there are informational deficits concerning companies' IPR management, unless companies report on it. This section describes some of the implications I find regarding the informational efficiency of capital markets.

Firstly, I find that CRAs are not likely to contribute to the informational efficiency of capital markets when it comes to intangibles – at least not in a way that will contribute to the fostering of technological innovation. This is because CRAs value intangible assets, and more specifically patents, from a debt market perspective. Theoretically, creditors are concerned with determining the bottom side of the distribution of economic returns, since they do not participate on the upside. For them, risks associated with patent lawsuits will therefore generally outweigh the potential economic benefits of growth opportunities. Accordingly, I find evidence suggesting that patents contribute to higher credit ratings not in terms of growth opportunities, but as insurance. This means that companies need to devote substantial financial resources to build and uphold a large patent portfolio to mitigate patent lawsuits or they will eventually face higher costs of debt. Hence, companies will experience higher costs of innovation through either increased costs of funding or increased patent portfolio costs – a finding that is especially problematic for smaller technology-driven firms.

Based on this finding, I argue that the financing of technological innovation through debt will be expensive either way – suggesting debt to be an inappropriate instrument for financing technological innovation. This has indeed also been suggested by various research scholars (see Section 2.7.5). Policy makers should therefore focus on enhancing the informational efficiency of stock markets in order to foster innovation. This is not to say that debt markets should be excluded from analytical frameworks regarding the financing of technological innovation. Research on the role of debt markets in this regard is relatively limited. Moreover, each company has its own financial requirements, and needs a particular mixture of equity and debt. Still, the fact that equity holders participate on the upside, while debt holders do not – leading to moral hazard complications for the financing of innovation by means of debt – makes a strong case for equity as the main source of innovation finance. I shall therefore focus my policy recommendations on equity markets, and how to make them more efficient in facilitating the allocation of financial capital towards technological innovation.

Secondly, my findings show that information which is likely to have been requested by investors and analysts, and thus is likely to have been published, is reflected in share prices, while information that has presumably remained private is not. On the whole, these findings provide a case for semi-strong stock market efficiency, meaning that prices adjust to reflect new IPR information made available in the public domain, at least as regards some indicators. However, there is no case for strong market efficiency, implying that prices also incorporate all information that is privately held (see, for example, Fama, 1970). As argued by Grossman and Stiglitz (1980), strong market efficiency may not be possible, but more information disclosures regarding companies' IPR management should, at least by such time as its value-relevance becomes better understood, contribute to more informationally efficient stock markets. This provides a strong case for encouraging the disclosure of more information regarding companies' IPR management.

Thirdly, from a stock market perspective, my findings show that IPR information is considered mainly in connection with important products – on the market as well as under development. For example, I find that patents being used for the protection of products have a positive impact on BHR. Moreover, reporting on the exclusivity situation around products under development reduces stock market uncertainty, as does reporting on secondary patents with the potential to extend the duration exclusivity in relation to products on the market. It thus seems plausible that IPR reporting should take place in relation to companies' products. This does not mean that the strategic aspects of IPR should be neglected in investment analysis and decisions. The uncertainty of FTO not being explicitly considered by investors could in fact pose problems for the financing of technological innovation. The same is true of the indicators related to IPR policies. Although these indicators contain information that is essential for assessments of the probability that investments will sufficiently materialise, or of the risks of patent lawsuits, they seem not to be reflected in share prices. This could also provide a source of stock market uncertainty. For example, I find a strong positive relationship between patent intensity on return volatility in some of my models. A challenge for policy makers is therefore, on the one hand, to make sure that the IPR information investors request is published, but also to create awareness among investors concerning other aspects of companies' IPR management, such as FTO. Creating a coherent structure for IPR reporting which connects companies' IPR management with its products would be a good starting point, not least as the exploratory study shows that analysts mainly consider IPR information in relation to companies' products.

Finally, and perhaps most alarming, is the finding that companies pursuing a licensing-based business model are found to be the losers in stock markets, systematically underperforming companies pursuing a product-based business model. For example, I find that the number of products a firm has on the market positively and significantly contributes to stock market returns, while out-licensing activity is found to be negatively associated with stock market returns. This is likely to provide an obstacle to the financing of technological innovation, not least because it is mainly smaller firms – often with constraints on internal funds and a higher need for external funding – that pursue a licensing-based business model. As they face higher costs of capital, their costs of innovation will be higher – potentially also leading to the abandonment of otherwise profitable R&D projects.

Presumably, the systematic underperformance of companies pursuing a licensing-based business model, can be traced to the high uncertainty attached to the markets for technology relative to product markets. As pointed out by Arora and Gambardella (2010): 'Economists have long identified uncertainty as a barrier to MFT (markets for technology)', which they argue in combination with risk aversion deters investment.

Similarly, it can be argued that this deters investment in companies pursuing a licensing-based business model. That information asymmetries in technology markets also have an impact on stock markets is suggested by the fact that additional reporting on licensing deals is associated with reduced return volatility. Policy makers should therefore be concerned with creating more transparent markets for technologies and also to lower the costs of financing of technological innovation.

Arora and Gambardella (2010) point to three main sources of uncertainty associated with technology markets that need to be overcome – namely, uncertainty about IPR, about the value of the technology, and about the transaction process. Uncertainty about IPR as a legal right recalls the point of Lemley and Shapiro (2005), who suggest that patents do not provide limited exclusion rights, but merely rights to try to exclude competitors, meaning that it is uncertain whether a company will be successful in doing so. Companies therefore tend to wait to license until a patent has been granted and both parties know its claims (Gans et al., 2008), and even then I find that companies conduct a comprehensive due diligence investigation of the patent before a licensing deal is closed (see Section 4.4.2.1).

As for uncertainty about the transaction process, a licensor can negotiate with several potential licensees. It is therefore not unlikely that a firm will end up overpaying, as each licensee may differ substantially in its subjective valuation. Uncertainty regarding the distribution of bids, which provides information about the value of the IPR, therefore provides a risk to the licensee in terms of overpaying, and thus a risk of adverse selection – something that could lead to an IPR market consisting mainly of lemons (see, for example, Pisano 1997; 2006).

Moreover, the value distribution of patents is highly skewed (see, for example, Gambardella et al., 2008; Harhoff et al., 2003), meaning that is essential to distinguish valuable patents from lemons. This, however, becomes less difficult as technologies mature. For example, Arora and Gambardella (2010) argue that the value of a technology is gradually revealed as time elapses, because R&D competition is more intense in the earlier phases. This means that the value of a technology becomes more certain as a dominant technology emerges. Furthermore, a relatively new project runs greater risks of infringing some existing patent. Accordingly, the closer the technology comes to being commercialised on the product market, the lower are the risks of failure.

From an investor perspective, value-related uncertainty seems to provide the main obstacle. To reduce legal uncertainty, a due diligence investigation is typically conducted upfront of a licensing deal. All companies participating in the exploratory study were found to do this. Accordingly, a licensing deal as such should signal a reduction in legal uncertainty about the IPR. Also the transparency of the negotiation process most likely poses less of a concern than the uncertainty attached to the value of the transaction. This is because if information about the financial aspects of the transaction is disclosed, it is easier to determine if a company has overpaid, by looking at comparable licensing deals. Additional reporting on licensing deal financial aspects should therefore also reduce uncertainty about the transaction process. Of course, the uncertainty attached to the value of the technology is not only a result of asymmetric information, but also of inherent uncertainty regarding R&D competition. A part of it, however, seems to be due to asymmetric information – something that is suggested by the finding that reporting on the financial aspects of an out-licensing deal is associated with reduced return volatility. Policy makers should therefore primarily look at ways of enhancing information flows related to licensing deal financial aspects. This would not only contribute to making technology markets more efficient, but also most certainly reduce innovative companies' costs of capital, and thus the overall costs of technological innovation.

In sum, there is a relatively strong case for policy makers, concerned with the fostering of technological innovation, to look at ways of enhancing the informational efficiency of capital markets by reducing IPR management-related asymmetric information. The next section will provide some recommendations on how they can do so.

6.4   OUTLOOK AND POLICY RECOMMENDATIONS

The literature is full of proposals on how to deal with intangibles from a financial reporting perspective – seeking to identify companies' hidden values – some of which have also been implemented in practice. The *Skandia Navigator* pioneered this field, systematising the difference between the Skandia corporation's book and market value (see Edvinsson, 1997). The catchword for explaining this difference – *intellectual capital* – comprises human capital and structural capital, which in turn are divided into different subcategories.[1] These categories also comprise intangible assets that are relatively soft compared with proprietary intangible assets. For example, is it easier to put a price tag on a legal right, such as a patent, than on a certain set of employee skills? Similar to the balanced scorecard concept of Kaplan and Norton (1992), this approach provided a way of identifying the value-drivers of companies, and finding measurements to assess the systematic management of assets that were not being recognised on firms' balance sheets. This has been followed by different proposals regarding introducing an additional statement on intangible values (Alwert et al., 2004; Maul and Menninger, 2004). Essentially, these aim to provide capital markets with additional information, enabling investors to make better assessments of firms' fundamental value.

Empirical research too has looked to identify the value-drivers of technology-driven companies. In a recent study, Hulten (2010), for example, examined the value-drivers of Microsoft. When R&D spending, sales and marketing expenditures, and expenditure on general administration are treated as investments, Hulten finds that the explained market value of the company increased from 17 to 45 per cent. Taking a similar approach, in a study of 617 technology-driven US companies, Hulten and Hao (2008) find that the explained value increased from 31 to 75 per cent when expensed R&D was treated as an investment. This suggests that capital market participants need to make adjustments to widely used financial measurements.

It has also been proposed that new accounting methods that better recognise internally developed technologies and brands should be established (see Hand and Lev, 2003). Lev and Zarowin (1999) argue that if historical financial information has an impact on the interpretation of new information, the continuous improvement of the information in past financial statements – in terms of enhanced matching between revenues and costs – should also enable investors to make better decisions about the future. This is suggested by empirical research findings that the stock market's valuation of FDA drug approvals, amongst other variables, is associated with the past operating performance of the firm (see, for example, Lev et al., 1998). Accordingly, Lev and Zarowin (1999) suggest that, if intangible investments materialise, both current and past financial statements should be adjusted to reflect the capitalisation of these investments, and the amortisation of the capitalised amount should be settled according to the duration of the economic benefits. This approach, they argue, is already used in the accounting for GDP, where figures are revised several years after the initial estimates.

Besides adjustments to current accounting practices, it has also been argued that capital markets, and especially stock markets, require more forward-looking information (see, for example, Upton, 2003). For example, the American Institute for Certified Public Accountants (AICPA) Special Committee on Financial Reporting recommends that companies supplement traditional financial statements with more forward-looking information (AICPA, 1994). This has been followed by a tendency towards more forward-looking reporting. Wasley and Wu (2006) note that, while cash-flow forecasts were rarely published before 2000, the number of cash-flow forecasts has since tripled. Financial statements, on the contrary, are backward-looking in focusing on transactions that have already occurred. This recalls the main purpose of accounting, which was to enable stakeholders to follow asset flows into and out of a firm, and thus track specific transactions. For businesses focused on trading physical goods, such practices may also be sufficient. The present study, however, focuses on companies that consist mainly of growth opportunities. When valuing technology-driven companies, asset flows are of less concern, although by no means unimportant. Even more, though, investors are interested in the profits a company can generate from its R&D investments. This suggests a high value-relevance of forward-looking information, implying a need for a new forward-looking financial reporting paradigm.

The present study therefore argues that although retrospective adjustment of financial statements,[2] or statements on intangible values, would presumably provide additional value-relevant information, capital markets most need more forward-looking information, at least for the valuation of technology-driven companies. For example, Ramb and Reitzig (2005a; 2005b) find forward-looking patent information to have a stronger correlation with the market value of firms than activated R&D investments on their balance sheet. My argument builds on corporate finance theory, stating that companies in principle consist of assets-in-place and growth opportunities (see, for example, Myers and Majluf, 1984). While the proposals described above look to enhance the value-relevance of companies' financial reporting, mainly to more comprehensively reflect assets-in-place, the exploratory study showed that analysts find growth opportunities most difficult to value, due largely to associated informational deficits. To bridge these, the present study argues that technology-driven firms should publish a *growth statement*, which can be provided as a supplement to its financial statement – that is, its balance sheet, income and cash-flow statement.

Before setting out what a growth statement might look like, however, some of its empirical and theoretical justifications ought to be mentioned. The present study has shown, alongside past research, that IPR information is not only relevant for assessments of firms' financial performance, but is also forward-looking. Patent information is disclosed as patents are filed up to three years before a new technology is commercialised and returns are generated (see, for example, Ernst, 2001), and its value-relevance has been confirmed empirically (see, for example, Neuhäusler et al., 2011; Ramb and Reitzig, 2005a; 2005b; Sandner and Block, 2011; Trautwein, 2007). In addition, Deng et al. (1999) find that several patent and technology indicators can be used as predictors of companies' stock market performance. It is thus reasonable that IPR reporting should take place within a forward-looking reporting framework. This is crucial, not least because the present study has shown that stock markets value IPR not as something in itself, but in relation to products and growth opportunities of the company. This means that IPR information ought to be provided in the context of the company's business, rather than separately. A growth statement would provide this context.

The proposed growth statement aims to link IPR information to a company's financial aspects or, more specifically, projected earnings. The statement is drafted in relation to the pharmaceutical industry, in which the empirical study was conducted and would not be applicable to every type of industry. However, its basic idea would presumably be useful to most technology-driven companies in terms of enabling investors to better assess the economic value of growth opportunities. More specifically, a growth statement consisting of the following aspects, some of which have already suggested by METI (2005), should help investors:

1. An explanation of the economic growth potential of each growth opportunity. This would include its expected market share, its market growth rate, and its competitive advantage within the market place.
2. An explanation of the commercialisation strategy for each growth opportunity, in terms of how the firm intends to convert its investments into profits.
3. A link between R&D investments and projected earnings, indicating their expected profitability. This would better enable investors to understand the purpose of the R&D, and the expected profitability of these investments.
4. A link between a company's IPR and the competitive advantage of its growth opportunities, enabling investors to assess whether the firm has been able to acquire the necessary IPR to protect and appropriate these.

The first two points are essential to reduce uncertainty about the economic value of IPR, and how they contribute to a firm's financial performance. For example, Seethamraju (2003) finds that this type information is considered by stock markets in relation to trademark acquisitions. Similarly, the financial analysts interviewed reveal that patents are valued in the context of the additional market share or premium price they can provide in relation to a product. Theoretical models for patent valuation also suggest that the value of a patent ought to be derived from the economic effect it can produce (see Wurzer and Reinhardt, 2009). If the economic effect, however, is generated through patent out-licensing, as opposed to product market commercialisation, this affects the context of the valuation and the economic value the company can generate through the patent. Companies should therefore provide information about the commercialisation strategy they intend to pursue regarding the growth opportunity. In addition, it is essential to indicate the profitability of investments in creating growth opportunities. This leads me to my third point. For example, Gu and Lev (2004) find that royalty income signals firms' ability to materialise future R&D investments. Hence, based on such information, investors can also draw conclusions about the future. Finally, the point of linking firms' IPR to projected revenues, but also to the competitive advantage of each growth opportunity, points to the findings of the present study – that is, that stock markets consider IPR mainly in relation to important products. Even more important, I find that companies which report on the type of patent protection they have obtained for their products under development reduce stock market uncertainty. Also theoretical patent valuation models argue that patents must be considered in relation to whether they protect a competitive advantage (see Wurzer and Reinhardt, 2010). These theoretical and empirical arguments provide a relatively strong case for a growth statement linking the information described above.

Turning to the structure of growth statement, it should be noted that pharmaceutical companies' growth opportunities are essentially the products in their pipeline. Each pipeline product is therefore one growth opportunity item in the statement. The information described above should be disclosed for each item, enabling investors to better value each growth opportunity separately. Furthermore, the statement is to be divided into two parts – the first part consisting of quantitative financial information which can easily be incorporated into asset pricing models by investors and analysts. More specifically, the projected costs and revenues of each growth opportunity should be disclosed. On the cost side, the growth statement contains the R&D budget for each growth opportunity, and how much of the budget has been used so far. The costs and revenues of the projects are divided between the years in which the investments will be conducted, so that the NPV of the growth opportunity can be derived more accurately. In addition, after a projected year has passed, the company ought to state both the projected and incurred costs and revenues. This way, corporate outsiders will be able to assess the accuracy of the company's forecasts ex post.

The second part consists of notes providing qualitative information, also linked to a specific growth opportunity. The purpose of this information is to enable investors to assess the plausibility of the projected financial outcome and of the assumptions behind the projections. More specifically, I propose a second part consisting of three sections. In the first section, companies quantify the assumptions behind their earnings projections, including a calculation of market size for the product, the market's expected growth rate, and the company's expected share of the market. This way, corporate outsiders are better able to make their own forecasts, by changing some of the underlying assumptions. The following section contains information about the commercialisation strategy the company intends to pursue regarding the growth opportunity. The purpose of this section is twofold. Firstly, it should create awareness among investors about how technology-driven companies materialise their intangible investments. As has been argued, the link between tangible investments and profits is relatively intuitive. A similar understanding is also needed in relation to intangible investments. Secondly, it ought to help clarify the projected earnings for the technology. For instance, the company may not have the financial means to pursue the development of a product, and may therefore plan to work within a strategic alliance. This will, on the one hand, limit the revenues that the company alone can generate, but, on the other hand, will increase the likelihood of successful commercialisation. As the present study shows that stock markets systematically undervalue companies pursuing a licensing-based business model, it seems to be important that these communicate the purpose and benefits of doing so.

The third section should clearly state the competitive advantage associated with each growth opportunity. This is essential if investors are to determine the plausibility of the market share the company expects to obtain, and to be able to distinguish the characteristics of the product from its competitors. In addition, investors will want to know if the company has sufficient isolation mechanisms in place to exclusively generate economic returns on this basis. To communicate this, companies will be asked to list the IPR related to the growth opportunity, and link this in with its competitive advantage. A short description of commercial relevance should be provided in relation to each IPR application for this purpose. In relation to patents, the description should state what the patent protects, and its economic purpose, in a language understandable by a person who is not necessarily skilled in the prior art. Moreover, companies should state whether each patent or trademark has been granted, its geographical scope, and expected expiry date (if a patent). This will give investors a better understanding of the IPR situation around each growth opportunity, and presumably reduce stock market uncertainty.

Information about the FTO situation will be more sensitive, in terms of disclosure, for competitor reasons (see Section 4.7.2). Therefore, no detailed information can be provided. It is, however, important that companies clearly state the potential FTO risks and how they may impact on their forecasts. Finally, measures taken to mitigate these risks should be listed, in terms of whether IPR policies are in place so that the company only pursues product development projects for which FTO can be obtained, and how often reassessments are made. This would presumably at least increase investor awareness about the potential financial consequences of not having secured FTO.

When implementing a growth statement, policy makers ought to consider some implications. These relate to:

- the accuracy and credibility of the information provided;
- associated moral hazard complications;
- the transparency of the reporting process;
- the costs of financial reporting;
- how to create incentives for companies to publish such a statement.

Firstly, of course, the future is uncertain, and so a growth statement will be uncertain, with implications for the accuracy of forward-looking reporting. Moreover, the credibility of such information is likely to be questioned by investors, not least because managers may have incentives to distort the information disclosed in order to maximise private benefits (Healy and Palepu, 2001). But studies show that management forecasts provide relatively accurate information. For example, past research finds that management forecasts are more accurate than contemporaneous analysts' forecasts (see, for example, Hassell and Jennings, 1986; Waymire, 1986), and that financial analysts revise their forecasts in response to management forecasts (see, for example, Hassell et al., 1988). Because corporate insiders normally possess more information than outsiders, their reporting should also be more accurate. Still, there is potential bias attached to such assessments, as managers are likely to be optimistic about their actions. Empirical research, however, shows management forecasts to be unbiased (see, for example, McNichols, 1989). Not without reason, they accordingly also provide credible information to investors. This is suggested by findings revealing positive stock market reactions to management forecasts of earnings increases, and negative reactions to forecasts of earnings decreases (Ajinkya and Gift, 1984; Waymire, 1984). Findings by Pownall and Waymire (1989) even suggest that management forecasts are more credible than audited financial information.

Secondly, it is crucial that IPR reporting is conducted in a transparent manner. My aim was therefore to propose a coherent structure for IPR reporting, in terms of a growth statement. The need for improved reporting transparency in an intangible economy has been noted by research scholars, such as Hand and Lev (2003), who argue that asymmetric information can stem from a lack of corporate disclosures, but also from a lack of transparency in the process of how investors obtain and process information about intangible assets (Blair and Wallman, 2003). Because IPR disclosures are widely dispersed, the process of gathering information is costly for corporate outsiders. For example, Healy and Palepu (2001) note that companies rely on new channels of investor communication, such as conference calls and the internet, to communicate with investors and financial intermediaries.[3] This suggests that, in order to capture most of the value-relevant IPR information, investors need to be more active in the research process, or rely on information intermediaries.

On the one hand, additional voluntary reporting has the advantage of providing more in-depth insights regarding the firm's business. The additional disclosure conducted by companies through a variety of reporting channels also suggests that companies perceive reduced costs of capital in doing so. On the other hand, however, IPR information is provided in an unstandardised manner, making it difficult to compare, and the dispersed manner in which it is disclosed makes its gathering more costly for corporate outsides. The proposed growth statement therefore intends to create a more coherent and transparent way of IPR reporting in the wider context of the firm's business.

Thirdly, while a growth statement would presumably reduce the costs of gathering information imposed on corporate outsiders, it could well increase the burden on companies in terms of corporate communication. At first sight, a growth statement might seem to put substantial burdens on companies in terms of financial reporting efforts. However, the exploratory study reveals that pharmaceutical companies conduct analysis on the basis of essentially the same information, in order to value their growth opportunities for internal purposes. These assessments are essential to give management an idea of the potential profitability of often substantial R&D investments. Most information is therefore already available internally and could easily be published.

Still, there are strong reasons to make the growth statement voluntary rather than a mandatory part of financial reporting – not least because the disclosure of forward-looking information, and especially IPR information, can be sensitive for competition reasons. Indeed, it has been found that managers are concerned about information disclosures damaging their competitive position in product markets (see, for example, Darrough and Stoughton, 1990; Verrecchia, 1983). Making the growth statement voluntary would allow managers to evaluate the marginal costs and benefits of adopting such a regime – that is, looking at the trade-offs between, on the negative side, the additional resources required for additional financial reporting and the potential damage to a company's competitive position and, on the positive side, a possible reduction in the firm's costs of capital.

Fourthly, it has been argued that companies' disclosure decisions are based on consideration of whether the information is favourable to the company, meaning that companies will not disclose bad information (see, for example, Dye, 2001), and only report when net private benefits are expected. There is some evidence to support this concern. For example, Cheng and Lo (2006) find that companies time voluntary disclosures to increase their trading benefits. Although the evidence of a direct link between managers' private benefits and voluntary information disclosures is relatively limited, this is something policy makers would need to consider. Hence, making the growth statement voluntary is problematic in terms of 'cherry picking' – that is, the risk that companies only report when information is positive. To deal with such moral hazard complications, the opt-in would need to be irrevocable to avoid future regulatory arbitrage. This means that once companies have published a growth statement, they must continue to do so – at least for a certain period of time.

Fifthly, to create incentives for management to publish a growth statement, or so as not to deter them from doing so, it would be advisable to establish a strong safe harbour in the disclosure regime so that managers are not held liable for reasonable and good faith projections. Already in the 1990s, shareholder lawsuits were most notable in technology-driven industries, raising concerns among mangers about litigation related to voluntary forward-looking information disclosures (see, for example, AICPA, 1994; Breeden, 1995). For this particular reason, private institutions, such as the AICPA Jenkins Committee, have been reluctant to advocate the expansion of financial reporting models to include forward-looking information (AICPA, 1994). In the US, Congress dealt with this through a revision of federal securities laws by enacting the Private Securities Litigation Reform Act of 1995, providing a safe harbour for financial forecasts and other forward-looking information. Before the 1995 Act, however, a safe harbour for reasonable and good faith projections had already been implemented. Still, the SEC perceived that companies were reluctant to disclose forward-looking information due to concerns about its effectiveness. Accordingly, the 1995 Act amended prior securities laws to create a safe harbour for both oral and written forward-looking information, provided that its disclosure met two conditions: (a) the information was clearly labelled as being of a forward-looking nature, and (b) supplementary to any forward-looking reporting, the management must state any essential factors which could cause actual results to diverge from the forecast.

The risk with such safe harbour provisions, as pointed out by several research scholars, is that, if the enforcement possibility of shareholder rights is limited and the threat of litigation is weak, the quality of disclosure tends to be poor (see, for example, Bhattacharya and Daouk, 2002; La Porta et al., 1997). Johnson et al. (2001), however, examine the consequences of the 1995 Act, addressing the essential questions of whether the reform contributed to more quantitative forward-looking reporting, and whether the quality of the information provided was affected. They find a significant subsequent increase in the number of forward-looking disclosures in the years after its implementation, implying that it created incentives for managers to commit to forward-looking reporting. Moreover, they do not find any support for the concern regarding misrepresentation for private benefits, reducing the quality of the information provided (Grundfest and Perino, 1997), nor did they find any evidence for subsequent projections being more optimistic or biased. On the contrary, they find subsequent forecasts to be less noisy than previous ones. Hence, the safe harbour did not provide a 'licence to lie'. A potential explanation is offered by Lev and Penman (1990), who argue for the credibility of forward-looking information since investors can verify it ex post. This is an aspect that the growth statement incorporates by advocating the disclosure of both projected and incurred costs and revenues.

In addition, companies can disclose additional supplementary information to enhance the credibility of their reporting. For example, Hutton et al. (2003) reveal that about two thirds of companies supplement their firms' earnings forecasts with verifiable forward-looking statements, of both a quantitative and a qualitative nature. While they find that bad news is always perceived as credible, positive forward-looking information was only credible when supplemented by verifiable quantitative statements. Qualitative supplementary disclosures, however, were not found to enhance the perceived credibility of the information for investors. Still, empirical studies, among them the present study, show that qualitative information too can be value-relevant. Guo et al. (2005) find that several product-related indicators explain biotechnology companies' share price performance. Similarly, Amir and Lev (1996) show that non-financial indicators better explain companies' stock market performance, in the wireless communications industry, than financial statement information. Finally, the present study has shown that some IPR management indicators also explain companies' share price performance in the pharmaceutical industry. Even more important, it has shown that reporting on qualitative IPR information can reduce stock market uncertainty. An essential aspect of the proposed growth statement is therefore the disclosure of the assumptions behind the forecasts, as well as related qualitative indicators, so that corporate outsiders can pass judgement on the statement's plausibility.

Finally, complementary to the growth statement, companies ought to disclose any IPR information of a precise nature which is expected to be relevant to capital market participants' investment decisions – in conformity with securities regulations. In order to be of a precise nature this information must indicate a set of circumstances or a particular event that has occurred or is expected to occur (see Section 2.8.2). Moreover, it needs to be specific enough for investors to determine its potential impact on the price of a financial instrument. Many patent licensing deals are likely to fulfil this criterion. However, I find that companies report on licensing deals mostly without providing much detailed information on the financial aspects or the exclusivity terms of the licence. At the same time, I find that these details reduce stock market volatility. This is information of a precise nature that also has an impact on companies' share price. It therefore seems that it should be disclosed, also according to present disclosure regimes. Either way, such reporting is found to be beneficial to companies pursuing a licensing-based business model, from the perspective of reducing their costs of capital, as investors tend to price protect for uncertainty. Accordingly, there are several reasons for policy makers and legislators to provide more detailed guidelines concerning the type of information that ought to be disclosed in relation to patent licensing deals. The benefits of doing so are obvious, in terms of enhanced informational stock market efficiency, improved allocation of financial resources, more efficient technology markets, and lower costs for the financing of technological innovation.

Taking the findings of past research and the present study together, there seems to be a strong case for a growth statement as well as more in-depth reporting on patent licensing deals. Although there is no empirical case for a growth statement in its proposed form and structure, empirical findings point in the direction of a need for a new paradigm of forward-looking reporting, of which IPR reporting forms an essential part. This section has suggested some guidelines for how this could be done – hopefully providing a starting point for forthcoming empirical research, to assess its benefits and limitations so as to adjust it in the best possible manner, if successively implemented by a number of companies. As empirical research can only examine models comprehensively after they have been implemented, this is obviously left to future research. In addition, further research is needed to develop conceptual frameworks for both IPR management and IPR reporting in other technology-driven industries.

In the end, however, the outlook for a new paradigm of forward-looking reporting will be determined by the commitment of policy makers and legislators to having a growth statement implemented and the willingness of companies to start to adopt such a regime.

NOTES

1. While human capital consists of the value companies' employees provide through their skills and expertise, structural capital refers to the infrastructure and processes that are created by employees who have become embedded company assets. Among these the firms' IPR is also found.
2. This would be especially problematic in the pharmaceutical industry, where it takes several years before R&D investments materialise.
3. For example, Tasker (1998) finds that 35 per cent of medium-sized companies held a conference call to mitigate the limitations of mandatory financial reporting.

Bibliography

Aaker, D.A. (1991), *Managing Brand Equity: Capitalizing on the Value of a Brand Name*, New York: Free Press.

Aaker, D.A. (1992), 'The Value of Brand Equity', *Journal of Business Strategy*, **13** (4), 27–33.

Aaker, D.A. (1995), *Building Strong Brands*, New York: Free Press.

Aaker, D.A. and R. Jacobson (1994), 'The Financial Information Content of Perceived Quality', *Journal of Marketing Research*, **31** (May), 191–201.

Aaker, D.A. and R. Jacobson (2001), 'The Value Relevance of Brand Attitude in High-technology Markets', *Journal of Marketing Research*, **38** (November), 485–93.

Aboody, D. and B. Lev (2000), 'Information Asymmetry, R&D, and Insider Gains', *Journal of Finance*, **55** (6), 2747–66.

Admati, A.R. and Pfleiderer, P. (1994), 'Robust Financial Contracting and the Role of Venture Capitalists', *Journal of Finance*, **49** (2), 371–402.

Aghion, P., S. Bond, A. Klemm and I. Marinescu (2004), 'Technology and Financial Structure: Are Innovative Firms Different?', *Journal of the European Economic Association*, **2** (2–3), 277–88.

AICPA (1994), *Improving Business Reporting: A Customer Focus*, New York: American Institute of Certified Public Accountants, Special Committee on Financial Reporting.

Ajinkya, B. and M. Gift (1984), 'Corporate Managers' Earnings Forecasts and Symmetrical Adjustments of Market Expectations', *Journal of Accounting Research*, **22**, 425–44.

Akerlof, G.A. (1970), 'The Market for Lemons: Quality Uncertainty and the Market Mechanism', *The Quarterly Journal of Economics*, **84** (3), 488–500.

Albert, M.B., D. Avery, F. Narin and P. McAllister (1991), 'Direct Validation of Citation Counts as Indicators of Industrially Important Patents', *Research Policy*, **20** (3), 251–9.

Alcacer, J. and M. Gittelman (2006), 'Patent Citations as a Measure of Knowledge Flows: The Influence of Examiner Citations', *Review of Economics and Statistics*, **88** (4), 774–9.

Alcacer, J., M. Gittelman and B. Sampat (2009), 'Applicant and Examiner

Citations in U.S. Patents: An Overview and Analysis', *Research Policy*, **38** (2), 415–27.

Alderson, M.J. and B.L. Betker (1996), 'Liquidation Costs and Accounting Data', *Financial Management*, **25** (Summer), 25–36.

Allegrezza, S. and A. Guarda-Rauchs (1999), 'The Determinants of Trademark Deposits: An Econometric Investigation', *Economie Appliqué*, **52** (2), 51–68.

Alwert, K., M. Bornemann and M. Kivikas (2004), 'Wissensbilanz – Made in Germany. Leitfaden 1.0', Herausgegeben durch das Bundesministerium für Wirtschaft und Technologie BMWi Berlin.

Amable, B., J. Chatelain and K. Ralf (2008), 'Patents as Collateral', University of Paris Working Paper.

Amir, A. and B. Lev (1996), 'Value-relevance of Nonfinancial Information: The Wireless Communications Industry', *Journal of Accounting and Economics*, **22** (1–3), 3–30.

Amir, E., B. Lev and T. Sougiannis (1999), 'What Value Analysts?', Tel Aviv University Working Paper.

Arora, A. (1997), 'Patents, Licensing, and Market Structure in the Chemical Industry', *Research Policy*, **26** (4–5), 391–403.

Arora, A. and A. Gambardella (1994), 'Evaluating Technological Information and Utilizing It: Scientific Knowledge, Technological Capability, and External Linkages in Biotechnology', *Journal of Economic Behavior & Organization*, **24** (1), 91–114.

Arora, A. and A. Gambardella (2010), 'Ideas for Rent: An Overview of Markets for Technology', *Industrial and Corporate Change*, **19** (3), 775–803.

Arora, A., A. Fosfuri and A. Gambardella (2002), *Markets for Technology: The Economics of Innovation and Corporate Strategy*, Cambridge, MA: MIT Press.

Arrow, K.J. (1962), 'The Economic Implications of Learning by Doing', *Review of Economic Studies*, **29** (3), 155–73.

Arundel, A. (2001), 'The Relative Effectiveness of Patents and Secrecy for Appropriation', *Research Policy*, **30** (4), 611–24.

Arundel, A. and I. Kabla (1998), 'What Percentage of Innovations are Patented? Empirical Estimates for European Firms', *Research Policy*, **27** (2), 127–41.

Arundel, A. and P. Patel (2003), 'Strategic Patenting', Background report for the Trend Chart Policy Benchmarking Workshop: New Trends in IPR Policy.

Ashbaugh-Skaife, H., D. Collins and R. LaFond (2006), 'The Effects of Corporate Governance on Firms' Credit Ratings', *Journal of Accounting and Economics*, **42** (1–2), 203–43.

Ashton, W.B. and R.K. Sen (1988), 'Using Patent Information in Technology Business Planning', *Research Technology Management*, **31**, 42–6.

Asquith, P. and D.W. Mullins Jr (1986), 'Equity Issues and Offering Dilution', *Journal of Financial Economics*, **15** (1–2), 61–89.

Audretsch, D. and E. Lehmann (2004a), 'The Effect of Experience, Ownership, and Knowledge on IPO Survival: Evidence from the Neuer Markt', Discussion Paper 04(10), Konstanz.

Audretsch, D. and E. Lehmann (2004b), 'Financing High-Tech Growth: The Role of Debt and Equity', *Schmalenbach Business Review*, **56** (4), 340–57.

Austin, D.H. (1993), 'The Value of Intangible Assets – An Event-Study Approach to Measuring Innovative Output: The Case of Biotechnology', *American Economic Review*, **83** (2), 253–8.

Bader, M.A. (2008), 'Managing Intellectual Property in Inter-firm R&D Collaborations in Knowledge-intensive Industries', *International Journal of Technology Management*, **41** (3), 311–35.

BaFin (2005), 'Emittentenleitfaden der Bundesanstalt für Finanz-dienstleistungsaufsicht', available at http://www.bafin.de/SharedDocs/Downloads/DE/Leitfaden/WA/dl_090520_emittentenleitfaden_2009.pdf?__blob=publicationFile (accessed 8 November 2012).

Bah, R. and P. Dumontier (2001), 'R&D Intensity and Corporate Financial Policy: Some International Evidence', *Journal of Business Finance & Accounting*, **5** (6), 671–92.

Ballow, J., R. Burgman, G. Roos and M. Molnar (2004), *A New Paradigm for Managing Shareholder Value*, Wellesley, MA: Accenture Institute for High Performance Business.

Barnes, P. (2008), *Stock Market Efficiency, Insider Dealing and Market Abuse*, Farnham: Gower Publishing.

Barney, J. (1991), 'Firm Resources and Sustained Competitive Advantage', *Journal of Management*, **17** (1), 99–120.

Barth, M.E., M.B. Clement, G. Foster and R. Kasznik (1998), 'Brand Values and Capital Market Valuation', *Review of Accounting Studies*, **3**, 41–68.

Bass, F.M. and D.G. Clarke (1972), 'Testing Distributed Lag Models of Advertising Effect', *Journal of Marketing Research*, **9** (August), 298–308.

Bass, F.M. and R.P. Leone (1983), 'Temporal Aggregation, the Data Interval Bias, and Empirical Estimation of Bimonthly Relations from Annual Data, Management Trial versus Advertising', *Journal of Marketing Research*, **20** (August), 257–67.

Basu, S. (1977), 'Investment Performance of Common Stocks in Relation to their Price-Earnings Ratios: A Test of the Efficient Markets Hypothesis', *Journal of Finance*, **32** (3), 663–82.

Bayus, B., G. Erickson and R. Jacobson (2003), 'The Financial Rewards of New-product Introductions in the Personal Computer Industry', *Management Science*, **49** (2), 197–210.

Bekkers, R., G. Duysters and Verspagen, B. (2002), 'Intellectual Property Rights, Strategic Technology Agreements and Market Structure – The Case of GSM', *Research Policy*, **31** (7), 1141–61.

Bennett, R. and S. Rundle-Thiele (2005), 'The Brand Loyalty Cycle: Implications for Marketers', *Journal of Brand Management*, **12** (4), 250–63.

Bergemann, D. and U. Hege (1998), 'Dynamic Venture Capital Financing and Learning', *Journal of Banking and Finance*, **22**, 703–35.

Berger, A. and G. Udell (1990), 'Collateral, Loan Quality, and Bank Risk', *Journal of Monetary Economics*, **25**, 21–42.

Berger, A. and G. Udell (1998), 'The Economics of Small Business Finance: The Roles of Private Equity and Debt Markets in the Financial Growth Cycle', *Journal of Banking and Finance*, **22** (6–8), 613–73.

Berger, A., I.K Hasan and F. Leora (2003), 'Further Evidence on the Link between Finance and Growth: An International Analysis of Community Banking and Economic Performance', The World Bank Development Research Group Finance, Policy Research Working Paper.

Bergmann, I., D. Butzke, L. Walter, J.P. Fuerste, M.G. Moehrle and V.A. Erdmann (2008), 'Evaluating the Risk of Patent Infringement by Means of Semantic Patent Analysis: The Case of DNA Chips', *R&D Management*, **38** (5), 550–62.

Bergmans, B. (1991), *Insider Information and Securities Trading: A Legal and Economic Analysis of the Foundations of Liability in the USA and European Community*, London: Graham & Trotman.

Bernstein, S., J. Lerner, M. Sørensen and P. Strömberg (2010), 'Private Equity and Industry Performance', National Bureau of Economic Research Working Paper No. 15632 and Harvard Business School Working Paper No. 10-045.

Bessen, J. (2008), 'The Value of U.S. Patents by Owner and Patent Characteristics', *Research Policy*, **37** (5), 932–45.

Bessen, J. and M.J. Meurer (2008a), *Patent Failure: How Judges, Bureaucrats, and Lawyers Put Innovators at Risk*, Hoboken, NJ: Princeton University Press.

Bessen, J. and M.J. Meurer (2008b), 'The Private Costs of Patent Litigation', Working Paper Series, Law and Economics Working Paper 7(8), Boston University School of Law.

Bester, H. (1987), 'The Role of Collateral in Credit Markets with Imperfect Information', *European Economic Review*, **31** (June), 887–99.

Bettman, J.R., E.J. Johnson and J.W. Payne (1991), 'Consumer Decision Making', in Robertson, T.S. and H.H. Kassarjian (eds.), *Handbook of Consumer Behavior*, Hoboken, NJ: Prentice-Hall, pp. 50–84.

Bhatia, V. and G. Carey (2007), 'Patenting for Profit', *MIT Sloan Management Review*, **7** (1), 15–16.

Bhattacharya, U. and H. Daouk (2002), 'The World Price of Insider Trading', *Journal of Finance*, **57** (1), 75–108.

Biel, A.L. (1992), 'How Brand Image Drives Brand Equity', *Journal of Advertising Research*, **32** (6), 6–12.

Bittelmeyer, C. (2007), *Patente und Finanzierung am Kapitalmarkt: Eine theoretische und empirische Analyse*, Wiesbaden: DUV-Verlag.

Black, B. and R. Gilson (1998), 'Venture Capital and the Structure of Capital Markets: Banks versus Stock Markets', *Journal of Financial Economics*, **47** (3), 243–77.

Blair, M. and S. Wallman (2003), 'The Growing Intangibles Reporting Discrepancy', in Hand, J. and B. Lev (eds.), *Intangible Assets: Values, Measures, and Risks*, New York: Oxford University Press, pp. 451–68.

Blind, K., K. Cremers and E. Mueller (2009a), 'The Influence of Strategic Patenting on Companies' Patent Portfolios', *Research Policy*, **38** (2), 428–36.

Blind, K., A. Cuntz, F. Köhler and Radauer, A. (2009b), 'Die volkswirtschaftliche Bedeutung des geistigen Eigentums und der Bedeutungsverlust klassischer Kapitalgüter für den Mittelstand in Deutschland', Study on behalf of the German Federal Ministry of Economics and Technology.

Blind, K., J. Edler, R. Frietsch and U. Schmoch (2003), 'Erfindungen kontra Patente: Schwerpunktstudie "zur technologischen Leistungsfäigkeit Deutschlands"', Final report for the Federal Ministry of Education and Research (BMBF), Karlsruhe.

Blind, K., J. Edler, R. Frietsch and U. Schmoch (2004), 'The Patent Upsurge in Germany: The Outcome of a Multi-motive Game Induced by Large Companies', Working Paper presented at the Eighth Schumpeter Conference in Milan, Fraunhofer Institute Systems and Innovation Research (ISI), Karlsruhe.

Blind, K., J. Edler, R. Frietsch and U. Schmoch (2006), 'Motives to Patent: Empirical Evidence from Germany', *Research Policy*, **35** (5), 655–72.

Bloom, N. (2009), 'The Impact of Uncertainty Shocks', *Econometrica*, **77** (3), 623–85.

Bloom, N. and J. Van Reenen (2002), 'Patents, Real Options and Firm Performance', *Economic Journal*, **112** (478), 97–116.

Bloom, N., S. Bond and J. Van Reenen (2007), 'Uncertainty and Investment Dynamics', *Review of Economic Studies*, **74**, 391–415.

Bogart, L. (1986), *Strategy in Advertising: Matching Media and Messages of Markets and Motivations*, Lincoln, IL: NTC Business.

Boisot, M.H., I.C. MacMillan and K.S. Han (2007), *Explorations in Information Space: Knowledge, Agents, and Organization*, New York: Oxford University Press.

Boone, J.P. and K.K. Raman (2003), *Off-Balance Sheet R&D Assets and Market Liquidity*, in Hand, J. and B. Lev (eds.), *Intangible Assets: Values, Measures, and Risks*, New York: Oxford University Press, pp. 335–65.

Boot, A.W. and A.V. Thakor (1994), 'Moral Hazard and Secured Lending in an Infinitely Repeated Credit Market Game', *International Economic Review*, **35** (4), 899–920.

Botosan, C.A. (1997), 'Disclosure Level and the Cost of Equity Capital', *The Accounting Review*, **72** (3), 323–50.

Boyd, J. and E.C. Prescott (1986), 'Financial Intermediary Coalitions', *Journal of Economic Theory*, **38**, 211–32.

Brealey, R.A. and S.C. Myers (2002), *Principles of Corporate Finance*, 7th edition, New York: McGraw-Hill Higher Education.

Breeden, R. (1995), Testimony before the Securities Subcommittee of the Senate Committee on Banking, Housing, and Urban Affairs, 6 April.

Brock, W.A. and B.D. Lebaron (1996), 'A Dynamic Structural Model for Stock Return Volatility and Trading Volume', *The Review of Economics and Statistics*, **78** (1), 94–110.

Brown, J.R. and B.C. Petersen (2009), 'Why has the Investment-cash Flow Sensitivity Declined so Sharply? Rising R&D and Equity Market Developments', *Journal of Banking and Finance*, **33** (5), 971–84.

Brown, J.R., S.M. Fazzari and B.C. Petersen (2009), 'Financing Innovation and Growth: Cash Flow, External Equity, and the 1990s R&D Boom', *Journal of Finance*, **64** (1), 151–85.

Brown, L. (1997), 'Analyst Forecasting Errors: Additional Evidence', *Financial Analysts' Journal*, **53**, 81–8.

Brown, L. and M. Rozeff (1978), 'The Superiority of Analysts' Forecasts as Measures of Expectations: Evidence from Earnings', *Journal of Finance*, **33**, 1–6.

Brown, L., G. Foster and E. Noreen (1985), 'Security Analyst Multi-year Earnings Forecasts and the Capital Market', Studies in Accounting Research, No. 23, American Accounting Association, Sarasota, FL.

Brown, S., S.A. Hillegeist and K. Lo (2004), 'Conference Calls and Information Asymmetry', *Journal of Accounting and Economics*, **37**, 343–66.

Burda, M. and C. Wyplosz (2005), *Macroeconomics: A European Text*, 4th edition, Oxford: Oxford University Press.

Burr, W. (2003), *Innovationen in Organisationen*, 1st edition, Stuttgart: Kohlhammer.

Buzzell, R.D. and B.T. Gale (1987), *The PIMS Principles*, New York: The Free Press.

Carpenter, M.P., F. Narin and P. Woolf (1981), 'Citation Rates to Technologically Important Patents', *World Patent Information*, **3** (4), 160–63.

Carpenter, R. and B. Petersen (2002), 'Capital Market Imperfections, High-tech Investment, and New Equity Financing', *The Economic Journal*, **112** (February), 54–72.

Casamatta, C. (2000), 'Financing and Advising: Optimal Financial Contracts with Venture Capitalists', Working Paper.

Ceccagnoli, M., A. Gambardella, P. Giuri and G. Licht (2005), 'Study on Evaluating the Knowledge Economy – What are Patents Actually Worth? The Value for Patents for Today's Economy and Society', Tender no. MARKT and 2004 and 09 and E Final Report for Lot 1, May 2005.

Chan, L., J. Lakonishok and T. Sougiannis (2001), 'The Stock Market Valuation of Research and Development Expenditures', *Journal of Finance*, **56** (6), 2431–56.

Chandler, A.D. (2005), *Shaping the Industrial Century: The Remarkable Story of the Evolution of the Modern Chemical and Pharmaceutical Industries*, Cambridge, MA: Harvard University Press.

Chaney, P., T. Devinney and R. Winer (1991), 'The Impact of New-Product Introductions on the Market Value of Firms', *Journal of Business*, **64** (4), 573–610.

Chang, J. (1998), 'The Decline in Value Relevance of Earnings and Book Values', University of Pennsylvania Working Paper.

Cheng, Q. and K. Lo (2006), 'Insider Trading and Voluntary Disclosures', *Journal of Accounting Research*, **44** (5), 815–48.

Chesbrough, H. and D. Teece (1996), 'When is Virtual Virtuous? Organizing for Innovation', *Harvard Business Review*, **74** (1), 65–73.

Chiang, C.C. and Y.M. Mensah (2004), 'The Determinants of Investor Valuation of R&D Expenditure in the Software Industry', *Review of Quantitative Finance and Accounting*, **22**, 293–313.

Christensen, C.M. (1997), *The Innovators Dilemma: When New Technologies Cause Great Firms to Fail*, Cambridge, MA: Harvard Business School Press.

Chung, K.H., M. Li and L.Q. Yu (2005), 'Assets in Place, Growth Opportunities, and IPO Returns', *Financial Management*, **34** (3), 65–88.

Chung, K.H., P. Wright and B. Kedia (2003), 'Corporate Governance and Market Valuation of Capital and R&D Investments', *Review of Financial Economics*, **12** (2), 161–72.

Clark, K.B. and Z. Griliches (1982), 'Productivity Growth and R&D at the Business Level: Results from the PIMS Data Base', NBER Working Papers 0916, National Bureau of Economic Research, Inc.

Coase, R.H. (1960), 'The Problem of Social Cost', *Journal of Law and Economics*, **3**, 1–44.

Cockburn, I. (2007), 'Is the Market for Technology Working? Obstacles to Licensing Inventions and Ways to Remove Them', presented at the Monte Verità Conference on the Economics of Technology Policy, Monte Verità, Ascona, 17–21 June.

Cockburn, I. and R. Henderson (1994), 'Racing to Invest? The Dynamics of Competition in Ethical Drug Discovery', *Journal of Economics & Management Strategy*, **3** (3), 481–519.

Cockburn, I. and R. Henderson (2001), 'Scale and Scope in Drug Development: Unpacking the Advantages of Size in Pharmaceutical Research', *Journal of Health Economics*, **20** (6), 1033–57.

Cohen, M.A., J. Eliashberg and T.H. Ho (1997), 'An Anatomy of a Decision-Support System for Developing and Launching Line Extensions', *Journal of Marketing Research*, **34** (1–2), 117–29.

Cohen, W.M. (2005), 'Patents and Appropriation', *Journal of Technology Transfer*, **30** (1), 57–71.

Cohen, W.M., R.R. Nelson and J.P. Walsh (2000), 'Protecting their Intellectual Assets: Appropriability Conditions and Why U.S. Manufacturing Firms Patent (or Not)', NBER Working Paper Series No. 7552), Cambridge MA: NBER (National Bureau of Economic Research).

Cohen, W.M., A. Goto, A. Nagata, R.R. Nelson and J.P. Walsh (2002), 'R&D Spillovers, Patents and the Incentives to Innovate in Japan and the United States', *Research Policy*, **31** (8–9), 1349–67.

Coller, M. and T. Yohn (1997), 'Management Forecasts and Information Asymmetry: An Examination of Bid–Ask Spreads', *Journal of Accounting Research*, **35** (2), 181–91.

Comanor, W.S. and F.M. Scherer (1969), 'Patent Statistics as a Measure of Technical Change', *Journal of Political Economy*, **77**, 392–8.

Cooper, R. (1985), 'Selecting Winning New Product Projects: Using the NewProd System', *Journal of Product Innovation Management*, **2**, 34–44.

Cooper, R. (1991), 'The Impact of Product Innovativeness on Performance', *Journal of Product Innovation Management*, **18** (4), 90–111.

Cotter, J.F., A. Shivdasani and M. Zenner (1997), 'Do Independent Directors Enhance Target Shareholder Wealth during Tender Offers?', *Journal of Financial Economics*, **43** (2), 195–218.

Czarnitzki, D. and K. Kraft (2004), 'Innovation Indicators and Corporate Credit Ratings: Evidence from German Firms', *Economic Letters*, **82** (3), 377–84.

Dall'Olmo, R.F., A.S. Ehrenberg, S.B. Castleberry, T.P. Barwise and N.R. Barnard (1997), 'The Variability of Attitudinal Repeat-rates', *International Journal of Research in Marketing*, **14** (5), 437–50.

Daniel, K. and S. Titman (2001), 'Market Reactions to Tangible and Intangible Information', NBER Working Paper No. 9743, Northwestern University.

Darrough, M. and N. Stoughton (1990), 'Financial Disclosure Policy in an Entry Game', *Journal of Accounting and Economics*, **12**, 219–44.

Davis, J.L. and S.S. Harrison (2001), *Edison in the Boardroom: How Leading Companies Realize Value from their Intellectual Assets*, 1st edition, New York: Wiley.

DeMeza, D. and D.C. Webb (1987), 'Too Much Investment: A Problem of Asymmetric Information', *The Quarterly Journal of Economics*, **102** (2), 282–91.

Demsetz, H. (1991), 'The Theory of the Firm Revisited', in Williamson, O.E. and S.G. Winter (eds.), *The Nature of the Firm*, New York: Oxford University Press, pp. 159–78.

Deng, Z., B. Lev and F. Narin (1999), 'Science and Technology as Predictors of Stock Market Performance', *Financial Analysts Journal*, **55** (3), 20–31.

Denicolo, V. and L.A. Franzoni (2004), 'Patents, Secrets, and the First-Inventor Defense', *Journal of Economics & Management Strategy*, **13** (3), 517–38.

Diamond, D. (1984), 'Financial Intermediation and Delegated Monitoring', *Review of Economic Studies*, **51**, 393–414.

Diamond, D. and R. Verrecchia (1991), 'Disclosure, Liquidity, and the Cost of Capital', *The Journal of Finance*, **66**, 1325–55.

Dietl, H.M. (1993), *Institutionen und Zeit*, Tübingen: Mohr Siebeck.

Dodgson, M. (1993), 'Organizational Learning: A Review of Some Literature', *Organization Studies*, **14** (3), 375–94.

Dres, J. and S.T. Ryser (1996), 'An Innovative Deficit in the Pharmaceutical Industry', *Drug Information Journal*, **30**, 19–108.

Duguet, E. and I. Kabla (1998), 'Appropriation Strategy and the Motivation to use the Patent System: An Econometric Analysis at the Firm Level in French Manufacturing', *Annales d'Economie et de Statistique*, **49/50**, 289–327.

DVFA (2005), 'Life Science am Kapitalmarkt: Biotechnologie im Fokus', Deutsche Vereinigung für Finanzanalyse und Asset Management.

Dybvig, P. and J. Zender (1991), 'Capital Structure and Dividend

Irrelevance with Asymmetric Information', *Review of Financial Studies*, **4** (1), 201–20.

Dye, R.A. (2001), 'An Evaluation of Essays on Disclosure and the Disclosure Literature in Accounting', *Journal of Accounting and Economics*, **32** (1–3), 181–235.

Dynkin, L., J. Hyman and V. Konstantinovsky (2002), 'Sufficient Diversification in Credit Portfolios', *Journal of Portfolio Management*, **29** (1), 89–114.

Easley, D. and M. O'Hara (2004), 'Information and the Cost of Capital', *The Journal of Finance*, **59**, 1553–83.

Eberhardt, A., W. Maxwell and A. Siddique (2004), 'An Examination of Long-Term Abnormal Stock Returns and Operating Performance Following R&D Increases', *The Journal of Finance*, **59** (2), 623–50.

Eckbo, E. (1986), 'The Valuation Effects of Corporate Debt Offerings', *Journal of Financial Economics*, **15** (1–2), 119–52.

Edvinsson, L. (1997), 'Developing Intellectual Capital at Skandia', *Long Range Planning*, **30** (3), 366–73.

Ehrat, M. (1997), 'Kompetenzorientierte, analysegestützte Technologiestrategieerarbeitung', Dissertation at University of St. Gallen, St. Gallen, No. 1981.

Eichner, M.P. (2008), *Insiderrecht und Ad-hoc-Publizität nach dem Anlegerschutzverbesserungsgesetz*, Baden-Baden: Nomos.

Eisenhardt, K.M. and M.E. Gräbner (2007), 'Theory Building from Cases: Opportunities and Challenges', *Academy of Management Journal*, **50** (1), 25–32.

Ernst, H. (1995), 'Patenting Strategies in the German Mechanical Engineering Industry and their Relationship to Firm Performance', *Technovation*, **15** (4), 225–40.

Ernst, H. (1996), *Patentinformationen für die strategische Planung von Forschung und Entwicklung*, Wiesbaden: DUV-Verlag.

Ernst, H. (2001), 'Patent Applications and Subsequent Changes of Performance: Evidence from Time-series Cross-section Analyses on the Firm Level', *Research Policy*, **30** (1), 143–57.

European Commission (2007), 'Mitteilung der Kommission an das Europäische Parlament und den Rat: Vertiefung des Patentsystems in Europa', Brussels.

European Commission (2009), 'Pharmaceutical Sector Inquiry', DG Competition Staff Report.

Fama, E.F. (1965), 'The Behaviour of Stock Market Prices', *Journal of Business*, **38** (1), 34–105.

Fama, E.F. (1970), 'Efficient Capital Markets: A Review of Theory and Empirical Work', *Journal of Finance*, **25** (2), 383–487.

Farag, H. (2009), *Collaborative Value Creation: An Empirical Analysis of the European Biotechnology Industry*, Heidelberg: Physica-Verlag.

Fluck, Z., D. Holtz-Eakin and H.S. Rosen (1997), 'Where Does the Money Come from? The Financing of Small Entrepreneurial Enterprises', New York University Working Paper.

Fornell, C., M. Sunil, V.M. Forrest and M.S. Krishnan (2006), 'Customer Satisfaction and Stock Prices: High Returns, Low Risk', *Journal of Marketing*, **70** (January), 3–14.

Francis, J. and L. Soffer (1997), 'The Relative Informativeness of Analysts' Stock Recommendations and Earnings Forecast Revisions', *Journal of Accounting Research*, **35** (2), 193–212.

Francis, J., D. Nanda and P. Olsson (2008), 'Voluntary Disclosure, Earnings Quality, and Cost of Capital', *Journal of Accounting Research*, **46** (1), 53–99.

Frey, C.B. and A.J. Wurzer (2009), *Intellectual Property Managers in Strategy Development: Integrating IP into Business Models*, in Wurzer, A.J. (ed.), *IP-Manager*, Cologne: Carl Heymanns Verlag.

Frey, C.B., S. Hundertmark and A.J. Wurzer (2008), 'IP Management – A Question of Perspectives', *Intellectual Asset Management Magazine*, **1**, 14–19.

Frietsch, R., U. Schmoch, B. Van Looy, J.P. Walsh, R. Devroede, M. Du Plessis, T. Jung, Y. Meng, P. Neuhäusler, B. Peeters and T. Schubert (2010), 'The Value and Indicator Function of Patents, Studien zum deutschen Innovationssystem', No. 15, Expertenkommission Forschung und Innovation (EFI).

Froot, K., D.S. Scharfstein and J. Stein (1992), 'Herd on the Street: Informational Inefficiencies in a Market with Short-Term Speculation', *Journal of Finance*, **47** (4), 1461–84.

Gambardella, A. (1995), *Science and Innovation in the US Pharmaceutical Industry*, Cambridge: Cambridge University Press.

Gambardella, A., D. Harhoff and B. Verspagen (2008), 'The Value of European Patents', *European Management Review*, **5** (2), 69–84.

Gans, J., D.H. Hsu and S. Stern (2008), 'The Impact of Uncertain Intellectual Property Rights on the Market for Ideas: Evidence from Patent Grant Delays', *Management Science*, **54** (5), 982–97.

Garcia-Vega, M. (2006), 'Does Technological Diversification Promote Innovation?: An Empirical Analysis for European Firms', *Research Policy*, **35** (2), 230–46.

Gassmann, O. and M. Bader (2010), *Patentmanagement: Innovationen erfolgreich nutzen und schützen*, 2nd edition, Berlin: Springer.

Gassmann, O. and M. Von Zedtwitz (2003), 'Trends and Determinants in Managing Virtual R&D Teams', *R&D Management*, **33** (3), 243–62.

Gassmann, O. and M. Von Zedtwitz (2004), *Leading Pharmaceutical Innovation: Trends and Drivers for Growth in the Pharmaceutical Industry*, 1st edition, Berlin: Springer.

Gassmann, O., E. Enkel and H. Chesbrough (2010), 'The Future of Open Innovation', *R&D Management*, **40** (3), 213–21.

Givoly, D. (1982), 'Financial Analysts' Forecasts of Earnings: A Better Surrogate for Market Expectations', *Journal of Accounting and Economics*, **4** (2), 85–108.

Goh, J.C. and L.H. Ederington (1999), 'Cross-sectional Variation in the Stock Market Reaction to Bond Rating Changes', *Quarterly Review of Economics and Finance*, **39**, 101–12.

Gompers, P.A. (1995), 'Optimal Investment, Monitoring, and the Staging of Venture Capital', *Journal of Finance*, **50** (5), 1461–89.

Gompers, P.A. and J. Lerner (1998), 'What Drives Venture Capital Fundraising?', Brookings Papers on Economic Activity (Microeconomics), pp. 149–92.

Gompers, P., L.H. Kovner, J. Lerner and D. Scharfstein (2008), 'Venture Capital Investment Cycles: The Impact of Public Markets', *Journal of Financial Economics*, **87** (1), 1–23.

Gottschalk, S., N. Janz, P. Peters, C. Rammer and T. Schmidt (2002), 'Innovationsverhalten der deutschen Wirtschaft', Hintergrundbericht zur Innovationserhebung, 2(3), Mannheim.

Grabowski, H. and J. Vernon (1992), 'Brand Loyalty, Entry and Price Competition in Pharmaceuticals after the 1984 Drug Act', *Journal of Law and Economics*, **35** (2), 331–50.

Graham, S. and D. Somaya (2006), 'Vermeers and Rembrandts in the Same Attic: Complementarity between Copyright and Trademark Leveraging Strategies in Software', Georgia Institute of Technology Working Paper.

Granstrand, O. (1999), *The Economics and Management of Intellectual Property: Towards Intellectual Capitalism*, Cheltenham, UK and Northampton, MA, USA: Edward Elgar Publishing.

Grant, R.M. (1991), 'The Resource-Based Theory of Competitive Advantages: Implications for Strategy Formulation', *California Management Review*, **33** (3), 14–35.

Grant, R.M. (1996), 'Toward a Knowledge-based Theory of the Firm', *Strategic Management Journal*, **17**, 109–22.

Greenhalgh, C. and M. Longland (2005), 'Running to Stand Still? – The Value of R&D, Patents and Trade Marks in Innovating Manufacturing Firms', *International Journal of the Economics of Business*, **12** (3), 307–28.

Greenhalgh, C. and M. Rogers (2006), 'Trade Marks and Market Value in UK Firms', Melbourne Institute Working Paper Series 4, University of Melbourne.

Greenhalgh, C. and M. Rogers (2010), *Innovation, Intellectual Property, and Economic Growth*, Hoboken, NJ: Princeton University Press.

Griffiths, W., P. Jensen and E. Webster (2005), 'The Effects on Firm Profits of the Stock of Intellectual Property Rights', Melbourne Working Paper 5(5).

Griliches, Z. and J. Mairesse (1981), 'Productivity and R&D at the Firm Level', in *R&D, Patents, and Productivity*, NBER Working Papers 0826, National Bureau of Economic Research, Inc.

Grindley, P. and D. Teece (1997), 'Managing Intellectual Capital: Licensing and Cross-licensing in Semiconductors end Electronics', *California Management Review*, **39** (2), 8–41.

Grossman, S.J. and Stiglitz, J.E. (1980), 'On the Impossibility of Informationally Efficient Markets', *American Economic Review*, **70** (3), 393–408.

Grundfest, J.A. and Perino, M.A. (1997), 'Securities Litigation Reform: The First Year's Experience', Working Paper No. 140, Stanford Law School.

Gu, F. and B. Lev (2004), 'The Information Content of Royalty Income', *Accounting Horizons*, **18** (1), 1–12.

Gulati, R. (1999), 'Network Location and Learning: The Influence of Network Resources and Firm Capabilities on Alliance Formation', *Strategic Management Journal*, **20**, 397–420.

Guo, R., B. Lev and N. Zhou (2005), 'The Valuation of Biotech IPOs', *Journal of Accounting, Auditing and Finance*, **21** (3), 423–59.

Hadlock, C. and C.M. James (1997), 'Bank Lending and the Menu of Financing Options', University of Florida Working Paper.

Hall, B.H. (1992), 'Research and Development at the Firm Level: Does the Source of Financing Matter?', NBER Working Papers 4096, National Bureau of Economic Research, Inc.

Hall, B.H. (1993), 'R&D Tax Policy during the Eighties: Success or Failure?', *Tax Policy and the Economy*, **7**, 1–36.

Hall, B.H. (1994), 'Corporate Capital Structure and Investment Horizons in the United States, 1976–1987', *Business History Review*, **68**, 110–43.

Hall, B.H. (2002), 'The Financing of Research and Development', *Oxford Review of Economic Policy*, **18** (1), 35–51.

Hall, B.H. and J. Lerner (2010), 'The Financing of R&D and Innovation', in Hall, B.H. and N. Rosenberg (eds.), *Handbook of the Economics of Innovation*, Amsterdam: Elsevier-North Holland.

Hall, B.H. and R. Ziedonis (2001), 'The Patent Paradox Revisited: An

Empirical Study of Patenting in the U.S. Semiconductor Industry, 1979–1995', *RAND Journal of Economics*, **32** (1), 101–28.

Hall, B.H., A. Jaffe and M. Trajtenberg (2005), 'Market Value and Patent Citations', *RAND Journal of Economics*, **36** (1), 16–38.

Hall, B.H., S.J. Graham, D. Harhoff and D.C. Mowery (2004), 'Prospects for Improving U.S. Patent Quality via Post-grant Opposition', in Jaffe, A.B., J. Lerner and S. Stern (eds.), *Innovation Policy and the Economy*, Vol. 4, NBER Books, Cambridge, MA: MIT Press.

Hamel, G. (2002), *Leading the Revolution*, 1st edition, New York: Plume.

Hand, J. and Lev, B. (2003), *Intangible Assets: Values, Measures, and Risks*, New York: Oxford University Press.

Hand, J., R. Holthausen and R. Leftwich (1992), 'The Effect of Bond Rating Agency Announcements on Bond and Stock Prices', *Journal of Finance*, **57** (3), 733–52.

Harhoff, D. (1998), 'Are there Financing Constraints for R&D and Investment in German Manufacturing Firms?', *Annales d'Economie et de Statistique*, **49/50**, 421–56.

Harhoff, D. (2005), 'Strategisches Patentmanagement', in Albers, S. and O. Gassmann (eds.), *Handbuch Technologie- und Innovationsmanagement: Strategie, Umsetzung, Controlling*, 1st edition, Wiesbaden: Gabler, pp. 175–92.

Harhoff, D. and Reitzig, M. (2001), 'Strategien zur Gewinnmaximierung bei der Anmeldung von Patenten: Wirtschaftliche und rechtliche Aspekte als Entscheidungsgrößen beim Schutz von Erfindungen', *Zeitschrift für Betriebswirtschaft*, **71** (5), 509–29.

Harhoff, D., F.M. Scherer and K. Vopel (2003), 'Citations, Family Size, Opposition and the Value of Patent Rights', *Research Policy*, **32** (8), 1343–63.

Hassell, J. and R. Jennings (1986), 'Relative Forecast Accuracy and the Timing of Earnings Forecast Announcements', *The Accounting Review*, **61**, 58–76.

Hassell, J., R. Jennings and D. Lasser (1988), 'Management Earnings Forecasts: Their Usefulness as a Source of Firm-specific Information to Security Analysts', *The Journal of Financial Research*, **11**, 303–20.

Healy, P. and K. Palepu (1993), 'The Effect of Firms' Financial Disclosure Strategies on Stock Prices', *Accounting Horizons*, **7**, 1–11.

Healy, P. and K. Palepu (1995), 'The Challenges of Investor Communications: The Case of CUC International, Inc', *Journal of Financial Economics*, **38**, 111–41.

Healy, P. and K. Palepu (2001), 'Information Asymmetry, Corporate Disclosure, and the Capital Markets: A Review of the Empirical Disclosure Literature', *Journal of Accounting & Economics*, **31** (1–3), 405–40.

Healy, P., A. Hutton and K. Palepu (1999), 'Stock Performance and Intermediation Changes Surrounding Sustained Increases in Disclosure', *Contemporary Accounting Research*, **16**, 485–520.

Hellmann, T. and J. Stiglitz (2000), 'Credit and Equity Rationing in Markets with Adverse Selection', *European Economic Review*, **44** (2), 281–304.

Helmers, C. and M. Rogers (2010), 'Innovation and the Survival of New Firms in the UK', *Review of Industrial Organization*, **136** (3), 227–48.

Henderson, R. and I. Cockburn (1996), 'Scale, Scope, and Spillovers: The Determinants of Research Productivity in Drug Discovery', *RAND Journal of Economics*, **27** (1), 32–59.

Henderson, R., L. Orsenigo and G.P. Pisano (1999), 'The Pharmaceutical Industry and the Revolution in Molecular Biology: Exploring the Interactions between Scientific, Institutional and Organizational Change', in Mowery, D.C. and R.R. Nelson (eds.), *Sources of Industrial Leadership*, Cambridge: Cambridge University Press.

Hens, T. and K.R. Schenck-Hoppé (2009), *Handbook of Financial Markets: Dynamics and Evolution*, Amsterdam: Elsevier-North Holland.

Herrmann, A., F. Huber, A. Shao and Y. Bao (2007), 'Building Brand Equity via Product Quality', *Total Quality Management & Business Excellence*, **18** (5), 531–44.

Higgins, M.J. and D. Rodriguez (2006), 'The Outsourcing of R&D through Acquisitions in the Pharmaceutical Industry', *Journal of Financial Economics*, **80** (2), 351–83.

Himmelberg, C.P. and B.C. Petersen (1994), 'R&D and Internal Finance: A Panel Study of Small Firms in High-Tech Industries', *Review of Economics and Statistics*, **76**, 38–51.

Hirschey, M. and V. Richardson (2001), 'Valuation Effects of Patent Quality: A Comparison for Japanese and US Firms', *Pacific-Basin Finance Journal*, **9** (1), 65–82.

Hirschey, M. and V. Richardson (2004), 'Are Scientific Indicators of Patent Quality Useful to Investors?', *Journal of Empirical Finance*, **11** (1), 91–107.

Hite, G. and A. Warga (1997), 'The Effect of Bond-rating Changes on Bond Price Performance', *Financial Analysts Journal*, **53** (3), 35–51.

Holthausen, R. and R. Leftwich (1986), 'The Effect of Bond Rating Changes on Common Stock Prices', *Journal of Financial Economics*, **17** (1), 57–89.

Hopf, C. (1995), 'Qualitative Interviews in der Sozialforschung: Ein Überblick', in Flick, U., E. von Kardorff, H. Keupp, L. von Rosenstiel and S. Wolff (eds.), *Handbuch Qualitative Sozialforschung: Grundlagen,*

Konzepte, Methoden und Anwendungen, 2nd edition, Weinheim, Beltz: Psychologie-Verlags-Union, pp. 177–82.

Hopt, K.J. and H.-C. Voigt (2004), *Prospekt- und Kapitalmarktinformationshaftung: Recht und Reform in der Europäischen Union, der Schweiz und den USA*, Tübingen: Mohr Siebeck.

Horrigan, J. (1966), 'The Determination of Long-Term Credit Standing with Financial Ratios', *Journal of Accounting Research*, **4**, 44–62.

Hoyer, W.D. and S.P. Brown (1990), 'Effects of Brand Awareness on Choice for a Common, Repeat-purchase Product', *Journal of Consumer Research*, **17**, 141–8.

Hudson, J. (2000), 'Generic Take-up in the Pharmaceutical Market Following Patent Expiry: A Multi-country Study', *International Review of Law and Economics*, **20** (2), 205–21.

Hull, J., M. Predescu and A. White (2004), 'The Relationship between Credit Default Swap Spreads, Bond Yields, and Credit Rating Announcements', *Journal of Banking and Finance*, **28** (11), 2789–811.

Hulten, C.R. (2010), 'Decoding Microsoft: Intangible Capital as a Source of Company Growth', National Bureau of Economic Research, NBER Working Papers No. 15799.

Hulten, C.R. and X. Hao (2008), 'What is a Company Really Worth? Intangible Capital and the "Market to Book Value" Puzzle', National Bureau of Economic, NBER Working Papers No. 14548.

Hurmelinna-Laukkanen, P. and K. Puumalainen (2007), 'Formation of the Appropriability Regime: Strategic and Practical Considerations', *Innovation, Management, Policy & Practice*, **9** (1), 2–13.

Hurwitz, M.A. and R.E. Caves (1988), 'Persuasion or Information? Promotion and Shares of Brand Name and Generic Pharmaceuticals', *Journal of Law and Economics*, **31** (2), 299–320.

Hussinger, K. (2006), 'Is Silence Golden? Patents versus Secrecy at the Firm Level', *Economics of Innovation and New Technology*, **15** (8), 735–52.

Hutton A.P., G.S. Miller and D.J. Skinner (2003), 'The Role of Supplementary Statements with Management Earnings Forecasts', *Journal of Accounting Research*, **41** (5), 867–90.

ICH Harmonized Tripartite Guideline (1997), *Timing of Nonclinical Safety Studies for the Conduct of Human Clinical Trials for Pharmaceuticals*.

Janz, N., G. Licht and T. Doherr (2001), 'Innovation Activities and European Patenting of German Firms – A Panel Data Analysis', ZEW Working Paper, Mannheim.

Jeng, L.A. and P.C. Wells (2000), 'The Determinants of Venture Capital

Funding: Evidence across Countries', *Journal of Corporate Finance*, **6** (3), 241–89.

Jennewein, K. (2005), *Intellectual Property Management: The Role of Technology-Brands in the Appropriation of Technological Innovation*, Heidelberg: Physica-Verlag.

Jensen, M. and W. Meckling (1976), 'Theory of the Firm: Managerial Behavior, Agency Costs and Ownership Structure', *Journal of Financial Economics*, **3**, 305–60.

Johnson, M.D., M. Hermann and H. Huber (2006), 'The Evolution of Loyalty Intentions', *Journal of Marketing*, **70**, 122–32.

Johnson, M., R. Kasznik and K. Nelson (2001), 'The Impact of Securities Litigation Reform on the Disclosure of Forward-Looking Information by High Technology Firms', *Journal of Accounting Research*, **39** (2), 297–327.

Jones, T.O. and W.E. Sasser Jr (1995), 'Why Satisfied Customers Defect', *Harvard Business Review*, November–December: 88–99.

Kalay, A. (1984), 'The Ex-Dividend Day Behavior of Stock Prices: A Re-examination of the Clientele Effect: A Reply', *Journal of Finance*, **39**, 557–61.

Kaplan, R.S. and D. Norton (1992), 'The Balanced Scorecard: Measures that Drive Performance', *Harvard Business Review*, January–February, 71–9.

Kaplan, R.S. and G. Urwitz (1979), 'Models of Bond Ratings: A Methodological Inquiry', *Journal of Business*, **52** (2), 231–61.

Kaplan, S. and P. Strömberg (2001), 'Venture Capitalists as Principals: Contracting, Screening, and Monitoring', *American Economic Review Papers and Proceedings*, **91** (2), 426–30.

Karpoff, J.M. (1987), 'The Relation between Price Changes and Trading Volume: A Survey', *Journal of Financial and Quantitative Analysis*, **22** (1), 109–26.

Keller, K.L. (2000), 'The Brand Report Card', *Harvard Business Review*, January–February, 147–57.

Kerr, W.R., J. Lerner and A. Schoar (2010), 'The Consequences of Entrepreneurial Finance: A Regression Discontinuity Analysis', Harvard Business School Entrepreneurial Management Working Paper No. 10-086.

Kim, K.S. (2005), 'Predicting Bond Ratings Using Publicly Available Information', *Expert Systems with Applications*, **29**, 75–81.

King, R.G. and R. Levine (1993), 'Finance and Growth: Schumpeter Might Be Right', *The Quarterly Journal of Economics*, **108** (3), 717–37.

Kingston, W. (2001), 'Innovation Needs Patent Reform', *Research Policy*, **30** (3), 403–23.

Kline, D. (2003), 'Sharing the Corporate Crown Jewels', *MIT Sloan Management Review*, **44** (3), 89–93.

Kodama, F. (1995), *Emerging Patterns of Innovation*, Boston, MA: Harvard Business School Press.

Köhler, F. (2010), 'Empirical Analyses of Company Patenting Behaviour – Essays on the Role of Strategic Patenting, Standardization, Technology Exchange and Product Piracy', Dissertation at TU Berlin, Chair of Innovation Economics.

Kortum, S. and J. Lerner (1999), 'What is behind the Recent Surge in Patenting?', *Research Policy*, **28** (1), 1–22.

Kortum, S. and J. Lerner (2000), 'Assessing the Contribution of Venture Capital to Innovation', *RAND Journal of Economics*, **31** (4), 674–92.

Kothari, S. (2001), 'Capital Markets Research in Accounting', *Journal of Accounting & Economics*, **31**, 105–231.

Kothari, S., T. Laguerre and A. Leone (2002), 'Capitalization versus Expensing: Evidence on the Uncertainty of Future Earnings from Capital Expenditures versus R&D Outlays', *Review of Accounting Studies*, **7**, 355–82.

Kraus, A. and R.H. Litzenberger (1973), 'A State-preference Model of Optimal Financial Leverage', *Journal of Finance*, **28** (4), 911–22.

Küting, K., C.P. Eber and C. Boecker (2006), *Die Bilanzanalyse. Beurteilung von Abschlüssen nach HGB und IFRS*, 8th edition, Stuttgart: Schäffer-Poeschel.

Kuusito, J. and S. Paallysaho (2007), 'Informal Ways to Protect Intellectual Property in Small and Medium Size Businesses', IPR Expert Group, DG Enterprise, European Commission.

La Porta, R., F. Lopez De Silanes, A. Shleifer and R. Vishny (1997), 'Legal Determinants of External Finance', *Journal of Finance*, **52**, 1131–50.

Landes, W.M. and R.A. Posner (1987), 'Trademark Law: An Economic Perspective', *Journal of Law & Economics*, **30** (2), 265–309.

Lane, V. and R. Jacobson (1995), 'Stock Market Reactions to Brand Extension Announcements: The Effects of Brand Attitude and Familiarity', *Journal of Marketing*, **59** (1), 63–77.

Lang, M. and R. Lundholm (1993), 'Cross-sectional Determinants of Analyst Ratings of Corporate Disclosures', *Journal of Accounting Research*, **31**, 246–71.

Lang, M. and R. Lundholm (2000), 'Voluntary Disclosure during Equity Offerings: Reducing Information Asymmetry or Hyping the Stock?', *Contemporary Accounting Research*, **17** (4), 623–62.

Lanjouw, J. (1998), 'Patent Value in the Shadow of Infringement: Simulation Estimations of Patent Value', *Review of Economic Studies*, **65**, 671–710.

Lanjouw, J. and M. Schankerman (2001), 'Characteristics of Patent Litigation: A Window on Competition', *RAND Journal of Economics*, **32** (1), 129–51.

Lanjouw, J. and M. Schankerman (2004), 'Patent Quality and Research Productivity: Measuring Innovation with Multiple Indicators', *The Economic Journal*, **114**, 441–65.

Leahy, J.V. and T.M. Whited (1996), 'The Effect of Uncertainty on Investment: Some Stylized Facts', *Journal of Money, Credit and Banking*, **28** (1), 64–83.

Lee, B.S. and O.M. Rui (2002), 'The Dynamic Relationship between Stock Returns and Trading Volume: Domestic and Cross-country Evidence', *Journal of Banking and Finance*, **26** (1), 51–78.

Lee, I., S. Lochhead, J. Ritter and Q. Zhao (1996), 'The Costs of Raising Capital', *Journal of Financial Research*, **19**, 59–74.

Lehman, B. (2003), 'The Pharmaceutical Industry and the Patent System', available at http://www.earthinstitute.columbia.edu/cgsd/documents/lehman.pdf (accessed 21 October 2008).

Lehner, F. (2009), *Wissensmanagement: Grundlagen, Methoden und Technische Unterstützung*, 3rd edition, Munich: Carl Hanser Verlag.

Leland, H.E. and D.H. Pyle (1977), 'Informational Asymmetries, Financial Structure, and Financial Intermediation', *The Journal of Finance*, **32** (2), 371–87.

Lemley, M. and C. Shapiro (2005), 'Probabilistic Patents', *Journal of Economic Perspectives*, **19** (2), 75–98.

Leonard-Barton, D. (1995), *Wellsprings of Knowledge: Building and Sustaining the Sources of Innovation*, Boston, MA: Harvard Business School Press.

Lerner, J. (1994a), 'The Importance of Patent Scope: An Empirical Analysis', *RAND Journal of Economics*, **25** (3), 319–33.

Lerner, J. (1994b), 'Venture Capitalists and their Decisions to Go Public', *Journal of Financial Economics*, **35**, 293–316.

Lerner, J. (2009), *Boulevard of Broken Dreams: Why Public Efforts to Boost Entrepreneurship and Venture Capital Have Failed – and What to do About it*, Hoboken, NJ: Princeton University Press.

Lerner, J., H. Shane and A. Tsai (2000), 'Do Equity Financing Cycles Matter? Evidence from Biotechnology Alliances', NBER Working Paper No. 7464.

Lerner, J., H. Shane and A. Tsai (2003), 'Do Equity Financing Cycles Matter? Evidence from Biotechnology Alliances', *Journal of Financial Economics*, **67** (3), 411–46.

Leuz, C. and R. Verrecchia (2000), 'The Economic Consequences of Increased Disclosure', *Journal of Accounting Research*, **38** (3), 91–124.

Lev, B. (2001), *Intangibles: Management, Measurement, and Reporting*, Washington, DC: Brookings Institution.

Lev, B. and S.H. Penman (1990), 'Voluntary Forecast Disclosure, Nondisclosure, and Stock Prices', *Journal of Accounting Research*, **28** (Spring), 49–76.

Lev, B. and P. Zarowin (1999), 'The Boundaries of Financial Reporting and How to Extend Them', *Journal of Accounting Research*, **37** (2), 353–85.

Lev, B., S. Radhakrishnan and C. Seethamraju (1998), 'FDA Drug Approvals and the Formation of Investors' Beliefs', New York University Working Paper.

Levin, R.C., A.K. Klevorick, R.R. Nelson and S.G. Winter (1987), 'Appropriating the Returns from Industrial Research and Development', *Brookings Papers on Economic Activity*, **3**, 783–831.

Levine, D. and A. Pritchard (1998), 'The Securities Litigation Uniform Standards Act of 1998: The Sun Sets on California's Blue Sky Laws', *The Business Lawyer*, **54** (1), 1–54.

Levine, R. and S. Zervos (1998), 'Stock Markets, Banks, and Economic Growth', *American Economic Review*, **88** (3), 537–59.

Levinthal, D.A. (1998), 'The Slow Pace of Rapid Technology Change: Gradualism and Punctuation in Technological Change', *Industrial and Corporate Change*, **7** (2), 217–47.

Li, X.-W. and M.-L. Zhang (2008), 'Relationship Benefit in Consumer Markets and its Role in Brand Image–Brand Loyalty Chain', International Conference on Management Science; Engineering.

Lichtenthaler, U. (2006), *Leveraging Knowledge Assets: Success Factors of External Technology Commercialization*, Wiesbaden: DUV-Verlag.

Linde, L. and A. Prasad (1999), 'Venture Support Systems Project: Angel Investors', MIT Entrepreneurship Centre Working Paper.

Lobo, G.J. and A.A. Mahmoud (1989), 'Relationship between Differential Amounts of Prior Information and Security Return Variability', *Journal of Accounting Research*, **27**, 116–34.

Long, J.S. and J. Freese (2001), *Regression Models for Categorical Dependent Variables Using Stata*, revised edition, College Station, TX: Stata Press.

Lourie, A.D. (1989), 'A Review of Recent Patent Term Data', *Journal of the Patent and Trademark Office Society*, February, 171–6.

Lys, T. and S. Sohn (1990), 'The Association between Revisions of Financial Analysts' Earnings Forecasts and Security Price Changes', *Journal of Accounting and Economics*, **13**, 341–64.

Macdonald, E. and B. Sharp (2003), 'Management Perceptions of the Importance of Brand Awareness as an Indicator of Advertising Effectiveness', *Marketing Bulletin*, **14** (2), 1–15.

Mahlich, J. (2005), 'Erfolgsfaktoren von forschungsintensiven Firmen am Beispiel der Pharmaindustrie', *Die Betriebswirtschaft*, **65** (4), 396–410.

Malerba, F. and L. Orsenigo (2001), 'Towards a History Friendly Model of Innovation, Market Structure and Regulation in the Dynamics of the Pharmaceutical Industry: The Age of Random Screening', KITeS, Centre for Knowledge, Internationalization and Technology Studies, Bocconi University, KITeS Working Papers 124.

Malkiel, B. (1973), *A Random Walk down Wall Street: The Time-tested Strategy for Successful Investing*, New York: W.W. Norton & Company, Inc.

Malmberg, C. (2005), 'Trademark Statistics as Innovation Indicators? – A Micro Study', CIRCLE Electronic Working Paper Series 2005-17, CIRCLE (Centre for Innovation, Research and Competence in the Learning Economy), Lund University.

Mansfield, E., M. Schwartz and S. Wagner (1981), 'Imitation Costs and Patents: An Empirical Study', *The Economic Journal*, **91**, 907–18.

Mansfield, E., J. Rapoport, A. Romeo, E. Villani, S. Wagner and F. Husic (1977), *The Production and Application of New Industrial Technology*, New York: W.W. Norton & Company, Inc.

March, J.G. (1991), 'Exploration and Exploitation in Organizational Learning', *Organization Science*, **2**, 71–87.

Mason, C. and R.T. Harrison (1990), 'Informal Risk Capital: A Review and Research Agenda', Venture Finance Research Project.

Matsumoto, D. (2000), 'Management's Incentives to Avoid Negative Earnings Surprises', Harvard Business School Working Paper.

Maul, K.H. and J. Mennigner (2000), 'Das "Intellectual Property Statement" – eine notwendige Ergänzung des Jahresabschlusses?', *Der Betrieb*, **11**, 529–33.

McNichols, M. (1989), 'Evidence of Informational Asymmetries from Management Earnings Forecasts and Stock Returns', *The Accounting Review*, **64**, 1–27.

Mendonca, S., T.S. Pereira and M.M Godinho (2004), 'Trademarks as an Indicator of Innovation and Industrial Change', *Research Policy*, **33** (9), 1385–404.

METI (2004), 'Reference Guideline for Intellectual Property Information Disclosure: In the Pursuit of Mutual Understanding between Companies and Capital Markets through Voluntary Disclosures of Information on Patent and Technology', Japanese Ministry of Economy, Trade and Industry, available at http://www.meti.go.jp/english/information/down loadfiles/cIPP0403e.pdf (accessed 11 October 2010).

Micu, M., E.M. Remolona and P. Wooldridge (2006), 'The Price Impact of Rating Announcements: Which Announcements Matter?', BIS Working Papers No. 207 (June 2006), available at http://www.bis.org/publ/work207.htm (accessed 9 June 2011).

Miles, M. and M. Huberman (1994), *Qualitative Data Analysis: An Expanded Sourcebook*, 2nd edition, Sage Publications Inc.

Miller, G. (2002), 'Earnings Performance and Discretionary Disclosure', *Journal of Accounting Research*, **40** (1), 173–204.

Miller, G. and J. Piotroski (2000), 'The Role of Disclosure for High Book-to-Market Firms', Harvard University Working Paper.

Ministry of Economic Development (2003), 'Review of the Pharmaceuticals Patent Act 1953, Pharmaceutical Patent Term in New Zealand', Discussion Paper, available at http://www.med.govt.nz/upload/4186/pharmaceutical%20patent.pdf (accessed 23 February 2009).

Mishkin, F. (2006), Weissman Center Distinguished Lecture, Lecture at Baruch College, New York, October 12, in Ferguson, N. (2008), *The Ascent of Money: A Financial History of the World*, 1st edition, New York: Penguin Press, p. 342.

Modigliani, F. and M.H. Miller (1958), 'The Cost of Capital, Corporation Finance and the Theory of Investment', *American Economic Review*, **48** (3), 261–97.

Moehrle, M.G., L. Walter, A. Geritz and S. Müller (2005), 'Patent-based Inventor Profiles as a Basis for Human Resource Decisions in Research and Development', *R&D Management*, **35** (5), 513–24.

Myers, S.C. (1977), 'Determinants of Corporate Borrowing', *Journal of Financial Economics*, **5**, 147–75.

Myers, S.C. (2003), 'Financing of Corporations', in Constantinides, G.M., M.S. Harris and M. René (eds.), *Handbook of the Economics of Finance*, Volume 1A Corporate Finance, Amsterdam: North-Holland, Elsevier.

Myers, S.C. and N. Majluf (1984), 'Corporate Financing and Investment Decisions when Firms Have Information that Investors do not Have', *Journal of Financial Economics*, **13** (2), 187–221.

Nadler, D. and M. Tushman (1987), *Strategic Organization Design*, Glenview, IL: Scott, Foresman.

Nakamura, L. (2001), 'What is the U.S. Gross Investment in Intangibles? (At Least) One Trillion Dollars a Year!', Federal Reserve Bank of Philadelphia Working Paper, 1(15).

Nakanishi, T. (2007), 'Financial Analyst Reports, Corporate Annual Reports, Investor Information, and IP', Northwestern University Working Paper.

Narin, F. and E. Noma (1987), 'Patents as Indicators of Corporate Technological Strength', *Research Policy*, **16** (2–4), 143–55.

Neuhäusler, P., R. Frietsch, T. Schubert and K. Blind (2011), 'Patents and the Financial Performance of Firms – An Analysis Based on Stock Market Data', Fraunhofer ISI Discussion Papers Innovation Systems and Policy Analysis, 28.

Nordhaus, W.D (1969), 'An Economic Theory of Technological Change', *American Economic Review*, **59** (2), 18–28.

OECD (1996), 'Venture Capital and Innovation', Synthesis Report, Organisation for Economic Co-operation and Development, Paris.

OECD (2008), 'Intellectual Assets and Value Creation', Synthesis Report, Organisation for Economic Co-operation and Development, Paris.

Opler, T.C. and S. Titman (1993), 'The Determinants of Leveraged Buyout Activity: Free Cash Flow vs. Financial Distress Costs', *Journal of Finance*, **48** (5), 1985–99.

Opler, T.C. and S. Titman (1994), 'Financial Distress and Corporate Performance', *Journal of Finance*, **49** (3), 1015–40.

Orsenigo, L., F. Pammolli and M. Riccaboni (2001), 'Technological Change and Network Dynamics: Lessons from the Pharmaceutical Industry', *Research Policy*, **30** (3), 485–508.

Pakes, A. (1986), 'Patents as Options: Some Estimates of the Value of Holding European Patent Stocks', *Econometrica*, **54** (4), 755–84.

Pakes, A. and Z. Griliches (1984), 'Patents and R&D at the Firm Level: A First Look', in Griliches, Z. (ed.), *R&D, Patents and Productivity*, Chicago: The University of Chicago Press, pp. 55–72.

Pangerl, S. (2009), *Defensive Publishing: Handlungsfreiheit und die Aneignung von Innovationsgewinnen*, 1st edition, Wiesbaden: Gabler.

Parchomovsky, G. and P. Siegelman (2002), 'Towards an Integrated Theory of Intellectual Property', *Virginia Law Review*, **88** (7), 1455–528.

Pastor, L. and P. Veronesi (2003), 'Stock Valuation and Learning about Profitability', *Journal of Finance*, **58**, 1749–89.

Pauwels, K., J. Silva-Risso, S. Srinivasan and D.M. Hanssens (2004), 'New Products, Sales Promotions and Firm Value, with Application to the Automobile Industry', *The Journal of Marketing*, **68** (4), 142–56.

Perez, C. (2003), *Technological Revolutions and Financial Capital: The Dynamics of Bubbles and Golden Ages*, Cheltenham, UK and Northampton, MA, USA: Edward Elgar.

Phillips, J. (2003), *Trade Mark Law: A Practical Anatomy*, New York: Oxford University Press.

Pinches, G. and K. Mingo (1973), 'A Multivariate Analysis of Industrial Bond Ratings', *The Journal of Finance*, **28** (1), 1–18.

Piotroski, J. (1999), 'Discretionary Segment Reporting Decisions and the Precision of Investor Beliefs', University of Chicago Working Paper.

Pisano, G. (1997), *R&D Performance, Collaborative Arrangements, and the Market for Know-How: A Test of the 'Lemons' Hypothesis in Biotechnology*, Cambridge, MA: Harvard Business School.

Pisano, G. (2006), 'Can Science Be a Business? Lessons from Biotech', *Harvard Business Review*, **84** (10), 114–24.

Pisano, G. and P. Mang (1993), 'Collaborative Product Development and the Market for Know-how: Strategies and Structures in the Biotechnology Industry', in Rosenbloom, R. and R. Burgelman (eds.), *Research on Technological Innovation, Management and Policy*, Vol. 5, Greenwich, CT: JAI Press, pp. 109–36.

Pitkethly, R.H. (2001), 'Intellectual Property Strategies in Japanese and UK Firms: Patent Licensing Decision and Learning Opportunities', *Research Policy*, **30** (3), 425–42.

Pitkethly, R.H. (2003), 'The Valuation of Patents: A Review of Patent Valuation Methods with Consideration of Option Based Methods and the Potential for Further Research', in *Intellectual Assets: Valuation and Capitalization*, Geneva: UNECE, United Nations.

Planès, B., M. Bardos, S. Avouyi-Dovi and P. Sevestre (2002), 'Financing Innovative Industrial Firms: Risk and Financial Constraints', Banque de France Bulletin Digest, No. 104.

Pogue, T. and R. Soldofsky (1969), 'What is in a Bond Rating?', *Journal of Financial and Quantitative Analysis*, **4** (2), 201–28.

Porter, M.E. (1985), *Competitive Advantage*, New York: Free Press.

Porter, M.E. (1991), 'Towards a Dynamic Theory of Strategy', *Strategic Management Journal*, **12** (Special Issue), 95–117.

Pownall, G. and G. Waymire (1989), 'Voluntary Disclosure Credibility and Securities Prices: Evidence from Management Earnings Forecasts', *Journal of Accounting Research*, **27**, 227–45.

Prahalad, C.K. and G. Hamel (1990), 'The Core Competence of the Corporation', *Harvard Business Review*, **68** (3), 79–91.

Pretnar, B. (2003), 'The Economic Impact of Patents in a Knowledge-based Market Economy', *International Review of Intellectual Property and Competition Law (IIC)*, **34** (8), 887–90.

Putnam, J. (1996), 'The Value of International Patent Rights', PhD thesis, Yale University.

PwC (2007), *Exploiting Intellectual Property in a Complex World, Technology Executive Connections*, PricewaterhouseCoopers, vol. 4.

Rajan, R.G. and L. Zingales (1995), 'What Do We Know about Capital Structure? Some Evidence from International Data', *Journal of Finance*, **50** (5), 1421–60.

Rajgopal, S. and M. Venkatachalam (2011), 'Financial Reporting Quality and Idiosyncratic Return Volatility', *Journal of Accounting and Economics*, **51** (1–2), 1–20.

Ramb, F. and M. Reitzig (2005a), 'Comparing the Value Relevance of R&D Reporting in Germany: Standard and Selection Effects', Discussion Paper Deutsche Bundesbank, Series 1, Economic Studies, 36.

Ramb, F. and M. Reitzig. (2005b), 'Who do You Trust while Shares are on Roller-Coaster Ride? Balance Sheet and Patent Data as Sources of Investor Information during Volatile Market Times', Working Paper Danish Research Unit for Industrial Dynamics, 05-15.

Rasmussen, B. (2004), 'Innovation and Industry Structure in the Biomedical Industry: Some Preliminary Results', Pharmaceutical Industry Project Working Paper Series No. 17.

Ravid, S.A. and M. Spiegel (1997), 'Optimal Financial Contracts for a Start-up with Unlimited Operating Discretion', *Journal of Financial and Quantitative Analysis*, **32** (3), 269–86.

Reichheld, F.F. (1996), 'Learning from Customer Defections', *Harvard Business Review*, **74** (2), 56–69.

Reitzig, M. (2002), *Die Bewertung von Patentrechten: Eine theoretische und empirische Analyse aus Unternehmenssicht*, Wiesbaden: DUV-Verlag.

Reitzig, M. (2004a), 'Strategic Management of Intellectual Property', *MIT Sloan Management Review*, **45** (3), 35–40.

Reitzig, M. (2004b), *A Comprehensive View on Corporations' Intellectual Property: Towards a Specific Strategy-Structure Contingency Framework*, Copenhagen: Copenhagen Business School.

Reitzig, M. (2004c), 'The Private Value of "Thickets" and "Fences": Towards an Updated Picture of the Use of Patents across Industries', *Economics of Innovation and New Technology*, **13** (5), 457–76.

Reitzig, M. (2007), 'How Executives Can Enhance IP Strategy and Performance', *MIT Sloan Management Review*, **49** (1), 37–43.

Rivette, K. and D. Kline (2000), 'Discovering the New Value in Intellectual Property', *Harvard Business Review*, January–February, 54–61.

Rogers, J.L., D. Skinner and A. Van Buskirk (2009), 'Earnings Guidance and Market Uncertainty', *Journal of Accounting and Economics*, **48** (1), 90–109.

Romer, P. (2003), 'The Soft Revolution: Achieving Growth by Managing Intangibles', in Hand, J. and B. Lev (eds.), *Intangible Assets, Values, Measures and Risks*, New York: Oxford University Press.

Rosenberg, B., K. Reid and R. Lanstein (1985), 'Persuasive Evidence of Market Inefficiency', *Journal of Portfolio Management*, **11** (3), 9–16.

Rothaermel, F.T. and D.L. Deeds (2004), 'Exploration and Exploitation Alliances in Biotechnology: A System of New Product Development', *Strategic Management Journal*, **25** (3), 201–21.

Rothschild, M. and J. Stiglitz (1976), 'Equilibrium in Competitive Insurance

Markets: An Essay on the Economics of Imperfect Information', *Quarterly Journal of Economics*, **90** (4), 629–49.

Rumelt, R.P. (1984), 'Towards a Strategic Theory of the Firm', in Lamb, R.B. (ed.), *Competitive Strategic Management*, Hoboken: NJ: Englewood Cliffs.

Sahlman, W. (1990), 'The Structure and Governance of Venture-capital Organizations', *Journal of Financial Economics*, **27**, 472–521.

Sandner, P. and J. Block (2011), 'The Market Value of R&D, Patents, and Trademarks', *Research Policy*, **40** (7), 969–85.

Sattler, H. (1997), 'Indikatoren für den Langfristigen Markenwert', *Zeitschrift für Markenführung*, **59** (6), 46–50.

Schankerman, M. (1998), 'How Valuable is Patent Protection? Estimates by Technology Field', *RAND Journal of Economics*, **29** (1), 77–107.

Schankerman, M. and A. Pakes (1986), 'Estimates of the Value of Patent Rights in European Countries during the Post-1950 Period', *Economic Journal*, **96** (384), 1052–76.

Scherer, F.M. (1965), 'Firm Size, Market Structure, Opportunity, and the Output of Patented Inventions', *American Economic Review*, **55** (5), 1097–125.

Scherer, F.M. and D. Harhoff (2000), 'Technology Policy for a World of Skew-Distributed Outcomes', *Research Policy*, **29** (4–5), 559–66.

Scherer, F.M., D. Harhoff and J. Kukies (2000), 'Uncertainty and the Size Distribution of Rewards from Innovation', *Journal of Evolutionary Economics*, **10** (1–2), 175–200.

Schilling, M. (2009), *Strategic Management of Technological Innovation*, 3rd edition, New York: McGraw-Hill and Irwin.

Schnell, R., P.B. Hill and E. Esser (2008), *Methoden der Empirischen Sozialforschung*, Munich: Oldenbourg Wissenschaftsverlag.

Schumpeter, J. (1939), *Business Cycles: A Theoretical, Historical and Statistical Analysis of the Capitalist Process*, New York: McGraw-Hill Book Company.

Schumpeter, J. (1962), *Capitalism, Socialism and Democracy*, rebound edition, New York: Harper Torchbooks.

Seethamraju, C. (2003), 'The Value Relevance of Trademarks', in Hand, J. and B. Lev (eds.), *Intangible Assets: Measures, Values and Risks*, New York: Oxford University Press, pp. 228–47.

Shapiro, C. (2001), 'Navigating the Patent Thicket: Cross Licenses, Patent Pools, and the Patent Law', in National Bureau of Economic Research (ed.), *Innovation Policy and the Economy*, Cambridge, MA: National Bureau of Economic Research: MIT Press, pp. 119–50.

Sheehan, J., E. Martinez and D. Guellec (2004), *Understanding Business Patenting and Licensing: Results of a Survey*, Paris: OECD.

Shyam-Sunder, L. (1991), 'The Stock Price Effect of Risky versus Safe Debt', *Journal of Financial and Quantitative Analysis*, **26** (4), 549–58.

Silverberg, G. and B. Verspagen (2007), 'The Size Distribution of Innovations Revisited: An Application of Extreme Value Statistics to Citation and Returns Measures of Patent Significance', *Journal of Econometrics*, **127** (2), 318–39.

Small Business Association (SBA) (2009), 'US Small Business Association press release', published March 2009, available at http: //www.sba.gov/opc/pubs/fs83.html (accessed 21 January 2010).

Solow, R.M. (1956), 'A Contribution to the Theory of Economic Growth', *Quarterly Journal of Economics*, **70**, 65–94.

Song, M., H. van der Bij and M. Weggeman (2006), 'Factors for Improving the Level of Knowledge Generation in New Product Development', *R&D Management*, **36** (2), 173–87.

Spence, M. (1973), 'Job Market Signaling', *Quarterly Journal of Economics*, **87** (3), 355–74.

Standard & Poor's (2006), 'Corporate Credit Rating Criteria', available at www.corporatecriteria.standardandpoors.com (accessed 4 April 2008).

Standard & Poor's (2008), 'Corporate Credit Rating Criteria', available at: www.corporatecriteria.standardandpoors.com (accessed 7 June 2011).

Standard & Poor's (2010), 'Refinancing Risk Remains: The Main Threat to the Credit Quality of European Speculative-Grade Companies', RatingsDirect.

STATA (2011), *Web Books*, Chapter 2, available at http://www.ats.ucla.edu/stat/stata/webbooks/reg/chapter2/statareg2.htm (accessed 5 September 2011).

Stiglitz, J. (1985), 'Credit Markets and the Control of Capital', *Journal of Money, Credit, and Banking*, **17** (2), 133–52.

Stiglitz, J. (2008), 'Economic Foundations of Intellectual Property Rights', *Duke Law Journal*, **57**, 1693–724.

Stiglitz, J. and A. Weiss (1981), 'Credit Rationing in Markets with Imperfect Information', *American Economic Review*, **71** (3), 393–410.

Tasker, S. (1998), 'Bridging the Information Gap: Quarterly Conference Calls as a Medium for Voluntary Disclosure', *Review of Accounting Studies*, **3**, 137–67.

Tauber, E.M. (1998), 'Brand Leverage: Strategy for Growth in a Cost-Control World', *Journal of Advertising Research*, **28**, 26–30.

Teece, D.J. (1986), 'Transaction Cost Economics and the Multinational Enterprise', *Journal of Economic Behavior and Organization*, **7**, 21–45.

Teece, D.J., G. Pisano and A. Shuen (1997), 'Dynamic Capabilities and Strategic Management', *Strategic Management Journal*, **18** (7), 509–33.

The Economist (2007), *The Value of Knowledge: European Firms and the Intellectual Property Challenge*, London: Economist Intelligence Unit.

The Economist (2011), 'Google's Takeover of Motorola Mobility: Patently Different', 20–26 August, p. 54.

Thumm, N. (2003), *Research and Patenting in Biotechnology: A Survey in Switzerland*, Bern: Swiss Federal Institute of Intellectual Property.

Thumm, N. (2004), 'Strategic Patenting in Biotechnology', *Technology Analysis & Strategic Management*, **16** (4), 529–38.

Tidd, J. and J. Bessant (1997), *Managing Innovation: Integrating Technological, Organizational and Market Change*, Chichester: John Wiley.

Tommsdorff, V. (1992), 'Multivariate Imageforschung und strategische Marketingplanung', in Hermanns, A. and V. Flegel (eds.), *Handbuch des Electronic Marketing – Funktionen und Anwendungen der Informations- und Kommunikationstechnik im Marketing*, Munich: Beck, pp. 321–37.

Trajtenberg, M. (1990), 'A Penny for Your Quotes: Patent Citations and the Value of Innovation', *RAND Journal of Economics*, **21**, 172–87.

Trautwein, A. (2007), *Werterelevanz von Patentinformationen im Kontext der Rechnungslegung: Eine empirische Betrachtung für börsennotierte Kapitalgesellschaften in Deutschland*, Wiesbaden: DUV-Verlag.

Trueman, B. (1986), 'Why do Managers Voluntarily Release Earnings Forecasts?', *Journal of Accounting and Economics*, **8**, 53–72.

Tsao, H.Y. and L.W. Chen (2005), 'Exploring Brand Loyalty from the Perspective of Brand Switching Costs', *International Journal of Management*, **22** (3), 436–41.

Ughetto, E. (2007), 'The Financing of Innovative Activities by Banking Institutions: Policy Issues and Regulatory Options', Innovation Studies Working Paper, No. 2.

Uncles, M. and G. Laurent (1997), 'Editorial', *International Journal of Research in Marketing*, **14** (5), 399–40.

Upton, W. Jr (2003), 'Challenges from the New Economy for Business and Financial Reporting', in Hand, J. and B. Lev (eds.), *Intangible Assets: Values, Measures, and Risks*, New York: Oxford University Press.

Urbig, D., R. Bürger, H. Patzelt and L. Schweizer (2011), 'Investor Reactions to New Product Development Failures: The Moderating Role of Product Development Stage', *Journal of Management* (online), 3 August.

Van Pottelsberghe, B. and A. Romain (2004), 'The Determinants of Venture Capital: Additional Evidence', Deutsche Bundesbank Discussion Paper No. 19.

Van Reekum, A.H. (1999), 'Intellectual Property and Pharmaceutical Innovation', Ridderkerk, Rijksuniversiteit Groningen.

Venture Economics (1988), *Exiting Venture Capital Investments*, Needham, MA: Venture Economics.

Venture Economics (2000), Press release, available at www.ventureeco nomics.com, (accessed 17 March 2011).

Verrecchia, R. (1983), 'Discretionary Disclosure', *Journal of Accounting and Economics*, **5**, 179–94.

Verrecchia, R. (2001), 'Essays on Disclosure', *Journal of Accounting and Economics*, **32**, 97–180.

Voet, M.A. (2008), *The Generic Challenge: Understanding Patents, FDA & Pharmaceutical Life-Cycle Management*, 2nd edition, Boca Raton, FL: Dissertation.com.

Wagner, S. (2007), 'Make-or-buy Decisions in Patent Related Services', *Zeitschrift für Betriebswirtschaft*, **4**, 47–68.

Wasley, C. and J. Wu (2006), 'Why Do Managers Voluntarily Issue Cash Flow Forecasts?', *Journal of Accounting Research*, **44** (2), 389–429.

Waymire, G. (1984), 'Additional Evidence on the Information Content of Management Earnings Forecasts', *Journal of Accounting Research*, **22**, 703–19.

Waymire, G. (1986), 'Additional Evidence on the Accuracy of Analyst Forecasts Before and After Voluntary Management Earnings Forecasts', *The Accounting Review*, **61**, 129–43.

Wernerfelt, B. (1984), 'A Resource-based View of the Firm', *Strategic Management Journal*, **5**, 272–80.

Wetzel, W.E. Jr (1994), 'Venture Capital', in Bygrave, W.D. and A.L. Zacharakis (eds.), *Portable MBA in Entrepreneurship*, New York: John Wiley & Sons: 172–94.

White, L. (2002), 'The Credit Rating Industry: An Organizational Analysis', New York University Working Paper, Leonard N. Stern School of Business, Department of Economics.

Wilbon, A. (2002), 'Predicting Survival of High-Technology Initial Public Offerings', *Journal of High Technology Management Research*, **13** (1), 127–41.

Williamson, O.E. (1971), 'The Vertical Integration of Production: Market Failure Consideration', *American Economic Review*, **61**, 112–23.

Williamson, O.E. (1979), 'Transaction Cost Economics: The Governance of Contractual Relations', *Journal of Law and Economics*, **22**, 233–61.

Williamson, O.E. (1981), 'The Modern Corporation: Origins, Evolution, Attributes', *Journal of Economic Literature*, **19**, 1537–68.

Williamson, O.E. (1988), 'Corporate Finance and Corporate Governance', *Journal of Finance*, **43**, 567–91.

Wilson, C. (1977), 'A Model of Insurance Markets with Incomplete Information', *Journal of Economic Theory*, **16** (2), 167–207.

WIPO (2004), 'Understanding Industrial Property', available at www. wipo.int/freepublications/en/intproperty/895/wipo_pub_895.pdf (accessed 10 October 2010).

Wong, A. (2002), 'Angel Finance: The Other Venture Capital', University of Chicago Working Paper.

Wooldridge, J. (2005), *Introductory Econometrics: A Modern Approach*, 3rd edition, Andover: Cengage Learning Services.

World Trade Organization (WTO) (2006), 'TRIPS und pharmazeutische Patente: Fact Sheet', http://www.wto.org/english/tratop_e/trips_e and factsheet_pharm00_e.htm (accessed 23 January 2009).

Wright, R.F. (2001), 'The Rational for Global Branding of Pharmaceuticals', *Journal of Pharmaceutical Marketing & Management*, **14** (2), 31–50.

Wurzer, A.J. and C.B. Frey (2009), 'Growth and Wealth Creation in a Knowledge Economy: The Role of IP-Managers', in Wurzer, A.J. (ed.), *IP-Manager*, Cologne: Carl Heymanns Verlag.

Wurzer, A.J. and L. Kaiser (2006), 'Patente, Produkte und Profite', *Harvard Business Manager*, March, 23–35.

Wurzer, A.J. and D. Reinhardt (2009), *Handbuch der Patentbewertung*, 2nd edition, Cologne: Carl Heymanns Verlag.

Zeithaml, V.A. (1988), 'Consumer Perceptions of Price, Quality, and Value: A Means–End Model and Synthesis of Evidence', *Journal of Marketing*, **52**, 2–22.

Zhang, H. (2005), 'Share Price Performance Following Actual Share Repurchases', *Journal of Banking & Finance*, **29**, 1887–901.

Zimmermann, K.F. and J. Schwalbach (1991), 'Determinanten der Patentaktivität', *Ifo-Studien*, **14**, 201–27.

ZVEI (2006), 'Mikroelektronik – Trendanalyse bis 2010, Wirtschaftliche und technische Aspekte', Working group for Electronic Components and System.

Index